David Clark has taught history fo   schools, colleges and universities. He has also worked as a senior tutor within HM Prison Service.

Recent titles in the series

A BRIEF GUIDE TO

BRITISH
BATTLEFIELDS

DAVID CLARK

ROBINSON

First published in Great Britain in 2015 by Robinson

A CIP catalogue record for this book
is available from the British Library.

ISBN: 978-1-47210-813-5 (paperback)
ISBN: 978-147210-828-9 (ebook)

Typeset in Stempel Garamond by TW Typesetting, Plymouth, Devon
Printed and bound in Great Britain by CPI Mackays

Robinson
is an imprint of
Constable & Robinson Ltd
100 Victoria Embankment
London EC4Y 0DY

An Hachette UK Company
www.hachette.co.uk

www.constablerobinson.com

CONTENTS

Part 5: The Seventeenth Century

Warfare in the Seventeenth Century   161

The Bishops' Wars

The English Civil Wars

FIRST CIVIL WAR

TIMELINE

British Battles in Context

1190   Massacre of Jews in York

1212   Childrens' Crusade
1215   Magna Carta
1249   University College, Oxford founded
1264   Lewes
1265   Evesham
1275   Marco Polo enters service of Kublai Khan
1284   Peterhouse College, Cambridge founded
1297   Stirling Bridge
1298   Falkirk

1307   Loudon Hill
1314   Bannockburn
1319   Myton
1322   Boroughbridge
1322   Byland
1332   Dupplin Moor
1333   Halidon Hill
1346   Battle of Crécy
        Neville's Cross
1348   First outbreak of Black Death in England
1356   Battle of Poitiers
1378   York Mystery Plays first performed
1381   Peasants' Revolt
1388   Otterburn

1402   Homildon Hill
1403   Shrewsbury
1408   Bramham Moor
1411   Reid Harlaw
1415   Battle of Agincourt
1431   Joan of Arc executed
1439   Gutenberg invents printing press
1455   1st St Albans
1457   James II of Scotland bans golf and football

1459	**Blore Heath**
1460	**Northampton**
	Wakefield
1461	**Mortimer's Cross**
	2nd St Albans
	Ferrybridge
	Towton
1464	**Hedgeley Moor**
	Hexham
1469	**Edgcote**
1470	**Empingham**
1471	**Barnet**
	Tewkesbury
1478	Spanish Inquisition established
1485	**Bosworth**
1487	**Stoke Field**
1492	Columbus discovers New World
1506	Leonardo Da Vinci completes *Mona Lisa*
1513	**Flodden**
1517	Martin Luther presents his ninety-five theses
1520	Field of Cloth of gold
1521	Cortez conquers Aztec Empire
1522	Magellan completes circumnavigation of the globe
1532	Pizarro conquers Inca Empire
1534	Act of Supremacy
1535	Thomas More executed
1536	Dissolution of the Monasteries
1542	**Solway Moss**
1545	**Ancrum Moor**
	Mary Rose sinks off Spithead
1547	**Pinkie Cleugh**
1568	**Langside**
1586	Sir Walter Raleigh introduces potato to England
1587	Execution of Mary, Queen of Scots
1588	Spanish Armada

1590   Shakespeare's first play (*Love's Labour's Lost*
         performed

1600   East India Company established
1601   Poor Law introduced in England
1605   Cervantes' *Don Quixote* published
         Gunpowder Plot
1607   Monteverdi's opera *L'Orfeo* performed
1611   Authorized Version of *The Bible* produced
1620   Pilgrim Fathers set sail for America
         First submarine constructed and trialed on River
         Thames
1639   Brig o' Dee
1640   Newburn
1642   Powick Bridge
         Edgehill
         Tadcaster
1643   Braddock Down
         Middlewich
         Hopton Heath
         Ripple Field
         Sourton Down
         Stratton
         Chalgrove Field
         Adwalton Moor
         Lansdown
         Roundway Down
         Gainsborough
         1st Newbury
         Winceby
         Alton
1644   Nantwich
         Cheriton
         Selby
         Cropredy Bridge
         Marston Moor

	Lostwithiel
	Tippermuir
	Aberdeen
	2nd Newbury
	Fyvie
1645	Inverlochy
	Auldearn
	Naseby
	Alford
	Langport
	Kilsyth
	Philiphaugh
	Rowton Heath
1646	Torrington
	Stow-on-the-Wold
1648	St Fagan's
	1st Preston
1649	Charles I executed
1650	Carbisdale
	Dunbar
1651	Inverkeithing
	Worcester
1660	Pepys begins his diary
1665	Great Plague of London
1666	Great Fire of London
1667	Milton's *Paradise Lost* published
	Racine's *Andromaque* performed
1679	Drumclog
	Bothwell Bridge
1685	Sedgemoor
1687	Newton's *Principia Mathematica* published
1689	Killiecrankie
1690	Cromdale
	Battle of the Boyne
1692	Glencoe Massacre
	Salem Witchcraft Trials

1701   Jethro Tull invents seed drill
1704   Battle of Blenheim
1707   Act of Union
1711   Ascot Races established
1715   2nd Preston
         Sheriffmuir
1719   Glenshiel
         Defoe's *Robinson Crusoe* published
1721   Robert Walpole Britain's first Prime Minister
         Guy's Hospital founded
1733   John Kay invents 'Flying Shuttle'
1741   Royal Military Academy established at Woolwich
1745   Prestonpans
         Clifton Moor
         Inverurie
1746   Falkirk
         Culloden
1755   Johnson's *Dictionary of the English Language*
         published

INTRODUCTION

Into battle!

I visited my first British battlefield (Stamford Bridge) in 1958. Since then, I have visited many more. This brief guide covers just over a hundred of them.

The book is divided into six historical periods, each prefaced by an outline of the nature of contemporary warfare. The battles within each period, presented in chronological order, are mainly grouped into campaigns. For each battle, the action is described, placed in context and illustrated with a sketch-map. Surviving features of interest for the prospective visitor are identified and a suggestion for detailed reading is included. The Select Bibliography section at the end of the book suggests avenues for deeper investigation.

One would hesitate to describe any battlefield guide as comprehensive because the more we learn about battlefields in Britain, the less confident we become about making precise judgements. So little is known about many of them as to render their inclusion impracticable. A case in point is the monumental battle against Roman occupation between Roman governor Suetonius Paulinus and Iceni queen, Boudica, in AD 60/61. Suggested locations include various sites throughout Leicestershire, Warwickshire, Oxfordshire and Northamptonshire.

Nor does contemporary documentation improve with the passage of time. Thus, Seacroft Moor (1643) is excluded. An important battle of the Civil Wars, it was described by the Parliamentarian, Sir Thomas Fairfax, as 'one of the greatest losses we ever received', and yet we cannot identify its exact location. It is known only that it was a running battle which took place on open ground some five miles to the east of Leeds.

Even when we think we are on relatively safe ground, problems arise, not least of all because of the fashion for rewriting history. Thus, 'alternative' locations are constantly being proposed for major battle sites. Stamford Bridge (1066), Hastings (1066), Bosworth (1485), Stow-on-the-Wold (1646) and Prestonpans (1745) are some of the victims. In each case, while noting the suggested alternative sites, I have adhered to the 'original' venues.

Other exclusions include battles that are not battles at all. Thus, Ludford Bridge (1459) and Turnham Green (1642), which are universally referred to as battles, were, in fact, merely stand-offs in which no fighting occurred. It is also customary to draw a distinction between battles and skirmishes – small-scale clashes that have little significance outside the locality in which they occurred. In short, a definitive list will always remain elusive.

On the practical side, by exploring the ground once trodden by kings and would-be kings, one can begin to experience more fully a sense of identity with the past, with half-formed images of battles that have shaped our history springing to life as we stand atop a hill or in a meadow where crowns were won and lost.

Most important of all, battlefield exploration is an enjoyable experience. It is an activity that you can undertake on your own at any time. Even on major battlefields like Towton (1461) or Marston Moor (1644), I find that I can still spend a day wandering around without meeting anyone else. For the less eccentric, there are developed, 'family friendly' battlefields like Hastings (1066), Shrewsbury (1403), Bosworth (1485) and Culloden (1746), ideal for day excursions. Similarly, explorations of urban battlefields such as St Albans (1455 and 1461), Worcester (1651) and Preston (1648 and 1715) can be built into town centre visits.

If I am already preaching to the converted, perhaps this book will serve as a source of reference on your bookshelf. If you are new to the subject, I hope it will encourage you to step out into a thousand years of colourful and exciting history. But do remember that battlefields in Britain are an endangered species, liable at any moment to be bulldozed for new roads, industrial estates, housing developments and, the new kid on the block, the HS2 rail link, so don't leave it too long . . .

David Clark

PART ONE:
THE DARK AGES

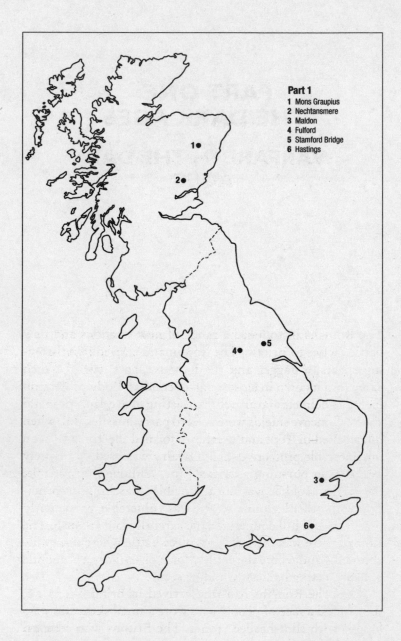

Part 1
1 Mons Graupius
2 Nechtansmere
3 Maldon
4 Fulford
5 Stamford Bridge
6 Hastings

WARFARE IN THE DARK AGES

The Romans introduced a range of new weapons and new battle tactics to Britain. The legionnaire carried two throwing spears, a dagger and the famous 'short' sword which came into its own in close-quarter combat. Body protection included helmets and armour consisting of overlapping metal strips. Concave shields were used to parry missiles and, when interlocked in front and overhead, formed the 'tortoise' – an impenetrable protective shell. Cavalry was used, but largely as a tool in pursuing a defeated foe. Although formidable, the Roman soldier was not invincible. Marching in formation with other legionnaires, he was vulnerable, particularly in forests and hill country, to the carefully laid ambush. The Roman forte was the large, set-piece battle where discipline counted – and where the earliest form of artillery, the mobile bolt-projecting ballista, could be seen.

When the Romans had first arrived in Britain in 55 BC, they found a race of people who wore animal skins and who fought with flint-headed spears. The Britons who rebelled against the Roman occupation were still often poorly armed, although the horse-drawn war chariot was in use and the more influential among them owned swords. Further north, the Romans identified present-day Scotland as Caledonia, referring to its tribes collectively as Caledonians – a naturally warlike people, impossible to subdue.

The Anglo-Saxons armed themselves with long (throwing) and short (thrusting) spears. Swords continued to be valuable possessions and were essentially cavalry weapons, borne by thanes (retainers of noblemen). There were several types of axe, possibly introduced by the Vikings; longbows were used, albeit sparingly, and the sling was still in use. Mail shirts were sometimes worn, as were helmets, designed to protect the nose as well as the skull. Shields were oval in shape. When interlocked, in a variation on the Roman 'tortoise', a shield-wall was formed, and battles often amounted to a trial of strength between opposing shield-walls, each pressing forward against the other. The best troops were the heavily armed house-carls, who also acted as bodyguards for royalty. The rank and file were the fyrd – locally raised levies of free men who were often indifferently armed and who lacked the commitment of the house-carls. Archers were uncommon, as was the use of cavalry.

Like the Anglo-Saxons, the Vikings usually fought on foot. They preferred the sword and battle-axe, with spears and bows coming a poor second. They wore armour of chain mail or reindeer hide and also used shield-walls. In attack, they often formed svinfylkings: wedge-shaped groups of men, with the thin end of the wedge pointing towards the enemy. They are best known for their legendary ferocity, particularly the wild warriors called berserks. (Hence the phrase 'going berserk'.)

Norman weaponry was also not dissimilar to that of the Anglo-Saxons and Vikings. Two spears, one for throwing and one for thrusting, were used. Their shields were kite-shaped and their mail shirts stretched below the knees. They placed more reliance upon bowmen than the Anglo-Saxons, and made greater use of horses – both of which factors were to stand them in good stead at Hastings.

I. Mons Graupius c. AD 84

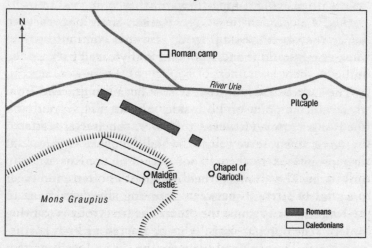

In either AD 83 or 84, Agricola, Roman governor of Britannia, was attempting to subdue the hostile Caledonians in the north of the province. Having abandoned a successful guerrilla campaign, the Caledonians amassed an army, reportedly 30,000 strong, and occupied 'Mons Graupius' – most probably within the Bennachie hills, to the west of present-day Inverurie in Aberdeenshire.

Agricola was camped a little to the north of Bennachie, at Durno. His army included several thousand auxiliary troops from Gaul. These auxiliaries, Agricola decided, would bear the brunt of the fighting. Accordingly, in preparation for battle, he deployed 8,000 foot soldiers, protecting the flanks with 3,000 horsemen. Another body of horse was held in reserve, while his legionnaires remained ready for action, if need be, in front of the camp. The Caledonians, allegedly under the leadership of one Calgacus, waited in tiered ranks on their hill and the immediate plain below, with charioteers forming their vanguard.

The battle began with an exchange of missiles, comprising javelins and sling-shot, neither side inflicting much damage upon the other. Then, Agricola ordered his auxiliaries on to the offensive. Rushing forward, they ploughed into the packed Caledonian lines. The Roman short swords with which they were armed proved, as always, very effective in close combat and the Caledonians were forced back up the hill.

The Caledonians to the rear now began to descend from their vantage point on both sides, threatening to outflank the Roman army. However, they were themselves scattered by Agricola's reserve cavalry, which he chose to release at this propitious moment. Soon, the Caledonians were in full flight. Those among their pursuers who were too eager paid dearly as their quarry used surrounding woodland to regroup and stage ambushes. It was left to Agricola to bring order to the pursuit, skilfully using the resources at his disposal to flush out pockets of resistance in an operation that went on throughout the day.

The Roman historian, Tacitus, claims that some 10,000 Caledonians were killed, as against 360 men of Agricola's army. While the victory may well have subdued the Caledonians temporarily, the problem of pacification would prove insurmountable, and by AD 122 Roman strategy had shifted from a policy of expansion to one of containment, with the construction of Hadrian's Wall.

The battlefield today

To reach Bennachie (OS Landranger 38 6825), first proposed as a probable site for the battle in 1978, take the A96 from Aberdeen. Two miles beyond Inverurie, take the minor road to Chapel of Garioch (founded by the Earl of Mar after the Battle of Reid Harlaw; see p. 76–8) and then the road to Bennachie Visitor Centre.

Further reading
Duncan B. Campbell, *Mons Graupius AD 83* (Osprey, 2010).

2. Nechtansmere, 685

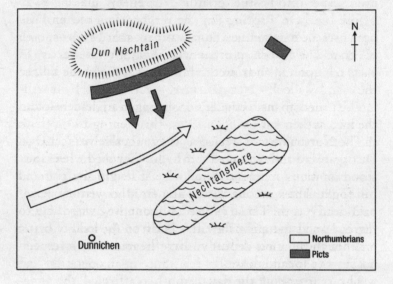

The Romans left Britain in about AD 400, and the land fell prey to other invaders, notably Angles and Saxons. At length, a number of kingdoms evolved: Wessex, Sussex, Kent, Essex, Mercia and Northumbria. The last named stretched northwards from the River Humber, and during the seventh century it was forcibly extended to the Firth of Forth, at the expense of the Picts. Beyond the Forth was the Pictish kingdom of Fortriu, over which the Northumbrian kings may also have claimed suzerainty.

In the year 685, the Northumbrian king, Egfrith, set out to curb the ambitions of a new Fortriu king, Brudei, sometimes described as his cousin. Egfrith had put down one Pictish rebellion in 671, at the Battle of Two Rivers. This had been a complete victory and Egfrith saw no reason why it should not be repeated. He was counselled against the move,

but went ahead with his plans. His experiences would set the
tone for the campaigns of invaders of Scotland for the next
millennium.

Egfrith led a substantial force beyond the Firth of Tay,
ever deeper into hostile territory, the enemy melting away
before him. On a spring day, he reached Dunnichen Hill,
near present-day Forfar, and it was here that Brudei sprang
his trap. The Northumbrians were caught unawares as the
Picts fell upon them from the hillside. Opposite the hill, to
the east, lay a loch – Nechtansmere – surrounded by marshland. Turning to meet Brudei's onslaught, the invaders found
the loch at their backs.

The Northumbrians reeled as they met the Picts' charge.
Disorganized and with nowhere to go, they died where they
stood or were forced into the loch. At length, Egfrith and
his bodyguard were cut down, and Brudei's victory developed into a rout. Those Northumbrians who were able to
flee did so, abandoning Egfrith's body on the field of battle
– although the Picts appear to have treated it with respect,
taking it to Iona for burial.

The outcome of the battle both reaffirmed the independence of the Southern Picts and marked the end of
Northumbria's attempts to extend its political influence.

The battlefield today
Dunnichen – the generally accepted location of the battlefield and the name by which the battle is sometimes known
– lies four miles to the east of Forfar, off the A932 (OS
Landranger 54 5149). A battlefield monument is adjacent to
Dunnichen Church, but a small piece of marshy ground is all
that remains of the loch. A Dunnichen Heritage Trail leaflet
is available for download from the Angus Council website.

Further reading
Graeme Cruickshank, *The Battle of Dunnichen* (Pinkfoot Press,
  1999).

3. Maldon, 991

A leading light among the Viking raiders who wreaked havoc on the east coast of Saxon England during the tenth century was the Norwegian folk hero, Olaf Tryggvason. In 991, he led a party of Norwegians and Danes in a raid on Ipswich. After sacking the settlement, the marauders followed the coastline to the River Blackwater and anchored at Northey Island. Although cut off from the mainland by the tidal river, the site was within easy striking distance of the flourishing settlement of Maldon.

A local alderman, Byrhtnoth, called out the militia to combat the threat. The force arrived on the scene at high tide, when the narrow causeway that formed a tenuous link between Northey Island and the mainland was submerged. When the tide began to ebb, the raiders asked Byrhtnoth for permission to cross to the mainland unmolested, so that a fair fight could take place. Unwisely, Byrhtnoth agreed, his men forming a shield-wall in preparation for the Viking onslaught.

Tryggvason was allowed to assemble his men, and the two forces locked horns, the Vikings hurling themselves against the Saxon shield-wall again and again. Then, one of Byrhtnoth's most trusted followers, Godric, son of Odda, tried to reach the cover of woodland to the rear. Astride one of Byrhtnoth's horses, a gift from the alderman, Godric was mistaken by many Saxons for Byrhtnoth himself. Thinking that their leader was quitting the field, they too sought to save themselves. As they fled, Byrhtnoth, having received several wounds, finally succumbed.

A hard core of Byrhtnoth's own retainers fought on to the death. The Saxons sold their lives dearly, for it is said that the raiders barely had enough survivors to man their ships. They decapitated Byrhtnoth, carrying away his head as a trophy. It was in the wake of the battle that regular payments of 'Danegeld', the annual tax levied to buy peace, began to be made to the Vikings. Byrhtnoth's defeat had, indeed, proved to be expensive.

The battlefield today

Maldon is situated on the A414, ten miles to the east of Chelmsford. To reach the battle site (OS Landranger 168 8605), walk from Promenade Park, where car parking is available, along the sea wall footpath – site of a bronze statue of Byrhtnoth. An information panel is situated by The Causeway. The Maeldum Heritage Centre in Market Hill houses the Maldon Embroidery, a tapestry based on the history of the town, which includes a panel depicting the Battle of Maldon.

Further reading

Donald Scraggs, *The Return of the Vikings: The Battle of Maldon 991* (Tempus Publishing, 2006).

WOMEN AT WAR

Britain's best known female warrior was the Iceni queen, Boudica, who directed and fought battles against the Romans. The tradition of the warrior queen was continued into Anglo-Saxon times by such leading ladies as Aethelberg of Wessex and Ethelfleda of Mercia. As late as the sixteenth century, women were still fighting openly on the battle-field, as suggested by the appearance of the legendary Maid Lilliard at Ancrum Moor (1545).

A century later, many women who would not normally have dreamt of taking up arms were drawn out of the closet by the Civil Wars. Jane Ingilby of Ripley Castle is believed to have fought for the Royalists at Marston Moor (1644), while Lady Brilliana Harvey of Brampton Bryan Castle was one of several Royalist wives who defended their places of residence in the absence of husbands away at the front. Henrietta Maria, queen to Charles I, contented herself with assuming the title of 'Her She-Majesty Generalissima' – thereby creating a situation to tax the diplomatic skills of more than one Royalist field commander.

Civil War sieges of towns and cities witnessed the involve-ment of women at many levels. Often they would have to provide board and lodging for the defending garrison, and in preparation for the Siege of Gloucester (1643) they dug earthworks to bolster the city defences. During the Siege of Leicester (1645), while under heavy fire, women laboured to repair breaches in the city walls. After Leicester had fallen, women possessed of firearms subjected the victorious Royalists to a steady fire from the windows of their houses and even pelted them with roof tiles.

Most women who wanted to fight in battle during the Civil Wars were compelled to do so *incognito*. If discovered, there was a problem, for the leadership of both sides took a dim view of cross-dressing. Charles I attempted to ban the practice as early as July 1643. The majority who wanted to make a contribution to the war effort did so in more conservative ways. In 1644, Lucy, wife of Parliamentarian Colonel John Hutchinson, helped to nurse the wounded in Nottingham Castle. She writes of the application of 'balsams and plasters' to several musket wounds, her ministrations resulted in the recovery of all the victims. Other women became involved in the peace movement. On 9 August 1643, a crowd of women wearing white ribbons in their hats marched on Parliament, to be dispersed – not without bloodshed – by armed guards. Some wives accompanied their husbands on campaigns, and there was rarely a shortage of camp followers, whose responsibilities, among other things, involved foraging for food, cooking and washing. The wives of senior officers travelled in coaches, those of the junior officers rode on horseback, while the women associates ('vermin on foot') of the common soldiers walked. In the wake of a battle, the women on the losing side could expect little sympathy. One of the worst atrocities on a British battlefield occurred at Naseby (1645), when over 100 Royalist wives and camp followers were slaughtered by the Parliamentarians – although others got off lightly, having their faces slashed.

The manner in which women were treated depended rather more on class than gender. During the Siege of Colchester (1648), 500 women and children tried to leave the town. The Parliamentarian besiegers fired blanks to drive them back inside. When this failed to have the desired effect, Lord-General Fairfax had four of the women stripped naked. The rest retreated. In contrast, after the 2nd Siege of Bradford (1643) when Fairfax's wife, Lady Anne, had been captured, the Royalist Duke of Newcastle used his own coach to send her on to her husband.

'1066'

4. Fulford, 20 September 1066

When Harold, Earl of East Anglia and Wessex, became King of England in 1066, his estranged brother, Tostig, was

living in exile in Flanders, where he passed his time plotting Harold's downfall. Seeking help, he approached the King of Norway, Harold Hardrada, who agreed to help him launch a challenge for the English throne.

Hardrada amassed a substantial force comprising Norwegians, Scots and Tostig's own followers. Setting sail in early September, 1066, the invasion fleet made for the River Humber. Pressing on into the Ouse, the long-ships finally came to rest at Riccall, ten miles to the south of York. On 20 September, Hardrada marched on the city.

Resistance was coordinated by Morcar, Earl of Northumbria and his brother Edwin, Earl of Mercia. Together, they gathered around 5,000 men, leading them along the banks of

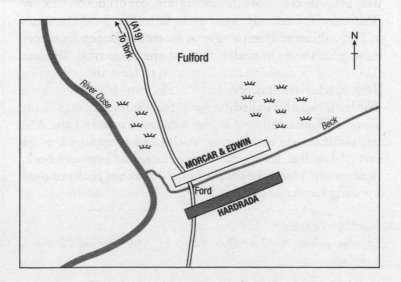

the Ouse to Fulford, a settlement between York and Riccall. Here, before Germany Beck, they deployed their men along a front stretching some 300 yards, flanked by the Ouse to their right and marshland to their left. When Hardrada arrived, he deployed his army – possibly 6,000 strong – opposite the Saxons, his most experienced men on his left wing, by the Ouse. By the marshland, on the right flank, his lines were thinner.

The Saxons made the first move, pressing forward along the entire length of the Viking line. The weaker section, by the marsh, was pushed back, but the Vikings took advantage of their strength on the other flank and in the centre. Slowly but surely, the Saxons were rolled back. Casualties were heavy on both sides but, with their backs to the marsh, the Saxons were cut to pieces – the few survivors retreating to the comparative safety of York.

Hardrada's peace terms were surprisingly generous. In exchange for hostages and supplies, the city would not be sacked. To meet their part of the bargain, the citizens agreed to rendezvous with the Norwegians on 25 September eight miles to the east of York, at Stamford Bridge. King Harold had been in the south, awaiting an expected invasion by William of Normandy. The Saxon failure to hold Hardrada at Fulford forced him to fight at Stamford Bridge, compromising his ability to deal with the danger posed by William.

The battlefield today

The battlefield (OS Landranger 105 6148) is two miles to the south of York, on the A19, between the city and the A64 bypass. It is believed that the Vikings were deployed to the east of Landing Lane; the Saxons, beyond Germany Beck. A memorial plaque is situated in the playing field opposite Landing Lane. Car parking is available along Landing Lane.

Further reading

Charles Jones, *The Forgotten Battle of 1066: Fulford* (Tempus, 2006).

5. Stamford Bridge, 25 September 1066

The Saxons who were vanquished by the Norwegians at the Battle of Fulford had not known that King Harold was marching from London to their aid. On 24 September, he reached Tadcaster. Early the following day, he was in York, but he

did not linger. After completing one of the most famous forced marches in history – 187 miles in four days – he moved straight on to Stamford Bridge, where Hardrada and Tostig were waiting to receive their tribute from York's citizens.

Harold's rapid approach on the morning of 25 September caught the allies at a disadvantage on the west bank of the River Derwent. Hardrada withdrew most of his men to a ridge on the east bank, leaving a smaller contingent on the bridge that crossed the river (about a quarter of a mile downstream from the present-day bridge) to cover his retreat. Eventually, all but one of the rearguard were cut down. The remaining Norwegian continued to stand fast until he was despatched by the upward thrust of a javelin, delivered by an enterprising Saxon who used a 'swine tub' to manoeuvre himself beneath the bridge.

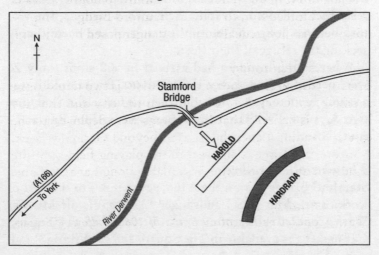

Hardrada managed to deploy his main body of troops in an area that came to be known as Battle Flat. They were drawn up in a horseshoe formation with Hardrada and Tostig, each with his personal retinue, occupying the centre. Harold launched his men at the defensive wall of shields. This was to be no replay of the Battle of Fulford, for Harold's house-carls – well-equipped, disciplined, highly trained professionals – were more than a match for the enemy. As the Saxons pressed forward, an increasing number of gaps appeared in the Viking defences, the concentrated fighting breaking up into small group and individual tussles.

With an occasional lull, this bruising contest went on for the better part of the day until men on both sides were dropping from exhaustion. An input of fresh troops could have proved decisive. Harold had no hope of receiving reinforcements, but the Vikings had summoned aid from their base camp at Ricall. Unfortunately, when they did arrive, the Viking reserves were so exhausted that they threw off their chain mail and so fell easy prey to sword and axe. At last, Hardrada was felled by one of the few Saxon archers on the field, while a house-carl's axe split Tostig's skull down to the jaw bone. With the death of their leaders, the Vikings' resistance collapsed. Despite their own weariness, the victors began a long and bloody pursuit of the enemy, now seeking the refuge of their fleet.

Whereas the invaders had arrived in 300 ships, only 24 were needed to ferry home the survivors. For Harold it was a stunning victory, yet he had little time for celebration. Just two days later, William of Normandy set sail for England's south coast.

The battlefield today

Stamford Bridge lies on the A166, seven miles to the east of York. Battle Flat (OS Landranger 105 7155) is off Minster Way. A battlefield monument can be found in The Square. Car parking is available in The Square and off Viking Road.

Alternative sites for the battle have been proposed, including nearby Low Catton (7053).

Further reading
Peter Marren, *The Battles of York,* *Stamford Bridge and Hastings*
  (Pen & Sword, 2002).

6. Hastings, 14 October 1066

William of Normandy landed in Pevensey Bay on 28 September 1066, just three days after King Harold's victory at Stamford Bridge. The next day, he moved on to Hastings where he established his army, content to let Harold come to him. For Harold, this meant another demanding march, first to London and then on to the south coast.

The Saxon army marched as far as Senlac Hill, eight miles short of Hastings. An army occupying this feature would command the road to London. A formidable obstacle, the western slopes were relatively gentle, but those to the south and east were steep. Harold deployed his men along this ridge at daybreak on 14 October. About 10,000 in number, they were tightly packed behind a single shield-wall, house-carls to the front, the weaker levies to the rear.

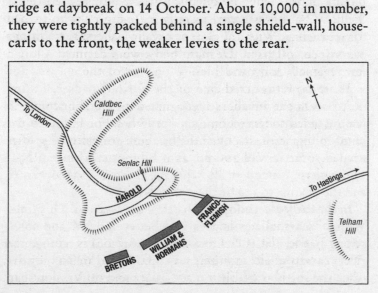

William was already marching to meet them. As the invaders, some 9,000 strong, descended Telham Hill, a mile to the south, they advanced in three divisions. In the centre, William commanded his Normans; to his right was a Franco-Flemish contingent; to the left were troops from Brittany. Each division was led by archers, followed by infantry and then cavalry – the horses having accompanied the invasion fleet in specially adapted transports.

The battle began at about 9.30 a.m. William had to assault Senlac Hill. With the armies about 500 yards apart, he sent forward his archers. Much of their impact was absorbed by the shield-wall. The infantry then advanced and, despite coming under fire from a variety of missiles, including arrows and spears, they fought their way up the hillside and came to grips with the house-carls. The defenders stood firm and the attack was beaten back. The Norman left wing gave ground first with the remainder following suit.

Harold had ordered his troops to stay where they were, but the men of his own right wing broke ranks and set off in pursuit of the fleeing Normans. It was a 'near run thing' for William, but he managed to rally his infantry, who turned to face their pursuers. When the cavalry were thrown in, the Saxons, cut off from the main body, were doomed. Only a few regained their own lines.

There now occurred one of the curious pauses, lasting up to an hour, which are recognized as a not uncommon feature of early battles. In such strength-sapping, toe-to-toe bludgeoning contests, even the hardiest professional soldier needed some respite and so, as if by mutual consent, hostilities were suspended, allowing the Normans to reorganize and the Saxons to repair their shield-wall.

In the early afternoon, the battle was restarted. This time, William marshalled his cavalry – between 3,000 and 4,000 strong – and led them forward. It was heavy going, the riders carefully picking their way up the hill. When they did reach the shield-wall, they made little more impression than their infantry. They regrouped but were still unable to force a path through. Again, they retreated and again some of the Saxons, this time on the left of the line, went after them. They, too, were cut down.

The light was beginning to fail as the Normans began yet another assault. Once more, a torrent of arrows rained down upon the Saxon shields before William advanced with every available man. Both sides had suffered heavy casualties, but the Saxon line was now shorter, making it possible to broaden the advance by attacking on both flanks. A foothold was established on the plateau, but the battle could still have gone either way. The Norman archers were still firing, having adjusted their aim so as to hit the rear of the Saxon ranks. One of these arrows struck Harold in his right eye. Mortally wounded, he was unable to fight on.

The news spread through the ranks, creating uncertainty among the fyrd, which began to waver. As men began to slip away, the house-carls fought on, gradually being pressed back until the Norman men-at-arms broke through to the dying king to administer the *coup de grâce*. The resistance of the fyrd collapsed entirely, the survivors taking refuge in the woods to the rear. Unwisely, the exhausted Norman cavalry followed, some horses stumbling in a ravine while other riders fell victim to small parties of Saxons with fight left in them.

Meanwhile, the victorious infantry stripped the dead and despatched the dying. Harold's body was identified and ultimately buried, but most of the Saxon corpses were left to rot. Their blanched bones, strewn across the ridge they had so heroically defended, could still be seen seventy years later. On 25 December 1066, in Westminster Abbey, the Conqueror was crowned King William I of England.

The battlefield today

The battlefield is situated near the town of Battle on the A2100, seven miles to the north of Hastings. Car parking is available at Battle Abbey Visitor Centre (OS Landranger 199 7415). The abbey was built by William I in atonement for the depredations committed during the campaign of conquest. The high altar of the abbey church was supposedly sited on the spot where Harold fell. The visitor centre houses a film and exhibitions and visitors can take a waymarked audio-tour of the battlefield. Various alternative sites for the battle have been proposed, including Caldbec Hill to the north.

Further reading
Jim Bradbury, *The Battle of Hastings* (History Press, 2010).

PART TWO:
THE EARLY MIDDLE AGES

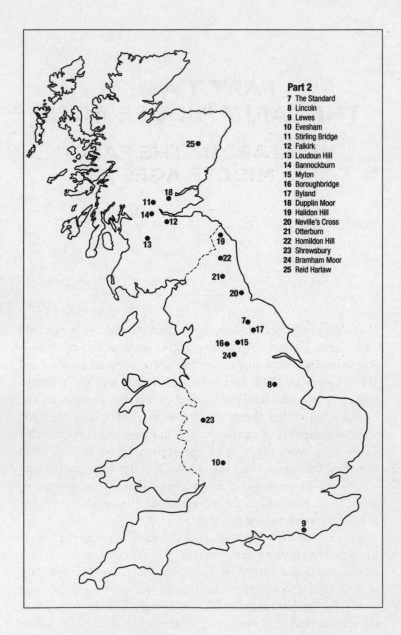

Part 2

7 The Standard
8 Lincoln
9 Lewes
10 Evesham
11 Stirling Bridge
12 Falkirk
13 Loudoun Hill
14 Bannockburn
15 Myton
16 Boroughbridge
17 Byland
18 Dupplin Moor
19 Halidon Hill
20 Neville's Cross
21 Otterburn
22 Homildon Hill
23 Shrewsbury
24 Bramham Moor
25 Reid Harlaw

WARFARE IN THE EARLY MIDDLE AGES

During the thirteenth century, experimental use was made of cannon. Little more than primitive tubes designed to project missiles over a distance, they were utilized by Edward III at Crécy in 1346. In England, Edward had put them to use twenty years earlier, in one of his forays against the Scots, who called them 'crakys of war'. The contraptions were not capable of causing much damage and their novelty value soon wore off. Critics entertained grave doubts as to whether the game was worth the candle, but combatants who were eager to grasp at anything that might give them an edge in battle kept the potential of gunpowder alive for exploitation by future generations.

This is not to say that no new weapons were being developed, albeit along more traditional lines. The most important of these was the longbow. An experienced archer could fire at least ten arrows per minute and would be able to aim accurately at distances of up to 220 yards. The downside was that he carried only twenty-four arrows, and during a lull in the fighting he might well have to run forward to retrieve any available shafts.

New tactics also developed from existing tried and trusted methods. For example, the early medieval period was the era of the famed Scottish 'schiltron'. In its classic form, this was a variation on the Saxon shield-wall, comprising a circle of spearmen, the front ranks kneeling with their spears fixed into the earth before them. Rear ranks, standing, would level their spears over the heads of their crouching comrades. It was superb in defence – less so when developed into an offensive measure.

Armour underwent a sea change. Norman mail armour permitted freedom of movement, but it was very heavy and could be penetrated by an arrow. Gradually, it was supplemented with plate armour: separate metal plates for the torso and limbs which led, inevitably, to what we would recognize as full suits of armour. Full plate armour, *cap-à-pie*, was heavy, although the weight was evenly distributed, dispensing with the 'dragging' effect of chain mail, and it has been argued that it weighed less than the kit carried by the modern infantryman. What had been lost in the transition was freedom of movement; it was difficult, if not impossible, for an armoured man on foot to escape capture if an army should be put to flight (assuming he had not already expired through exhaustion or suffocation).

The composition of armies also changed. This was brought about by necessity rather than choice, the baronial rebellions encouraging monarchs to place a greater reliance on paid troops than on service through feudal obligation. Knights and professional men-at-arms, fighting mounted or on foot, were the elite of an army, but the lower classes grew in importance – particularly the archers, who could decimate heavy cavalry at a distance. And the cost of equipping and employing an archer was a tiny fraction of what was required to put his social superiors into the field.

Despite developments in weaponry and armour, tactics

remained very basic. King Robert I of Scotland ('The Bruce') did take the trouble to visit prospective fields of battle, e.g. Loudoun Hill (1307) and Bannockburn (1314), with a view to using natural features of the landscape. More often than not, however, medieval armies merely brayed, lowered their heads and charged at one another.

Before this happened, there were certain preliminaries to be observed. There might be a gentlemanly agreement to fight at an appointed time and place. So, Robert I (not playing with a straight bat) was able to get the lie of the land at Loudoun Hill because his foe had offered to give battle there. Again, there might be a preliminary exchange of heralds with a view to discussion of peace terms although, more often than not, the participants were merely going through the motions. Sometimes, as at Bannockburn, a battle would be preceded by single combat or, on other occasions, jousting. After a battle, persons of high rank were willingly given quarter, albeit owing to their ransom value. This was, after all, the Age of Chivalry.

The Anarchy

7. The Standard, 22 August 1138

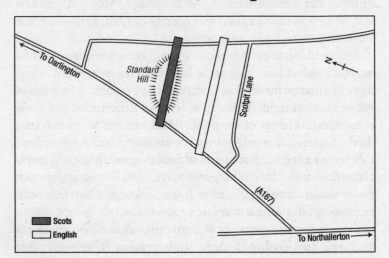

On the death of Henry I in 1135, the English crown was seized by his nephew, Stephen of Bois, who became King Stephen I. Henry's daughter, Matilda, was Henry's legitimate heir and, with the active support of her uncle, King David I of Scotland, she pursued her claim.

Early in 1138, David crossed the border and began terrorizing the northern counties of England. Preoccupied with a baronial rebellion, Stephen was in no position to deal with the problem, and it was left to Archbishop Thurstan of York, who also held the office of Lord Lieutenant of the North, to coordinate resistance. While an army was assembled, Bernard de Balliol, Bearer of the King's Commission, was sent to parlay with the Scots. The earldom of Northumbria was offered to David's son, Prince Henry, as an inducement to the Scots to withdraw, but David refused.

Some 10,000 men had gathered at York. Under the leadership of William le Cros, Earl of Albermarle, they marched to Thirsk and then to Northallerton and beyond, to an area of gently rising ground to the north of the town. Here, they awaited David's army, advancing from the neighbourhood of the River Tees.

At dawn on 22 August, the English raised their standard, from which the battle takes its name. A curious contraption, it consisted of a ship's mast fixed to a cart. On top of the mast, a consecrated wafer was enclosed in a pyx; from cross-pieces nailed to the lower mast hung the banners of St John of Beverley, St Peter of York, St Wilfred of Ripon, and probably that of St Cuthbert of Durham. Thus, the standard served a dual purpose: as a rallying point for the English army and to symbolize the crusading nature of the enterprise. Detailed accounts of the troop formations vary, but it is likely that archers formed the English front line, with spearmen directly behind and unmounted knights in the rear.

David's army, some 12,000 strong, arrived in the early morning and deployed along high ground to the north of the English positions. Lightly armed Galwegians (men of Galway) formed the front line; behind them was Prince Henry, with a mix of lowland English archers and Norman cavalry; a third line comprised foot soldiers from Lothian; King David occupied the rear, with a reserve of infantry and cavalry.

The battle opened with a charge by the Galwegians. They had insisted on leading the attack and now they paid dearly for the privilege. The English lines withstood the onslaught and the English archers discharged volleys of arrows into their ranks. Resulting casualties included the chieftains Ulgeric and Dunewald.

As the now leaderless Galwegians wavered, Prince Henry tried to turn the tide by leading a charge through the English lines. Unsupported by the men of Lothian, his party was surrounded. Only with difficulty did the prince manage to extricate himself. Now in full retreat, the Galwegians recoiled upon their own lines, creating widespread confusion and panic. Within two hours of the start of the battle, most of the Scots were in full flight, both King David and Prince Henry making good their escape.

There was no sustained pursuit, although stragglers and the wounded were shown no mercy. Those who fell were buried in an area to the rear of the English lines, subsequently known as The Scots Pits. The English army failed to follow up its success and immediately disbanded, leaving the border counties undefended, thus enabling the Scots to continue to raid at will.

The battlefield today
The battlefield is on the A167, three miles to the north of Northallerton (OS Landranger 99 3697). There is a roadside monument to the battle, with an interpretation panel, and a lay-by for parking. Scotpit Lane, marking the site of the burial pits, although readily identifiable, is now a mass of tangled undergrowth.

Further reading
Jim Bradbury, *Stephen and Matilda: The Civil War of 1139–53* (History Press, 2005).

8. Lincoln, 2 February 1141

During the civil war of King Stephen's reign – a period of English history known as 'The Anarchy' – a great deal of the fighting between Stephen's supporters and those of Matilda, daughter of Henry I, consisted of sieges and indecisive skirmishes. An important gain for Matilda was the seizure of Lincoln Castle by earls Ranulf of Chester and William de Roumare, in 1140. At the beginning of 1141, Stephen arrived with an army to take control of the prosperous town of Lincoln and lay siege to the castle.

Soon after, Ranulf contrived to slip away to raise a relief force. He appealed to the Earl of Gloucester – his

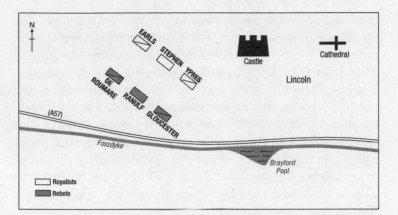

father-in-law and Matilda's half-brother – whose followers, together with a band of knights disinherited by Stephen and a contingent of Welsh mercenaries, created an army of over 1,000 men. By 1 February, they were approaching Lincoln.

Their appearance was a surprise to Stephen, and the fording points of Fossdyke were inadequately guarded, enabling the earls to effect a crossing. Faced with a choice of withstanding a siege or making a stand, Stephen chose to fight, descending the following morning to meet the opposition via Lincoln's West Gate. He arrayed his men, also numbering around 1,000, in three divisions. On the left was the Flemish cavalry of William Ypres; in the middle were Stephen's men-at-arms and locally raised foot soldiers; on the right were several earls with their mounted knights.

The precise rebel deployment is unclear, but the cavalry division of the Earl of Gloucester probably occupied the right wing with the disinherited knights under de Roumare on the left and the infantry, including dismounted knights, commanded by Ranulf in the centre. The Welsh, lightly armed, were deployed on the flanks.

Stephen's earls expected the battle to open with a round of preliminary jousting, and were shocked when de Roumare's knights attacked and immediately set to fighting at sword point. Thoroughly discomfited, the earls were put to flight, enabling de Roumare to turn in on Stephen's centre. As the earls galloped away to the north, Ypres charged, scattering the Welsh on the rebel right flank, before coming to grips with Gloucester's cavalry. With the help of Ranulf's infantry, however, Ypres was checked. Thus deprived of its cavalry support, Stephen's infantry division was now surrounded as rebel cavalry and infantry closed in. The king himself fought bravely, wielding a two-handed battle-axe and, when this broke, a sword. He was eventually captured by a knight, William de Chesney, after being felled by a stone – perhaps a slingshot from one of the lightly armed Welshmen.

Stephen was taken to Bristol Castle and imprisoned. Following the capture of Robert of Gloucester by Stephen's supporters in September 1141, the two men were exchanged. The civil war would continue for thirteen more years.

The battlefield today
Lincoln Castle is open to the public, enabling one to look out over the field of battle, West Common, adjoining the A57 (OS Landranger 121 9671).

Further reading
Rupert Matthews, *The Siege of Lincoln: 1141* **(Bretwalda Books, 2013).**

Simon de Montfort's Rebellion

9. Lewes, 14 May 1264

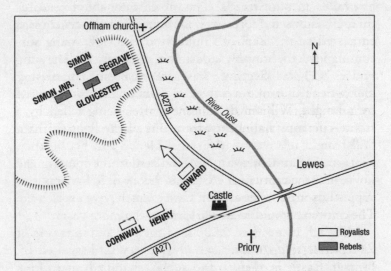

King Henry III was regarded by many as an incompetent wastrel. One of his most outspoken critics was his own brother-in-law, Simon de Montfort, Earl of Leicester, who emerged as leader of a powerful group of disaffected barons who resented Henry's contempt for the principles of government as enshrined in Magna Carta.

By the spring of 1264, both factions had amassed armies. On 11 May 1264, Henry and his son, Prince Edward, arrived at Lewes, following a march across The Weald to gather support. Determined to bring Henry to battle, Simon and the rebel barons marched out from London in pursuit, making camp eight miles from Lewes, at Fletching.

In the early morning of 14 May, the rebel barons quitted their camp. Morale was high but their army, 5,000 strong, was outnumbered by two to one – and with only 600 cavalry, it was important for Simon to seek out an advantageous position. He found it in Offham Hill, which overlooked Lewes from a height of some 400 feet. On its broad plateau, Simon deployed his troops with confidence, aided by intelligence gleaned from an enemy lookout who had fallen into his hands. The rebels were able to muster three divisions and a reserve. Command of the centre was entrusted to the Earl of Gloucester; the right wing was commanded by Simon's eldest son, Henry; the left wing under Nicholas Segrave was the weakest, comprising inexperienced men recruited in London. Simon himself commanded the reserve.

The king must have been aware of the activity on Offham Hill from a relatively early stage. Henry and his brother, Richard, Earl of Cornwall, were billeted to the south of the town, in the vicinity of the Cluniac Priory of St Pancras, but Prince Edward was located in Lewes Castle, from which the rebel movements could be observed.

Although Henry had 9,000 foot soldiers and in excess of 1,000 cavalry, his numerical advantage was dissipated by the fact that Prince Edward took the field in advance of his father. Henry occupied the centre, with the Earl of Cornwall to his left. Prince Edward was on the right wing. Advancing from Lewes Castle, he led a cavalry assault on Offham Hill as his father and uncle, emerging from the town, were deploying their troops on rising ground to the north of the present-day jail.

Edward directed his cavalry towards Segrave's Londoners, who broke and fled towards Offham, with Edward in hot pursuit. Henry and Cornwall were left with no option but to follow up this success by crossing Landport Bottom and labouring up Offham Hill to close with the rebel centre and right wing. As they approached the plateau, Gloucester and Henry de Montfort launched their own charges. Cornwall's men were scattered almost immediately, but the king's division held until it was finally overcome when Simon committed his reserves.

The royal army fell back towards Lewes, seeking refuge

in the castle and the priory. Cut off from his command and unable to reach the town, Cornwall was reduced to barricading himself inside a windmill. When Prince Edward returned to the battlefield, sporadic fighting was still taking place, but it was clear that the battle was lost. He sought out the king in the priory and it was arranged that they would seek an accommodation with the rebel barons.

An agreement, known as the 'Mise of Lewes', provided for further talks about the introduction of a progressive form of government, while Prince Edward was to be held hostage to guarantee the king's participation. In fact, Simon de Montfort's victory at Lewes was a turning point in English history, for it enabled him to convene what would be the very first elected Parliament.

The battlefield today
Landport Bottom is to the north-west of Lewes (OS Landranger 198 3911) and is accessible via public footpaths. Car parking is available in the town. Lewes Castle is open to the public and a battlefield monument can be found in the recreation area adjacent to the Cluniac Priory of St Pancras.

Further reading
John Sadler, *The Second Barons' War: Simon De Montfort and the Battles of Lewes and Evesham* **(Pen & Sword, 2008).**

10. Evesham, 4 August 1265

Simon de Montfort's first faltering steps towards the introduction of a rudimentary form of representative government, following his victory at the Battle of Lewes, were not to everyone's liking. A number of barons, including his old ally, the Earl of Gloucester, grew resentful of his power; his sons were rumoured to be amassing personal fortunes, and efforts were being made to raise a French army to come to the aid of King Henry III.

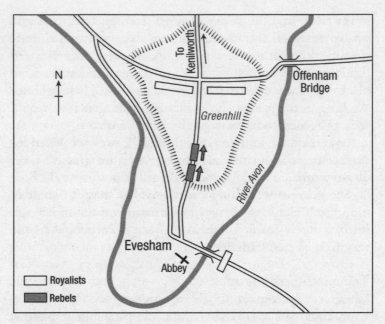

Early in 1265, Simon's erstwhile supporter, the Earl of Gloucester, withdrew to the Welsh Marches, where he joined forces with Roger Mortimer, with a view to plotting Simon's downfall. Simon and his supporters marched west, taking with them King Henry and Henry's son, Prince Edward. On 28 May 1265, at Hereford, Edward managed to slip his leash and joined the opposition. There followed several weeks of manoeuvring as both sides built up their strength, Simon securing the services of 5,000 spearmen from Llewellyn ap Gruffyd in Wales.

Soon, the most pressing problem facing Simon was how to cross the River Severn. He found his passage blocked at every turn and at the end of July, he was still stranded in Hereford. His plan was to link up with his son, Simon junior, who was at Kenilworth Castle with his own army. However, in a bold move, Edward made a lightning attack on Kenilworth and succeeded in disabling the younger Simon's forces. In Edward's absence, the elder Simon did at least manage to break out, crossing the Severn on 2 August to the south of Worcester, at Kempsey. The next day, he marched on to Evesham, arriving in the early hours of 4 August.

Simon has been criticized for his choice of campsite, but the town, bounded on three sides by the River Avon, seemed to offer good natural defences. Simon did not anticipate Edward's night march which brought him to Evesham the following morning, but his real mistake lay in not keeping open the back door: the only bridge over the river at nearby Bengeworth.

The rebels made a comparatively late start to the day. The captive Henry, playing for time, persuaded Simon to let him attend mass in Evesham Abbey. A lookout posted on the abbey tower had reported troops advancing towards the town, but identification proved difficult as Edward carried rebel banners taken at Kenilworth, and Simon could well have been expecting Simon junior. By the time the situation became clear, Edward had occupied high ground at Greenhill to the north, while a cavalry detachment under Roger Mortimer held the bridge. Simon took the decision to break out, beginning his march towards Greenhill at around 9.00 a.m.

The force facing him was split into two divisions: Prince Edward to his right and Simon's old ally, Gloucester, to his left. Simon planned to advance in a single column, using his cavalry in the vanguard to punch a hole in the centre, following through with his English infantry and Welsh spearmen. Somewhere in their midst was King Henry, cunningly clad in rebel colours.

Simon's spearhead drove forward into the enemy front lines, which buckled under the pressure, but the rear lines held firm. Although the rebels were outnumbered (6,000 men against Edward's 10,000), they should have had the weight to break through but, at this crucial moment, the Welshmen lost heart and retreated in disorder. Deprived of this support, Simon was doomed.

The enemy right and left wings closed in around those rebels who stood their ground, and the ensuing action was described by the Earl of Gloucester as 'murder'. Even though Simon and his remaining supporters fought fiercely, they were overcome by sheer weight of numbers. Much of the fighting took place during a thunderstorm and, according to tradition, when the storm was at its height and the battlefield swathed in darkness, Simon de Montfort fell.

The battle had lasted two hours. About 2,500 rebels were killed, including one of Simon's sons, Henry. Another son, Guy, survived although severely wounded. Many corpses were dismembered. It is said that Roger Mortimer made his wife a gift of Simon's head and genitals, although Henry, who had managed to escape serious injury, did permit the abbey's Franciscan monks to give the mutilated torso a Christian burial.

Prince Edward's victory at Evesham re-established the authority of the crown and established his own reputation as a commander in the field. The lessons he had learned would stand him in good stead when he succeeded to the throne as King Edward I, 'hammer of the Scots'.

The battlefield today

The battlefield is at Greenhill, to the north of Evesham's town centre (OS Landranger 150 0345). The Almonry Museum in Vine Street houses a model of the battle and is a good starting point for a visit. Opposite is Abbey Park, with a memorial marking the approximate spot of Simon de Montfort's burial. St Lawrence's Church has a stained-glass window commemorating the battle. Towards the top of Greenhill, a track to the right ('Blaneys Lane'), leads to Offenham ferry, where many of the fleeing Welshmen were cut down as they tried to cross the river via a long-vanished crossing. Almost opposite, a road to the left, The Squires, gives access to a parking area and a footpath leading to Leicester Tower, erected in memory of Simon de Montfort

– and, a little further on, to a battlefield monument. The main features of the battlefield are included within a short battlefield trail (with battlefield information panels en route) available via the Simon de Montfort website. This is a battlefield that ranks high on any 'must visit' list.

Further reading
John Sadler, *The Second Barons' War: Simon De Montfort and the Battles of Lewes and Evesham* (Pen & Sword, 2008).

Wars of Scottish Independence

11. Stirling Bridge, 11 September 1297

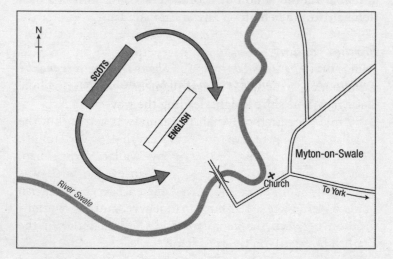

In 1296, King Edward I declared himself King of Scotland and installed a governor, the Earl of Surrey. Widespread dissatisfaction culminated in a revolt. The most conspicuous leaders were Andrew Moray in the north and William Wallace in the south. In response, from his base at Berwick, Surrey led an army northwards.

When Wallace received the news that Surrey was on the march, he and Moray descended on Stirling. Wallace was familiar with the local topography and secured the high ground above Cambuskenneth, overlooking the narrow bridge spanning the River Forth, which Surrey would have to cross in order to reach him.

Surrey reached Stirling on 10 September. The next morning, an attempt was made to parlay. Surrey would have preferred a peaceful resolution, if only because he was concerned about the strength of Wallace's position, but Wallace remained obdurate. In fact, Wallace commanded only around 2,300 men – 2,000 foot soldiers and 300 light cavalry – as opposed to Surrey's 8,000 infantry and 1,000 heavy horse.

Surrey received sound advice from a friendly Scot, Sir Richard Lundin, who spoke of an alternative fording point downstream, where up to sixty men at a time could cross. However, Hugh Cressingham, the administration's treasurer in Scotland, persuaded Surrey to waste no time in giving battle. Accordingly, the English began filing over the wooden structure, Cressingham and Sir Marmaduke Twenge, a Yorkshire knight, leading the way.

By mid-morning, only half the army was across, but the impulsive Twenge ordered the heavy cavalry forward uphill. The advance was met resolutely by Wallace's spearmen. Furthermore, Twenge failed to keep an eye on what was happening behind him, which enabled a party of Scottish horse to complete a flanking manoeuvre, cutting communication between the vanguard and the remainder of the English force still on the west bank.

With the enemy's line of retreat blocked, Wallace ordered his men to charge down from the high ground, creating confusion in the English ranks. The Scottish horse between the bridge and the English rear joined in the mêlée – but so narrow was the bridge that insufficient numbers of men could be moved across in time to make a difference. At some point, the bridge collapsed under the strain. Those who did attain the east bank did not have the space to form up and simply added to the confusion. The slaughter among the English was great as they turned tail and ran in search of safety. Many were driven into the river. By making use of the ford that Surrey had rejected, the Scots were able to engage in a merciless pursuit.

English casualties could be counted by the thousand. Remarkably, Sir Marmaduke Twenge managed to fight his way back to the bridge and effect his escape. Hugh Cressingham, who had accompanied Twenge in the van, was killed. Allegedly, his skin was used to make a sword belt for Wallace. On the

Scottish side, casualties were light, although they did include Moray. Twenge made his way to Stirling Castle, where he was eventually captured by Wallace, but the majority of English soldiers fled to Berwick and beyond – leaving Scotland, for the time being at least, firmly in the hands of the Scots.

The battlefield today

The bridge of the battle probably lay about sixty yards upstream of Stirling's surviving medieval bridge (OS Landranger 57 7994). Almost all of the battlefield area has been built over. The William Wallace Monument (with car park) on Hillfoots Road adorns Abbey Craig, the vantage point from which Wallace watched the approach of the English army. The monument's visitor centre has an audio-visual presentation of the battle, while a panoramic view of the battlefield can be obtained from the top. (A complementary visit to Stirling Castle, on Castle Esplanade in the centre of Stirling, is also appropriate.)

Further reading

Peter Armstrong and Graham Turner, *Stirling Bridge and Falkirk 1297–98: William Wallace's Rebellion* (Osprey Publishing, 2003).

12. 1st Falkirk, 22 July 1298

In the summer of 1298, Edward I set about bringing the rebellious Scots, led by William Wallace, to heel. Having mustered a substantial force of 2,500 heavy cavalry and up to 15,000 infantry, he took personal charge and crossed the border in early July. Wallace was eventually located at Falkirk and, on the morning of 22 July, the two armies met.

The strength of Wallace's army is unknown, but it is certain that the Scots were heavily outnumbered. They were drawn up to the south of Falkirk, on the southern slopes of Callendar Wood, the pikemen assuming schiltron

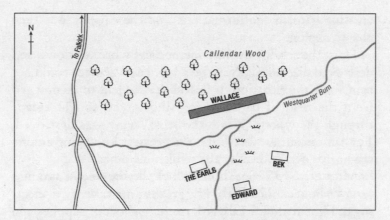

formations. Archers were deployed between the schiltrons, while cavalry under John Comyn occupied the rear. Topographically, the position was far inferior to that of Stirling Bridge the previous year, but some protection was afforded by a morass, with the addition of a row of long stakes driven into the ground.

The English advanced in three divisions: the first, comprising cavalry, was led by the Earl Marshall and the Earls of Hereford and Lincoln; the second, also of cavalry, was led by Anthony Bek, Bishop of Durham; the third, in the rear, comprising cavalry and infantry was led by Edward. In order to avoid boggy ground before them, the earls moved to their left, Bek to his right. The defensive stakes were trampled down as the heavy horse bore down upon each wing. Comyn, taking a pessimistic view of his own chances in the face of such opposition, led his light cavalry from the field almost immediately.

The Scottish archers proved easy targets for the English horse, but not so the pikemen. Even though they were left isolated, the schiltrons could not be broken by heavy horse alone. They held firm, the English horse failing in attempts to break up the circles or ride the defenders down. It proved necessary for Edward to bring up his own infantry, volleys of arrows from his bowmen supported by sling-shot creating gaps in the formations that the cavalry was then able to exploit.

Thus, the schiltrons were methodically broken down and destroyed piecemeal. Even the presence of Wallace could not transform the situation. It is said that he had to be dragged from the field of battle to join those who sought escape through the woods. While the Scots' army was destroyed, English casualties were light, the greatest loss being among the horses despatched by the schiltrons' pikes.

After Edward's success at Falkirk, Wallace ceased to be a force to be reckoned with. His greatest mistake lay in electing to fight at all, for Edward, running short of supplies and with mutiny breaking out in the ranks of his army, had been on the verge of abandoning the campaign. Wallace remained at large until 1305 when he was handed over to the English to suffer a barbarous execution.

The battlefield today

Callendar Wood is to the west of Falkirk, off the A803, Callendar Road (OS Landranger 65 9078). Callendar House, with car parking, is a useful starting point for a site visit. A battlefield memorial cairn is located within the grounds. An alternative location proposed for the battle is a little to the north, in the present-day Falkirk suburb of Grahamston (OS Landranger 64 8880).

Further reading

Peter Armstrong and Graham Turner, *Stirling Bridge and Falkirk 1297–98: William Wallace's Rebellion* (Osprey Publishing, 2003).

13. Loudoun Hill, 10 May 1307

The prestige of William Wallace was destroyed by his defeat at Falkirk and, that same year (1298), Robert Bruce became Guardian of Scotland. In 1306, he was crowned

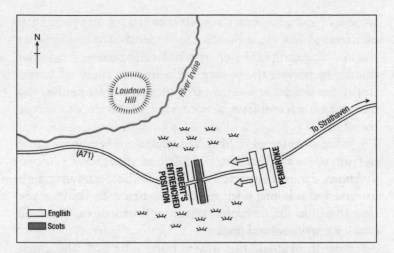

king, becoming Robert I. Militarily, he did not impress and spent months in hiding, suffering a number of defeats by the English and those loyal to Edward I. During his time as a fugitive, he benefited from his celebrated experience of watching a spider succeed in spinning a web against all the odds. Determined to emulate the arachnid, he reappeared in Ayrshire early in 1307 and set about gathering support.

At the head of a poorly equipped force of some 600 men, Robert harassed the English army commanded by Aymer de Valence, Earl of Pembroke, through a concerted guerrilla campaign. Pembroke sent him a message taunting him with cowardice and offering to give battle on 10 May at Loudoun Hill, to the east of Kilmarnock. Robert accepted.

The pair had met in open battle before, at Methven, where the Scots were speedily routed. This time, Robert had ample opportunity to survey the ground. The road from the north, the most likely line of Pembroke's approach, wound over open meadows that would facilitate the deployment of heavy cavalry. At some distance from the road, on either side, were two tracts of marshland that would, at least, hamper flank attacks. To limit the strength of a frontal assault, a line of three trenches was dug from the marshes across the firm ground – a gap being left in the middle to permit the passage of a limited body of horse. The Scots would be able to position themselves behind the forward trench and then, if necessary, withdraw to the rear trenches.

On the morning of 10 May, as anticipated, Pembroke came in from the north, his army of 3,000 men advancing in two divisions. He had expected the Scots to be occupying high ground and was surprised to see them below the hill, on the flat. It would be a simple matter to finish them. A single cavalry charge should do it.

Given the signal, the heavy horse charged, the earth trembling at the pounding of hooves. Perhaps Pembroke expected Robert's nerve to break. If so, then he was disappointed, for the Scottish spearmen stood firm. Finally, the two sides locked horns. Both men and horses became the target as the Scots sought to check the onslaught. The ditches, too wide for the horses to jump, prohibited any outflanking manoeuvre. The defensive line held and the attack faltered. Eagerly, Robert grasped at the opportunity to go on to the offensive.

It was a brave – some might say foolhardy – move for foot soldiers to attack heavy cavalry, but the gamble paid off. The van was completely overcome and the rear division fled without striking a blow. Despite his utmost endeavours to rally his troops, Pembroke was driven from the field. At least 100 English lost their lives. Casualties among the Scots were low, but their weakness necessarily limited the speed and intensity of the pursuit that followed their stunning victory.

The battle transformed Robert's situation, turning him from a fugitive into a formidable foe, but the greatest fillip to his cause was an event over which he had no control: the death of King Edward I.

The battlefield today

Loudoun Hill is off the A71, three miles to the east of Darvell (OS Landranger 71 6037). Although the precise location of the battle is unknown, it is generally accepted that the action occurred to the south of the River Irvine. Quarrying has disfigured the local landscape, but the development of a wildlife park has facilitated exploration. Make an initial visit to the Loudoun Hill Visitor Centre, adjacent to the Loudoun Hill Inn on the A71. Alternatively, take the minor road to Drumboy and Meadowfoot and you will arrive at a car park on your left. There is a modest monument to the battle, but the area is dominated by the William Wallace Arch memorial, lying in the shadow of the hill, where Wallace supposedly enjoyed an earlier victory over the English.

Further reading

Chris Brown, *The Scottish Wars of Independence* **(History Press, 2006).**

14. Bannockburn, 23/24 June 1314

The timely death of Edward I in July 1307 provided Robert I of Scotland with the leeway he needed to consolidate his position. It took him seven years to conquer the kingdom he claimed as his own, and the late English king's son, the weak, vacillating Edward II, allowed him the opportunity to do it.

As time passed, Edward's unpopularity among his own subjects increased until he became convinced that his salvation lay in bringing the Scots to book. Accordingly, on 17 June 1314, at Wark, he mustered an army 20,000 strong. The primary objective was the relief of Stirling Castle, still in English hands, and under nominal siege for many months. Thus, the site of any battle would be fixed in the vicinity of Stirling, leaving Robert free to choose his ground as at Loudoun Hill, seven years earlier.

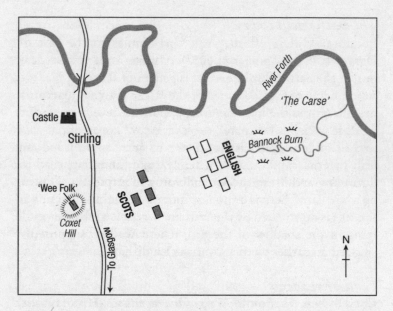

The governor of Stirling Castle had agreed to surrender if relief had not arrived by 24 June 1314. With his ponderous army, accompanied by a substantial baggage train, Edward had his work cut out to reach it within a week. The weather was hot and the English must have been weary as the castle finally hove into view on 23 June.

Although he commanded only about 7,000 men, Bruce, as at Loudoun Hill, had the luxury of choosing his ground. He drew up his army at The Borestone – literally, a bored stone that held his standard – about two miles to the south of the castle, roughly on the present-day A872. His front was protected by man-made pits, his right flank by high ground (Gillies Hill and Coxet Hill) and his left flank by marshland.

As Edward approached Bruce's position, he sent in his vanguard, commanded by the Earls of Hereford and Gloucester, to attack. A second contingent, led by Sir Robert Clifford and Sir Henry Beaumont, were despatched to the right, on a course that would take them towards boggy ground known as The Carse.

There now occurred the famous episode in which Hereford's nephew, Sir Henry de Bohun, charged forward from the English van to meet Robert in single combat. The odds appeared to be in de Bohun's favour, armed as he was with a lance against Robert's battle-axe. In the heat of the moment, however, de Bohun's aim went awry and Robert shattered his skull with a single blow. Nevertheless, the English van surged forward, only to falter when it reached the defensive pits. After a fierce fight, the English were forced to withdraw, the Scots holding their position. Taking this as a cue to advance, the Scots put the English column to flight. Clifford and Beaumont were repulsed likewise and also retreated. Edward decided that he needed to review the situation and gave orders to pitch camp on The Carse, thus ending the first act of the English tragedy.

The baggage train had fallen behind and the English passed but a poor night, wallowing in the mud. At daybreak on 24 June, the Scots, still ahead of the game, advanced upon the English camp. Their deployment took the form of four divisions. Edward Bruce occupied the right wing, with Sir James Douglas on the left and the Earl of Moray in the centre. Robert, commanding a fourth division, stood to the rear, with the light cavalry of Sir Robert Keith also uncommitted. Edward seems to have been taken by surprise, and the English hurried to make themselves ready. Crammed together, they were unable to deploy effectively, standing their ground in several massed divisions, the Earl of Gloucester in the van and Edward in the rear.

On the previous day, the English heavy horse had come to grief against Robert's entrenched positions. Now they faced the formidable schiltrons, which they found to be just as impenetrable. Gloucester was among the first to be killed. Time and again, the cavalry hurled themselves at the sea of Scottish pikes and, on each occasion, were beaten back. At length, Edward introduced his archers on the Scottish left, but they were scattered by a charge of the Scottish light horse.

When it became clear that the unthinkable had happened and the day was lost, individuals and then small groups in the rear began to slip away, creating space for the Scots to push further forward. Soon, Edward himself was at risk and his bodyguard, perceiving that the tide of battle had turned against them, forced him to pull back. As they witnessed the Royal Standard disappearing, his demoralized troops saw what they thought were Scottish reinforcements about to enter the fray. In fact, this was a rag-tag group of itinerants referred to as the 'wee folk' and in some manner attached to Robert's army. On their own initiative, they came hurtling down from Coxet Hill. The unexpected sight, coupled with that of their king in flight, was enough to create panic in the English lines. They scattered in all directions, hotly pursued by the enemy.

Miraculously, Edward evaded Robert's clutches. Refused entry to Stirling Castle, he made his way to Dunbar, from where he took a small boat to Berwick. Much of his army was not so fortunate, sustaining very heavy casualties, although the Scottish pursuit was hampered by the victors' interest in Edward's abandoned baggage train, valued at roughly £200,000.

Robert had won a great victory for Scottish nationalism, but his subsequent attempts to reach an understanding with Edward fell on deaf ears. There followed years of devastating raids by the Scots, striking deep into the northern shires of England, laying waste tracts of Northumberland, County Durham and Yorkshire.

The battlefield today

The battlefield lies off the A872, two miles to the south of Stirling (OS Landranger 57 7990). Exit the M80/M9 at Junction 9. The National Trust for Scotland's new Visitor Centre is the focal point for any visit. The value of the fifty-eight-acre site is largely symbolic, owing to the fact that the main battle may have taken place to the north-east on land engulfed by warehousing and distribution development. Yet, the landscaped grounds do include the Borestone (see above) and Pilkington Jackson's famous bronze statue of Robert I, unveiled in 1964. Coxet Hill, to the rear of which the 'wee folk' were hidden, is now covered with housing. The Bannock burn runs to the south of the heritage centre.

Further reading
Aryeh Nusbacher, *The Battle of Bannockburn 1314* **(History Press, 2000).**

The Earl of Lancaster's Rebellion

15. Myton, 20 September 1319

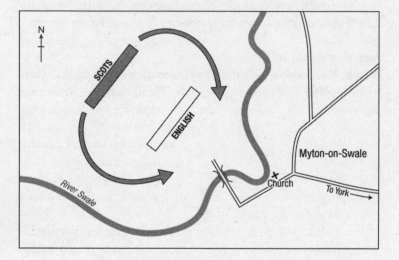

In 1318, the Scots captured Berwick-upon-Tweed, an important border stronghold on the east coast. In August of the following year, Edward II, having recovered from his disastrous campaign of 1314, marched north and laid siege to the town.

By way of an attempt to raise the siege, the Earl of Moray and Lord James Douglas led a diversionary raid across the border, creating havoc as far south as Yorkshire. Furthermore, Edward's queen, Eleanor, was staying in York, and the Scots hoped to take her captive. She was removed to Nottingham while William Melton, Archbishop of York, assembled an army to put the invaders to flight. In this task, he was aided by John Hotham, Bishop of Ely, and Sir Nicholas Fleming, the Mayor of York. The scratch English force included citizens of York, noblemen, peasants, beggars and a good many monks and priests, but hardly any experienced fighting men.

They set off on the morning of 20 September 1319, following the River Ouse, until they reached Myton-on-Swale, near Boroughbridge, where they knew Douglas and Moray were camped. The plan was to catch the Scots unawares, but in this they failed. A narrow bridge spanned the River Swale at Myton and the English, having proceeded along the east bank, were enticed across to the opposite bank where the Scots were waiting for them.

It is said that the Scots set fire to three haystacks, thus blinding the English with smoke. Then, dividing into two separate wings, they enveloped the hapless expedition, cutting off the line of retreat across the bridge. There appears to have been little in the way of organized resistance among the English, enabling the Scots to indulge in an orgy of killing. The waters of the Swale, into which the panic-stricken English threw themselves in their frantic efforts to escape, also accounted for many lives.

It is difficult to estimate the size of the armies involved – perhaps in the region of 10,000 apiece – but Scottish losses would have been light, while between 2,000 and 4,000 English, including Fleming, died. Such was the slaughter among the monks and clergy that the victors referred to the battle as 'The Chapter of Myton' and 'The White Battle'.

Douglas and Moray certainly achieved their major objective in that the siege of Berwick was raised, while relations between Edward and one of England's most powerful barons, the Earl of Lancaster, already strained, were stretched to breaking point by the latter's insistence on abandoning the siege and returning home.

The battlefield today

Myton-on-Swale is three miles to the east of Boroughbridge (OS Landranger 99 4366). The road terminates in the village and roadside parking is available by the Church of St Mary. At the end of the road, a track branches off to the right. This leads to an iron footbridge spanning the River

Swale. A plaque by the bridge provides information about the battle. The medieval bridge of the battle was about 200 yards downstream.

Further reading
Graham Bell, *Robert the Bruce's Forgotten Victory: The Battle of Byland 1322* **(Tempus, 2005).**

16. Boroughbridge, 16 March 1322

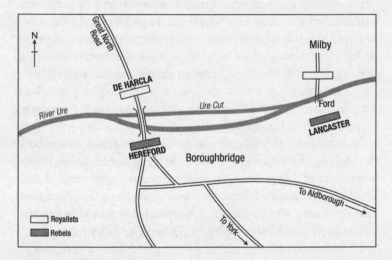

The working relationship between Edward II and the barons, always threatened by baronial desires to limit the power of the monarchy, finally broke down in 1321, through the excesses of the king's current favourite, Hugh Despenser. Resistance to Edward was led by the influential Earl of Lancaster, who attracted the support of the similarly powerful Earl of Hereford, Hugh Audley the Younger and Sir Roger Clifford.

As luck would have it, the mass support which Lancaster and his adherents had hoped to attract failed to materialize. By the middle of March 1322, with only a modest force at their command, they had left Lancaster's own stronghold, Pontefract Castle, and were on their way north to seek more help in Scotland. An army raised by the king was on their trail, but on 16 March they reached Boroughbridge, where they planned to rest in safety until the next day.

Lancaster's scouting arrangements must have left much to be desired, for, after his army had begun to settle in, he learned that the bridge over the River Ure at the north end of the town was already in Royalist hands. This had come about through the intervention of the Warden of Carlisle and the Western Marches, Sir Andrew de Harcla, who had been instructed to muster northern manpower on behalf of the king. Learning of Lancaster's progress towards Boroughbridge, de Harcla made a detour to reach the town ahead of him.

Faced with the dread prospect of being caught between de Harcla and the main Royalist army advancing from the south, the rebels were compelled to try to take the bridge. De Harcla's force of up to 4,000 men dwarfed Lancaster's 1,000-strong army, and the bridge would not be an easy objective. A narrow, wooden structure, it spanned sixty yards of water, and de Harcla deployed his men well: knights and men-at-arms before the bridge, with archers to the rear, on higher ground.

At first, Lancaster tried to win over de Harcla, reminding him of past favours – de Harcla had received his knighthood from the earl – but de Harcla would have none if it and, albeit late in the day, battle commenced. At first, the contest was limited to volleys of arrows which the archers of each side projected across the river. While this may have suited de Harcla, the rebel barons could not afford to allow themselves to be pinned down. In an effort to break the deadlock, therefore, the Earl of Hereford led a charge on the bridge while Lancaster, with a party of horse, tried to outflank the Royalists by crossing at a ford a little downstream, at Milby.

To Lancaster's dismay, he arrived at the ford to find it

well defended by more archers who resisted all his attempts to cross over. After suffering heavy losses, he was forced to retire. At the bridge, Hereford made good progress before allegedly meeting his end at the hands of a Welsh spearman who, having climbed beneath the bridge, disembowelled the fearless earl with an upwards thrust of his spear – a story that may owe something to the tale of the Norwegian who met a similar end at Stamford Bridge (1066). The rebel offensive faltered. When Roger Clifford was felled by an arrow, it broke down entirely, the rebels withdrawing in disorder.

In the knowledge that the battle was lost, Lancaster concluded a temporary truce with de Harcla, by which he agreed to surrender the following morning, or suffer the consequences. This led to the extraordinary situation of the vanquished retiring into Boroughbridge to sleep soundly while the victors remained on stand-by throughout the night, guarding the bridge and the ford. It may have been that de Harcla, mindful of his debt to Lancaster, wanted to provide him with an opportunity to slip away, but although many rebels did melt into the countryside, the earl remained. Dawn heralded the arrival of Sir Simon Ward, High Sheriff of Yorkshire, with royal reinforcements, and de Harcla was compelled to enter the town.

Lancaster tried to claim sanctuary in a chapel that stood in St James's Square. Dragged from the altar, he was stripped of his armour and forced to wear servant's apparel. Later, he was shipped to York, where he was pelted with mud by the citizens, the same folk who would gladly have adorned him with garlands had his revolt been successful. On 22 March 1322, he was beheaded on a hill close to his own Pontefract Castle.

The royal victory did nothing to quell dissatisfaction among Edward's subjects, and in 1327 he suffered the indignity of being deposed by his wife, Isabella, and her lover, Roger Mortimer.

The battlefield today

Boroughbridge is located on the B6265, off the A1, seventeen miles to the west of York. Parking is available at the picnic site by the bridge on the north bank of the river (OS Landranger 99 3967). A riverside path leads to Milby Cut, site of the ford. A blue plaque on the bridge commemorates the battle and a commemorative cross is located in nearby Aldborough.

Further reading

William Grainge, *The Battles and Battlefields of Yorkshire from the Earliest Times to the End of the Great Civil War* **(British Library Historical Print Editions, 2011).**

BAD MEDICINE

When the future Henry V was wounded in the face by an arrow at Shrewsbury (1403), he received the best medical attention available at the time. Royal physician, John Bradmore, removed the arrow's wooden shaft and widened the entry hole by using carefully constructed wedges. Then he inserted a specially crafted pair of tongs into the arrowhead. The tongs screwed apart until they gripped the head, allowing it to be extracted. The patient was so impressed that he arranged for surgeons to accompany him on his Agincourt campaign.

In the wake of Barnet (1471) Gerhard von Wesel, a Hanse merchant visiting London, spoke of wounded survivors as being hurt mostly in the lower portion of the body and in the face. In other words their armour had protected them from fatal wounds, enabling them to emerge with their lives, but with disfiguring injuries, such as the loss of their noses, which, according to von Wesel, kept them indoors.

'Gentlemen' always stood the best chance of recovery. The Duke of Exeter, stripped and left for dead at Barnet, lay badly wounded throughout much of the day. Eventually, he was discovered and taken to the nearby house of one of his servants, where he received medical attention and recovered sufficiently to enable him to survive four years' incarceration in the Tower of London. Sir Thomas Fairfax had his own doctor. Wounded in the wrist at Selby (1643), he would have bled to death but for the aid of his surgeon who 'came seasonable and bound up the wound, so stopped the bleeding'.

Often, it was insufficient for wounds to be dressed. When Sir Phillip Skippon was hit by a musket ball at Naseby (1645), a chunk of armour and pieces of clothing were driven into the resulting hole in his left side. The metal was removed, but the cloth festered in the wound. Eventually, in what must have been literally a painstaking operation, it was extracted by a London surgeon and Skippon made a full recovery. A grateful Parliament awarded him the sum of £200 to cover his medical bills.

In the absence of a standing army, the provision of treatment for the wounded was always going to be a hit-or-miss affair although, during the Civil Wars, some hospitals, such as the Savoy and St Bartholomew's, were put to military use. One common soldier, George Robinson, is recorded as spending six months in St Bartholomew's after being wounded in the lower limbs at 1st Newbury (1643), during which time eighty bone splinters were removed from one of his legs. St Bartholomew's had a survival rate of around 85 per cent – one of the most successful among the London hospitals.

At best, the treatment of wounds was a grim affair. At worst, it was positively gruesome. At Aberdeen (1644), an Irishman's leg was nearly blown off by a cannonball. Resorting to DIY, he produced his dirk, cut away the lower portion of the limb and passed it to a colleague. At Culloden (1746), while English army surgeons cared for their own men, the wounded Highlanders were simply despatched with bayonet thrusts.

For all this, it is worth bearing in mind that disease usually carried off a great many more men than injuries sustained in battle. During the seventeenth century, for example, as few as 10 to 25 per cent of military deaths resulted from violence. 'Camp fever' (probably typhoid) was a great killer, as were dysentery and bubonic plague. Life was tough and warfare made it just that little bit tougher.

17. Byland, 14 October 1322

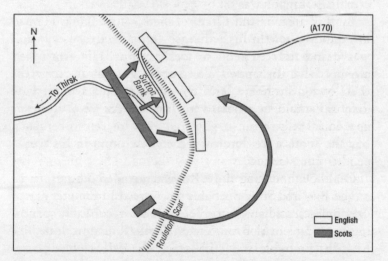

The defeat of the Earl of Lancaster and the rebel barons at Boroughbridge in March 1322 enabled Edward II to turn his attention once more to the Scots, whose border raids were increasing in frequency and severity.

Towards the end of July 1322, Edward despatched his fleet to the Firth of Forth and, on 1 August, he set out for Scotland with an army in excess of 20,000 men. As he crossed the border, all opposition melted before him. The retreat was tactical for, in pursuing a scorched-earth policy, the Scots ensured that no supplies fell into English hands. As he advanced towards Edinburgh, Edward's men became weak from hunger. To cap it all, the English fleet, lacking favourable winds, was unable to penetrate the Firth of Forth. The grand army turned about and began the long march home.

Meanwhile, Robert I of Scotland was planning to go on to the offensive. He did not attempt to tackle the English as they retreated, but decided instead to follow at a respectful distance and wait for an opportune moment to strike. On 30 September, he reached Carlisle and by 13 October, a forced march had brought him and his army, up to 4,000 strong, to Northallerton.

By this time, Edward had reached Sutton Bank. He had lost many men through disease (notably dysentery) and was desperately in need of fresh troops. His army may already have disbanded, the survivors striving to make their own way home, and the number at his immediate disposal would have been very limited. Aware of Robert's approach, he sent out urgent requests for reinforcements, but the Scots were determined to catch him in his weakened circumstances.

On 14 October, therefore, Robert moved in. The remnants of the English army, probably encamped in the vicinity of Old Byland, attempted to block his path, probably assuming a strong position on Sutton Bank/Roulston Scar. The English leadership was still intact, the defence being conducted by John of Brittany (3rd Earl of Richmond), Aymer de Valence (2nd Earl of Pembroke) and Henry Beaumont (4th Earl of Buchan).

As expected (and hoped for), the Scots, led by Sir James Douglas and Thomas Randolph (1st Earl of Moray), led a charge up the steep face of the escarpment. They took severe punishment, showered with arrows and rocks hurled from above as they tried to scale the heights. Nevertheless, they clawed their way to the top, and a fierce struggle ensued. The English were doomed, but they may have been able hold on for longer had not Robert outwitted them. A contingent of Highlanders was included within the Scottish ranks, and Robert despatched them to find another way up the hill, and so outflank the defenders.

The flanking party may have taken some time, but when they did finally appear to the rear of the English position, the fighting was soon over. Richmond, Pembroke and Buchan were taken prisoner, while those who could find a way out did so. It may well have been that the English commanders were aware of the possibility of being outflanked, but that they just did not have the manpower to cover all eventualities.

Sir Walter Stewart and the Scottish horse lost no time in advancing to search for Edward, having learned from captives that he was at Rievaulx Abbey. When Stewart arrived there, he found that Edward had already gone. The king is said to have been dining when news of the defeat reached him. That he fled in some confusion, first to Bridlington and then to the safety of York, is attested by the fact that he abandoned his treasure and privy seal. The Scots had been hoping to take him captive, but had to make do with ransacking both Rievaulx and Byland abbeys, before moving on to pillage as far south as Beverley before retreating to Scotland, unmolested, a week later.

The blame for the English defeat was laid at the door of Sir Andrew de Harcla, the hero of the Battle of Boroughbridge. Suspected of collusion with the Scots, he made his own peace treaty with them the following year, for which he was arrested, tried and executed. However, in the end, Edward was compelled to conclude a truce with Scotland, leading to thirteen years of comparative peace.

The battlefield today
A number of sites have been proposed for the battle, but one of the most probable is the high land between Roulston Scar and Sutton Bank (OS Landranger 100 5181). Car parking is available at Sutton Bank National Park Centre, on the A170,

mid-way between Thirsk and Helmsley. There is no monument, but visitors can spend a superb day exploring the area via the public footpath system.

Further reading
Graham Bell, *Robert the Bruce's Forgotten Victory: The Battle of Byland 1322* **(Tempus, 2005).**

18. Dupplin Moor, 10/11 August 1332

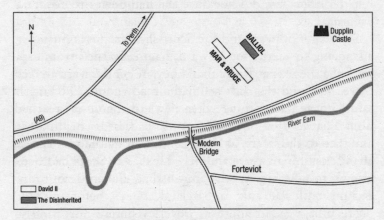

When Robert I of Scotland died in 1329, he was succeeded by his five-year-old son, David II. Old rivalries and festering resentments soon surfaced, in particular the dissatisfaction of the 'Disinherited' – mainly Englishmen who had fought at Bannockburn (1314) and who had been dispossessed of their Scottish estates as a consequence of their defeat.

The Disinherited put together a small army, led by Henry de Beaumont and Edward Balliol, son of John Balliol, the great rival of Robert I. About 1,500 in number, the force consisted of men-at-arms, infantry, archers and a complement of German mercenaries. With the support of Edward III, King of England since 1327, it made its way by sea to Fife. After resting for a few days, Beaumont and Balliol advanced towards Perth.

On 10 August 1332, they reached the River Earn, camping at Forteviot, some seven miles to the south-west of Perth. In full view, drawn up on high ground on Dupplin Moor, on the north bank of the river was the army (perhaps 4,000 strong) of David II, commanded by the Earl of Mar, who had been appointed Guardian for the period of David's minority. With another army, commanded by Patrick, Earl of Dunbar, approaching from the south, the Disinherited deemed it necessary to give battle.

The rickety bridge over the Earn had been disabled and a guard placed upon it. Fortunately, Beaumont and Balliol learned of an unguarded ford and decided to risk making a crossing during the night. It was not easy and one man is recorded as having drowned. Once safe on the north bank, they attacked what was thought to be the main Scottish camp, but it turned out to be an isolated band of infantry. Even so, the Disinherited should not have been able to cross the river at all, but the overconfident Mar had not taken the precaution to set a general watch. This led to sharp criticism from his colleague, Lord Robert Bruce, illegitimate son of Robert I.

The Disinherited just had time to assume a good defensive position on high ground at the head of a narrow valley. The infantry was flanked by bowmen, while the German mercenaries remained mounted in the rear. The Scots were soon upon them, advancing in two divisions, but there was no attempt at coordination, Mar and Bruce vying with one another to be first to get to grips with the enemy. Bruce won the race, his spearmen forcing the English to give ground. However, the bowmen on the English wings kept up a continuous fire so that the Scots on each flank converged on their own centre. When Mar's division came up in the rear, the pressure on Bruce's division became unbearable. The English line stabilized and many of the Scots in the van were suffocated. It is said that most of the Scottish casualties occurred in this manner. Efforts to make an orderly withdrawal collapsed as the English men-at-arms, supported by the German mercenaries, set off in pursuit.

The English dead could be counted in tens, the Scottish dead, which included Bruce and Mar, in thousands. The battle had been an object lesson in the power of the longbow and heavily dented the confidence of the Scots, who were still living on the reputation acquired at Bannockburn. The victory also enabled Edward Balliol to have himself crowned King of Scotland – an office he held for four months before being forced out of the country.

The battlefield today

Dupplin Moor is seven miles to the south-west of Perth on the B934, off the A9 (OS Landranger 58 0419). A ninth-century cross, traditionally marking the site of the battle, is to be seen in St Serf's Church in nearby Dunning. Miller's Acre, on the eastern edge of Forteviot, supposedly marks the English campsite. The precise battle site cannot be identified, a possible alternative being Upper Cairnie (0319). On-road car parking can be found in Forteviot.

Further reading

Pete Armstrong, *The Battle of Dupplin Moor 1332* (Lynda Armstrong, 2000).

19. Halidon Hill, 19 July 1333

Although his victory at Dupplin Moor (1332) enabled Edward Balliol to be crowned King John I of Scotland, his new status did not guarantee him the support of his subjects. A few months after his coronation, supporters of his rival, David II, forced him to flee to England. In return for a promise from Balliol to hand over Berwick, held by Scotland since 1318, King Edward III led an army north.

In Scotland, Sir Archibald Douglas, the new Guardian of the Realm for the juvenile David II, blocked Edward's path

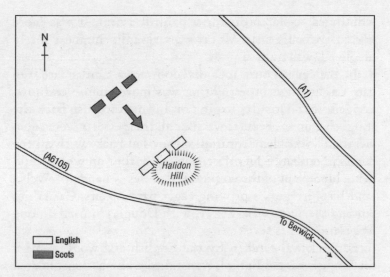

into Scotland by arranging for Berwick's defence. On 1 May 1333, Edward arrived outside Berwick and laid siege to the town, but it was not until July that Douglas made his move to lift the siege.

While a token force remained before Berwick, the English army, in expectation of an attack by Douglas, deployed on Halidon Hill, two miles to the north-west. As if on cue, at 9.00 a.m. on 19 July, Douglas was seen approaching. The English army, comprising some 9,000 men, was drawn up in three divisions: Edward in the centre, with the Earl of Norfolk on the right and Balliol on the left. The Scots, possibly 13,000 strong, approaching from Witches Knowe to the north-west, also probably deployed in three divisions: the Earl of Moray on the right, Douglas on the left and Robert Stewart in the centre.

The Scots had to negotiate a bog and then attack uphill. Hoping that the English might descend to meet them, they did nothing until noon. When they finally advanced, they steered themselves towards the English left wing and the hated Balliol. As they laboured through the marshy ground, a hail of arrows rained down upon them and continued to do so during a painful ascent. It was more than they could bear. Moray's division, its numbers sorely depleted, was routed.

In the centre, Stewart's division met a similar fate. On the English right, the fighting was more intense and prolonged, with Douglas urging on his men to push back the English and reach the town. But all their efforts were to no avail and, like their comrades, they fell back. With all the Scots in retreat, Edward's troops embarked on what would be a bloody pursuit over several miles – bands of Welsh and Irish irregulars proving eager participants. Casualties among the Scots were heavy, with Douglas himself among the slain.

Berwick was retaken by the English and would remain in English hands. Balliol, reinstalled as king, consolidated his unpopularity by also ceding the fortresses of Dunbar, Roxburgh and Edinburgh. The battle is considered to be particularly significant because it demonstrated to Edward the potential of the longbow – a lesson he would remember on the foreign field of Crécy.

The battlefield today

Halidon Hill is two miles to the west of Berwick, off the A6105 (OS Landranger 75 9654). Take the first minor road to the right beyond the A1. (The battlefield is signposted.) A car park, with an information panel, is along here on the left-hand side. A footpath leads to the top of the hill. A battlefield monument is by the roadside. The ruins of Berwick Castle are in the care of English Heritage.

Further reading

Chris Brown, *The Second Scottish Wars of Independence* (History Press, 2006).

20. Neville's Cross, 17 October 1346

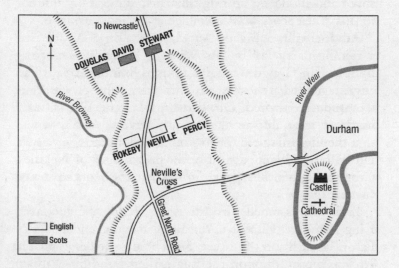

By 1346, England was nine years into The Hundred Years' War with France. On 26 August of that year, Edward III won one of Western Europe's most decisive battles, at Crécy.

Philip IV of France begged the Scots for help. Edward Balliol, sponsored by Edward III, had been ousted for good as King of Scotland in 1336. The alternative claimant, David, son of Robert I, now securely installed as King David II, was only too happy to oblige the French. On 7 October, he led an army of some 12,000 men across the border. They laid waste everything in their path; Lanercost Priory was plundered, as was Hexham Abbey. At length, they reached Durham, camping two miles to the west of the city, at Bearpark.

The 'auld alliance' plan was to draw English troops away from French soil, but in this respect it failed. Resistance was coordinated by the Archbishop of York, William Zouche. Those who answered the call included Henry Percy and Ralph Neville, representatives of the two great rival families that bore the brunt of border warfare. With remarkable speed and efficiency, an English army, numerically inferior to that of the Scots, was assembled at Bishop Auckland.

Advancing from Bishop Auckland, the English surprised a raiding party led by Sir William Douglas. Reporting back to King David, Douglas advised him to retreat to an advantageous battle site, but this wise counsel was contemptuously ignored, David dismissing the English as a horde of 'miserable monks and pig-drivers'. And so it was that the English chose the ground, sweeping to the west of Durham to take up a position in the vicinity of Neville's Cross, in sight of Bearpark, from where the Scots advanced to meet them.

Each side assumed three divisions: Ralph Neville faced King David in the centre; the English right, under Henry Percy, faced Robert Stewart; Sir Thomas Rokeby and the Archbishop of York on the English left faced Sir William Douglas. It was Douglas who made the opening move. As his men, with characteristic impetuosity, charged forward, they found their progress hampered by a small ravine and were forced to swerve to their left, into the Scottish centre. The English bowmen, quick to capitalize on the situation, poured destructive volleys of arrows into the congested enemy ranks. Cognisant of the damage being wreaked, a Scottish nobleman (named by some sources as William Graham) led a cavalry charge into the body of archers and succeeded in scattering them. Robert Stewart followed up this piece of individual heroism with a more organized assault on Percy's wing. Once more, the English front line wavered. In the centre, King David's men were more than holding their own.

While the battle raged, something rather curious was happening on the crest of a hill known as Maiden's Bower, to the east of the Scottish position. Here, a number of ecclesiastics from Durham Cathedral had gathered to pray, the focus of their devotions being a relic (the sacred corporas cloth of St Cuthbert). Affixed to a spear in order to function as a sacred banner, it was used to send news of the conflict to monks looking out from the cathedral tower. The priests remained at their outpost, unmolested, for the duration of the battle, employing their own semaphore to keep their colleagues within the cathedral walls informed of progress.

Just as it was beginning to look as if the Scots might carry the day, concerted English cavalry charges transformed the situation, both Scottish flanks being forced back and, ultimately, put to flight. David and a human shield of devoted knights may have fought on until the exhausted survivors were forced to yield. According to one story, after a badly wounded David was taken prisoner, he struck his captor, John Copeland, Governor of Roxburgh Castle, in an attempt to goad him into killing him. Another, less edifying version of events has David slipping away, unwounded, only to be discovered skulking beneath a bridge.

The slaughter of the vanquished was great, the constrictions imposed by the ravine and the River Browney making them an easy mass target for their eager pursuers. Perhaps 1,000 Scots, including many nobles, were slain. On the English side, the only person of rank to lose his life was Randolph, Lord Hastings.

King David was imprisoned in the Tower of London, although the conditions of his captivity were not particularly onerous. During the eleven years he spent there, it is said that he acquired a taste for such comforts of life as were missing north of the border.

The battlefield today

Neville's Cross is one mile to the west of the centre of Durham (OS Landranger 88 2642). The remains of a cross, erected by Ralph Neville in celebration of the English victory, is situated on the Durham side of the A690, close to the A690–A167 crossroads. An information panel can be found on the A167, at the point where it crosses the railway line. There is also a waymarked battlefield trail. Car parking is available on Toll House Road, a little further along the A167, or in Durham town centre.

Further reading
David Rollason and Michael Prestwich (eds), *The Battle of Neville's Cross 1346* (Shaun Tyas, 1998).

Border Wars

21. Otterburn, 19 August 1388

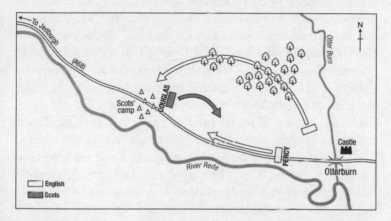

After Neville's Cross in 1346, no major battle was fought on British soil for forty-two years. The English victory had been comprehensive and King David II was a spent force. In addition, in 1348, the 'Black Death' found its way to the British Isles, via the port of Weymouth.

Manpower may not have been quite so plentiful, but Edward III did manage to mount his 'Burnt Candlemas' campaign of 1356, in which the Lothians were laid waste. Routine border warfare also continued. The 'Border Reivers' – families on both sides of the western borders, for whom lawlessness was a way of life – went on raiding regardless of national concerns.

On the eastern borders, there was intense Anglo-Scottish rivalry between two powerful Houses: those of Percy and Douglas. By 1388, each family was representing the interests of the crown on its 'patch'. James, 2nd Earl of Douglas, owed his allegiance to King Robert II of Scotland, who had succeeded David II in 1371, while the Earl of Northumberland served Richard II, King of England since Edward III's death in 1377.

In the summer of 1388, Douglas led a raid into England, crossing the Tyne at Corbridge and penetrating as far south as Brancepeth, to the south-west of Durham. Following the customary orgy of pillage and destruction, the Scots retreated northwards, with a view to sacking Newcastle on the way home. Thanks to a stout defence conducted by the Earl of Northumberland's sons, Sir Henry Percy (the celebrated 'Hotspur') and Sir Ralph Percy, the attack came to naught, and Douglas continued his homeward march, along the Redesdale corridor.

On 18 August, Douglas pitched camp at a spot identified today as Greenchesters, about a mile to the west of Otterburn. The following day, an unsuccessful attempt was made to take Otterburn Tower. It may be that the Scots, laden down with booty, considered a confrontation inevitable, and were seeking to strengthen their position. In fact, the Percy brothers were already on the move. After a forced march at the head of over 3,000 men – rather more than the Scots – they arrived on the scene towards evening on 19 August.

A detachment of men was ordered to work its way around to the north of the Scottish position, while Henry and Ralph with the main body made a frontal assault. When they attacked, however, they found that they had surprised a campsite of servants and attendants, the fighting men being encamped to the rear. The error gave the latter time to rouse themselves, although not to don full armour, which, in Douglas's case, would prove fatal.

Having scouted the land roundabout, the Scots were able to mount an outflanking manoeuvre of their own. Instead of meeting the attack head-on, they skirted the high ground to the north of the camp. Missing the English flanking party, which had taken too wide a sweep, they worked their way around to the Percy right flank and descended upon it.

The English quickly overcame their confusion and regrouped. Neither side was going to enjoy an easy victory. At length, the Scots were pushed back – perhaps with the aid of the English flanking party – and Douglas attempted to retrieve the situation by wading into the thick of the fighting, where he was cut down by English men-at-arms. Neither side seems to have been aware that he had fallen.

The Percys had been counting on a quick result, for their men were both hungry and tired, having marched over thirty miles. Now it was dark, the scene illuminated only by fitful moonlight, and the Scots began to get the upper hand. As the English were, in their turn, pushed back, Ralph Percy was captured. Then his brother was forced to yield and English resistance was broken, the survivors retreating towards Newcastle.

The next day, English reinforcements led by the Bishop of Durham were en route between Newcastle and Otterburn when they encountered survivors seeking the comparative safety of Newcastle's walls. Ultimately, after reconnoitring the Scottish positions, the bishop erred on the side of caution and decided to withdraw.

In total, English losses numbered over 1,000, with the Scots losing, perhaps, half as many men. Although it settled nothing in terms of local rivalries, the battle certainly caught the popular imagination, becoming endowed with a significance that far outweighed its actual consequences.

The battlefield today

The battlefield is located one mile to the west of Otterburn on the A696 (OS Landranger 80 8793). A car parking area includes an information panel and Percy's Cross, a battlefield monument that originally stood 150 yards to the west. The Otterburn Tower Hotel, in Otterburn itself, was developed from the original tower besieged by Douglas into a privately owned country house before conversion to its present use.

Further reading

Stephen Walsh, *Otterburn 1388: Bloody Border Conflict* (Osprey Publishing, 2006).

22. Homildon Hill, 14 September 1402

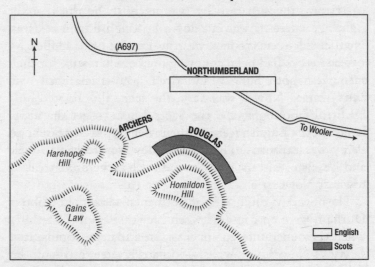

Between the Battles of Otterburn and Homildon Hill, both England and Scotland gained new rulers. In 1390, Robert II of Scotland died and was succeeded by Robert III. In 1399, Henry Bolingbroke deposed Richard II, seizing the English throne as Henry IV.

In the borders, warfare fuelled by fierce rivalries continued unabated until in August 1402, Archibald, 4th Earl of Douglas, led several thousand men in a major raid across the border. They laid waste to Northumberland and proceeded as far as Newcastle before retiring, with the Earl of Northumberland and his son, Sir Henry Percy, in pursuit.

In many respects, the general situation resembled that which had resulted in the Battle of Otterburn, fourteen years previously. Then, too, a Douglas had raided as far as Newcastle and had been challenged by the Percy family on the way home.

This time, the Earl of Northumberland and Sir Henry Percy contrived to cut off Douglas's line of retreat, reaching Millfield, to the south of Coldstream, while the Scots (laden with booty and slow-moving cattle, as they had been at Otterburn) had progressed only as far as Wooler.

Douglas chose to stand and fight at Homildon Hill, just beyond the town, probably deploying his men along the lower slopes. The main body of the English army, outnumbering the Scots, drew up to the north in an area known as Red Riggs.

Instead of charging the Scots, the English sent forward a detachment of archers. From the lower slopes of Harehope Hill, adjacent to Homildon Hill, they were able to wreak great damage on the stationary foe. Such archers as the Scots had among them returned fire, but their bows were less powerful and the English longbowmen were able to keep out of range.

Small groups of Scottish horsemen attempted to disperse the archers, but their armour was easily penetrated by the English arrows, and they were compelled to withdraw. Finally, discipline collapsed and the Scots began to disperse, forgetting about their plunder in a flight towards Coldstream. Many must have been intercepted by the English, who pursued them to the River Tweed. A hard core of Scottish knights did remain and, charging the main English position, fought fiercely. Archibald Douglas was wounded several times and lost an eye, but his men were eventually killed or captured.

It can be safely assumed that Scottish losses were heavy while English casualties were light. The main significance of the battle, however, lay with the high-value prisoners, particularly Douglas, who fell into English hands. King Henry IV's demand that Douglas be handed over to him was one of the causes of the Percy rebellion of the following year.

The battlefield today

Homildon Hill, now known as Humbleton Hill, is one mile to the north-west of Wooler, on the A697. The field of battle is marked by the Bendor Stone, which lies in a field by the

A697, near the hamlet of Bendor (OS Landranger 75 9629). On-road car parking is available in Humbleton, from where it is possible, via a public footpath, to walk to the top of the hill.

Further reading
A. W. Boardman, *Hotspur* (The History Press, 2003).

The Percy Rebellion

23. Shrewsbury, 21 July 1403

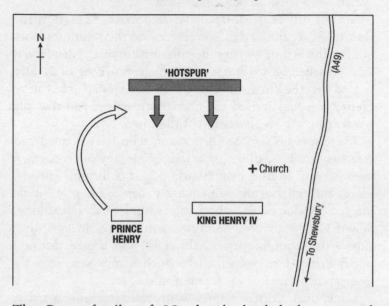

The Percy family of Northumberland had supported
Henry Bolingbroke in his dispute with Richard II, which
left Richard deposed and Henry crowned as Henry IV.
As guardians of the king's interests on the borders with
Scotland, they wielded considerable power, but the inevitable battles with the Scots were costly, Henry Percy, 1st Earl
of Northumberland, claiming that he was £60,000 out of
pocket. At the Battle of Homildon Hill, Archibald, 4th Earl
of Douglas, had been taken prisoner and, rather than hand
him over to the king as they should have done, the Percys
decided to keep him. His ransom value, they argued, would
help cover their expenses.

The sum total of slights, real or imagined, aimed at the
House of Percy was enough to lead the earl's son, Sir Henry
Percy, 'Hotspur', into open rebellion. The earl himself did

not participate, citing illness as the cause, but Hotspur could call on the Earl of Worcester (Thomas Percy, his uncle), the Earl of Douglas, who agreed to join his faction, and the Welsh nationalist, Owen Glendower.

In early July 1403, Hotspur marched south. At Stafford, he was joined by the Earl of Worcester, and their joint force set out for Shrewsbury where they planned to meet Glendower. They reached Shrewsbury early on the morning of 21 July to find that the king, with his son, Prince Henry – the future Henry V – had arrived the previous evening, and that the royal army was in possession of the town.

There was no sign of Glendower, who later blamed bad weather for his failure to arrive, and Hotspur retreated northwards, to the neighbourhood of Albright Hussey. Here, the rebel army subsequently deployed, in a single massed division on slightly rising ground, to await the king. When Henry arrived, he drew up his army in two divisions – the major, his own, to the right, with a lesser division under Prince Henry on the left. Both armies were roughly numerically equal, at 14,000 men apiece.

Some, unsuccessful efforts were made to secure a truce, but finally, in the late afternoon of 21 July, the royal vanguard attacked the rebel position. This assault was halted in its tracks by Hotspur's archers. The king's archers replied and it appeared that the outcome might be decided by the longbow. Hotspur's archers initially had the better of the exchange and the king led forward his main battle. Impetuously, Hotspur advanced, accompanied only by a small detachment of cavalry, in an attempt to kill Henry. In this, he failed, allegedly because several knights, wearing replica sets of the royal armour, had been deployed to act as decoys. Now surrounded by the enemy, it was Hotspur who was cut down.

It suited the victors to claim that the intervention of the Prince of Wales was decisive in securing a royal victory, and he may have led a charge that succeeded in turning the rebel right flank. Without Hotspur to rally them, many of the rebels fell back in disarray, although others continued to put up stout resistance. The Prince of Wales and Douglas both suffered serious wounds. In total, there were some 5,000 casualties.

In some respects, Henry reacted with magnanimity: Douglas was released, while the Earl of Northumberland (who would pose a threat for the next six years) was absolved of guilt. Henry also endowed a chapel on the battlefield itself, which developed into the surviving Church of St Mary Magdalene. As a warning to future malcontents, Hotspur's head was placed on York's Micklegate Bar; that of the executed Earl of Worcester, on London Bridge.

The battlefield today

The battlefield lies three miles to the north of Shrewsbury (OS Landranger 126 5117). Long gone are the days when a visitor would arrive at Battlefield Church, provisioned with a flask of tea in preparation for a day's investigative exploration. A bespoke car park and viewing point now adorn the south of the battlefield, at the A5124/Battlefield Way roundabout – starting point of a battlefield trail; the half-timbered sixteenth-century Albright Hussey Manor has been transformed into a prestigious hotel and restaurant; Battlefield 1403, occupying Battlefield Farm to the north of the church, comprises a battlefield exhibition centre and café, where a key can be obtained for the church.

Further reading

John Barratt, *War for the Throne: The Battle of Shrewsbury 1403* (Pen & Sword, 2010).

24. Bramham Moor, 19 February 1408

In the aftermath of the Battle of Shrewsbury, the Earl of Northumberland had been lucky to escape censure, but

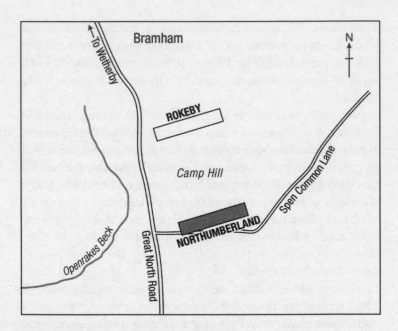

instead of entering into retirement, he continued to plot against Henry IV. In particular, he was involved in the rebellion of Richard Scrope, Archbishop of York, in 1405. Although Scrope assembled several thousand men on Shipton Moor, he was tricked into laying down his arms and afterwards executed with other ringleaders. Northumberland, in company with Thomas Bardolph, 5th Baron Bardolph, escaped to Scotland.

At the beginning of 1408, Northumberland embarked on what would be his last challenge to Henry when he and Bardolph led an army of Scots into England. As far as the Scots were concerned, the venture was mainly another opportunity for pillage, and the fighting qualities of such adherents as were picked up along the way, during a march to the Yorkshire town of Thirsk, left much to be desired.

The intention was to take possession of the bridge at Knaresborough, but the High Sheriff of Yorkshire, Sir Thomas Rokeby, had moved quickly to occupy the bridge with a force of militia – thereby blocking the route south. The rebels proceeded via Boroughbridge, Wetherby and Tadcaster, with Rokeby now in pursuit, until they stopped on Bramham Moor at a spot known as Camp Hill.

The two sides clashed at about 2.00 p.m. on the afternoon of 19 February in a battle that was short and sharp. The rebels had adequate time to arrange their deployment, but they must have been outnumbered by Rokeby who had gathered, en route, much of the local support for which Northumberland had hoped. Furthermore, the rebels lacked the training and discipline of Rokeby's force.

Archers may have played a preliminary role in the battle, but it is believed that the issue was decided by close combat, savage and bloody, following a charge by Rokeby. The end was hastened by the fact that Bardolph fell at an early stage. Northumberland was killed, either in a rearguard action, or while attempting to escape.

Casualties on the rebel side were heavy. The dead were interred in mass graves in the churchyard of All Saints, Bramham. Many Scots must have been apprehended while attempting to reach home. Not surprisingly, the king was not inclined to be merciful and a good number of rebels were executed. For his services, Sir Thomas Rokeby received Spofforth, one of the Earl of Northumberland's Yorkshire estates.

The battlefield today

The village of Bramham lies off the A1M, three miles south of Wetherby. A service road, Paradise Way, runs from the junction. Follow this down to Spen Common Lane. A new battlefield monument and information panel (with a little off-road car parking) overlooking Camp Hill is at the corner (OS Landranger 105 4341). It is not possible to pinpoint the exact site of the battle, which probably raged over a wide area. Indeed, the neglected Percy's Cross, supposedly marking the spot of the Earl of Northumberland's death, is well to the north in a copse on York Lane (4443).

Further reading

William Grainge, *The Battles and Battlefields of Yorkshire from the Earliest Times to the End of the Great Civil War* (British Library, Historical Print Editions, 2011).

Clan Wars

25. Reid Harlaw, 24 July 1411

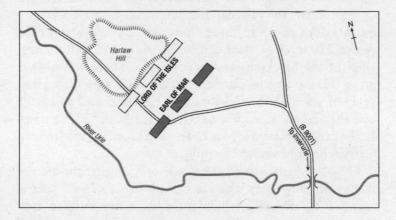

The Battle of Harlaw cannot be neatly pigeon-holed within any classification scheme. It was one of a number of internal Scottish battles arising from clan disputes, although it does reflect the growing tension between the Highlands and Lowlands of Scotland. The bone of contention in this case was ownership of the vast lands of the Earldom of Ross in the far north of Scotland. Robert Stewart, Duke of Albany, and Donald, Lord of the Isles, both had claims.

In the summer of 1411, Donald gathered 6,000 men and marched through Ross to Dingwall, where he won a victory over the MacKays. He then marched on to Inverness, where he burned the castle. With his numbers having swelled to perhaps as many as 10,000, Donald set out for Aberdeen, which he intended to sack. On 23 July he paused, setting up camp to the north of Inverurie, where Alexander, Earl of Mar, was gathering an army to repel the Highlanders.

Mar's force would have been several thousand strong, though probably smaller than that led by Donald. At dawn on 24 July, he marched out of Inverurie and drew up before

Donald's camp. It is probable that he deployed his men in three divisions: himself in the centre, Sir Alexander Forbes on the right, with men of Angus under Sir Alexander Ogilvy (the Sheriff of Angus) and Sir James Scrymgeour on the left.

Apparently, the Highlanders were caught unawares, but quickly formed up in three divisions: Donald was in the centre, Hector Roy MacLean on the right and Callum Beg, chief of the Mackintoshes, on the left. There was always great rivalry among clan chieftains over who was given pride of place on the right wing. This continued to be the case through the Civil Wars and into the Jacobite rebellions. In the present instance, MacLean ceded some of his lands to Callum Beg to sweeten the pill.

The MacLeans opened the battle by charging the men of Angus, although they failed to make headway. In the centre, Mar led his division, which included many knights, into Donald's Islesmen, but with no more success. There seemed to be no limit to the reserves of Highlanders. Mar also had fresh men arriving, but it seems that he did not use them to advantage.

The fighting continued throughout the day until, with the onset of darkness, both sides withdrew, exhausted. Indeed, neither side wanted a continuation of the battle and it was with immense relief the following morning that Mar discovered the clansmen had gone home to lick their wounds. Nine hundred of them, including Hector Roy MacLean, had died on the battlefield, but then so had 600 of the Lowlanders: the provost of Aberdeen, Robert Davidson, Sir James Scrymgeour, Sir Alexander Irvine and many knights of note had fallen.

Later in the year, the Duke of Albany regained the lands that Donald had overrun. In 1412, further pressure compelled Donald to renounce his claim on Ross all together.

The battlefield today
The battlefield (signposted) lies two miles to the north-west of Inverurie, on a minor road off the B9001 (OS Landranger

38 7524). There is a little off-road car parking near an impos-
ing battlefield monument with an interpretation panel. A
Battle of Harlaw leaflet is available for download from the
Aberdeen City Council website.

Further reading
John Sadler, *Clan MacDonald's Greatest Defeat: The Battle of
Harlaw 1411* **(Tempus Publishing, 2005).**

PART THREE:
THE LATER MIDDLE AGES

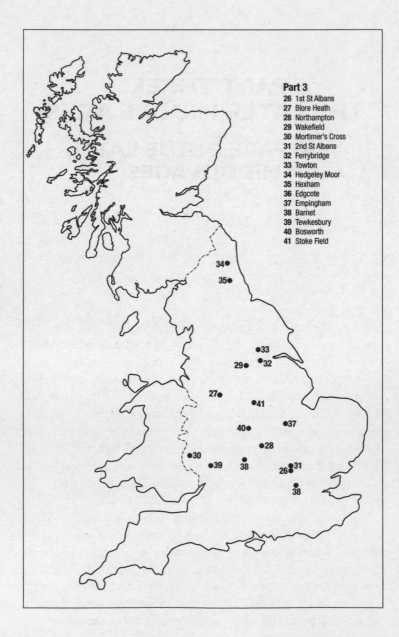

Part 3
26 1st St Albans
27 Blore Heath
28 Northampton
29 Wakefield
30 Mortimer's Cross
31 2nd St Albans
32 Ferrybridge
33 Towton
34 Hedgeley Moor
35 Hexham
36 Edgcote
37 Empingham
38 Barnet
39 Tewkesbury
40 Bosworth
41 Stoke Field

WARFARE IN THE LATER MIDDLE AGES

Warfare in Britain during the Later Middle Ages revolved around the Wars of the Roses – a fight to the death between two rival claimant families to the throne.

The facts available to the military historian, even with regard to major Roses battles, are limited. This paucity of information is particularly troublesome in terms of the size of armies, given the tendency for contemporary/near-contemporary commentators to exaggerate. Thus, the size of the Yorkist army at Northampton (1460) was variously estimated at anything between 50,000 and a colossal 160,000, when the actual size was probably 20,000 or less.

With the exception of Towton (1461), casualties were usually comparatively light, most deaths continuing to be sustained during the pursuit of a defeated army. In the past, noblemen stood a fairly good chance of survival, owing to their ransom value. In Roses battles, they were transformed into particular targets, for the aim of each side was to gain supremacy by destroying the leading lights of the other.

Armies were increasingly divided into 'battles' (the ante-cedents of battalions) comprising vanguard, middle guard and rearguard. If deployed horizontally, the van occupied the right with the rearguard on the left. Tactical use of cav-alry still lay in the future, and horses continued to be used largely as a means of transport to reach the battlefield and, afterwards, as an aid to escape or pursuit.

Numbers were occasionally supplemented with gun-toting foreign mercenaries. The 300 mercenaries who accompanied Edward IV on his return to England in 1471 possessed 'hand-gonnes'. In its earliest form, this weapon comprised an iron barrel with a three-quarter-inch (two-centimetre) bore attached to a straight piece of wood. Weighing up to sixteen pounds (seven kilograms), it was fired from a rest and required two men for its management. Slow and inaccurate at the best of times, the handgun, in its embryonic stages, was notoriously unreliable. At 1st St Albans (1455), the 'hand-gonnes' of Warwick's Burgundians blew up in their faces. It is a wonder that they were ever used at all.

Light artillery also made regular appearances on the battlefield – probably culverins firing seven-pound (three-kilogram) stone balls, although larger cannon were available. A monstrous example was 'Mons Meg', weighing in at over four tons (4,000 kilograms) and with a calibre of twenty inches (fifty centimetres), made for James II of Scotland. An enthusiastic artilleryman, James was killed by an exploding cannon in 1460. None of the guns used during this period were home-grown, the first English cannon-foundry being established in 1521.

The longbow was still the most reliable long-range weapon. Traditionally, the best bows were made of yew, many staves being imported from Spain and Italy. However, foreign mer-chants responded to the surge in demand during the Roses campaigns by increasing their prices, so that inferior English wood was often substituted for the quality product.

Plate armour was still developing, and during the Roses period it achieved its maximum efficiency in terms of invulnerability. It was also at its most cumbersome, and any fully armoured individual without a horse – such as Richard III at Bosworth (1485) – had a serious mobility problem. Arms included the long sword, short sword and dagger, and the infantryman's pike which, by this time, incorporated so many cunningly appended hooks and spikes that the horrific injuries they caused led to efforts being made to ban them.

The Wars of the Roses

Opening phase

26. 1st St Albans, 22 May 1455

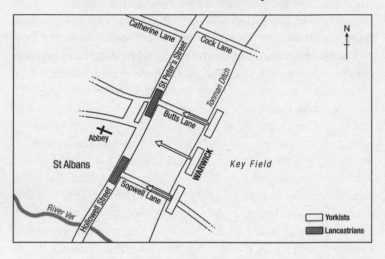

The long conflict between the Houses of Lancaster and York – the Wars of the Roses – first manifested itself as a struggle between Richard, Duke of York, and the staunch Lancastrian, Edmund Beaufort, 2nd Duke of Somerset, cousin to King Henry VI. The king was not of sound mind, a condition both York and Somerset wanted to exploit for their own ends. Although Henry had a strong-willed queen, Margaret of Anjou, he would remain a pawn in the game until his death.

In May 1455, York and Somerset finally came to blows. Having raised an army in the north of England, York marched on London. By the time he reached Royston on 20 May, his force, augmented by the Earl of Salisbury and his son, the Earl of Warwick, had swelled to 3,000 men. On 21 May, the Lancastrians, including King Henry, the Duke of

Somerset and Humphrey Stafford, 1st Duke of Buckingham, marched out of London to give battle.

The two armies met at St Albans, the Yorkists deploying on ground to the east, known as Key Field, as early as 7.00 a.m. on 22 May. The Lancastrians arrived in the city to find themselves outnumbered by a thousand men, but, peace overtures having failed, the Duke of Somerset resolved to fight.

The London road at that time entered St Albans from Key Field by Sopwell Lane, and here there was a wooden bar which could be swung across the street, as required. Another bar existed at Butts or Shropshire Lane (now Victoria Street) and both these were closed and guarded by the Lancastrians, who deployed along the city's main thoroughfare, comprising St Peter's Street and Hollowell Street.

From Tonman Ditch, fronting Key Field, the Yorkists attacked along Sopwell Lane and Shropshire Lane, but the defenders absorbed the pressure, being able to repulse all assaults, which were funnelled into the narrow passages. However, between Tonman Ditch and the houses along St Peter's and Hollowell Streets were certain gardens known as 'The Town Backsides'. Warwick thought that it might be possible to batter his way through one of the houses between Sopwell and Shropshire Lanes.

This is exactly what he did, hacking through the walls of a house said to be between 'the signe of the Keye and the sygne of the Chekkere'. Emerging into Hollowell Street, he cut the Lancastrian defensive line in half, attacking them in the rear to both right and left. Assaults on the Lanes were pressed home and, within half an hour, the Yorkists had secured victory.

Not more than a hundred or so Lancastrians perished, because the Yorkist rank and file were under orders to smite only the leaders. Buckingham was wounded but others, notably Somerset and Thomas, Lord Clifford, were killed. As soon as the fighting was over, the victors sought out the king (who had been wounded by an arrow) in a tanner's cottage, where he had sought refuge, and tendered their allegiance.

The battle sealed the fate of the kingdom, fixing the two parties in a blood feud and shutting out all hope of a peaceable permanent solution. For the moment, the House of York held sway, the Duke of York becoming Constable of England – an office rendered vacant by Somerset's demise.

The battlefield today

St Albans is twenty-two miles to the north of London (Junction 9 of the M1 or Junction 22 of the M25) (OS Landranger 166 1407). Use the city centre car parks. The main thoroughfare through the town, Holywell Hill/Chequer Street/St Peters Street (A1081) remains, as does Sopwell Lane, Shropshire/Butts Lane (now Victoria Street) and Cock Lane (now Hatfield Road). The present-day London Road did not exist in 1455. Warwick broke through into the town at a point roughly indicated by The Cheltenham & Gloucester Building Society. A plaque on the wall of the Skipton Building Society commemorates the death on that spot of the Duke of Somerset.

Further reading

Peter Burley, Michael Elliott and Harvey Watson, *The Battles of St Albans* (Pen & Sword, 2007).

SECOND PHASE

27. Blore Heath, 23 September 1459

By 1459, the Houses of Lancaster and York were once again arming for war. The Yorkist plan was for the Earl of Salisbury, the Earl of Warwick and the Duke of York to join forces at Ludlow in Staffordshire.

Salisbury raised a force of over 4,000 men at the Yorkist stronghold of Middleham Castle in North Yorkshire. His

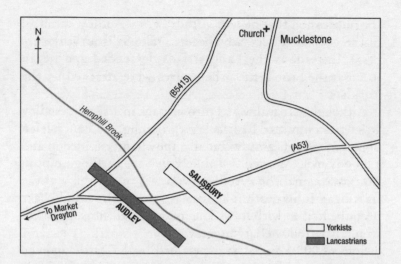

march south took him through Lancashire, Cheshire and
the north of Shropshire. Queen Margaret was at Eccleshall,
ten miles to the south-east of Market Drayton, where James
Touchet, 5th Lord Audley, was based with a newly mustered
Lancastrian army. Margaret instructed Audley to oppose
the earl at the earliest possible opportunity.

On the morning of 23 September, the two armies met
to the east of Market Drayton on what is today the A53.
Salisbury was marching from Newcastle-under-Lyme when
he learned that Audley was blocking his path. Accordingly,
he deployed his 3,000-strong army to the north of Blore
Heath on rising ground beyond Hempnill Brook. Audley,
whose army may have been twice the size of Salisbury's, had
selected a good defensive position along a ridge to the south
of the brook – possibly to the rear of a high hedge.

Salisbury had to take the initiative, but it would have
been suicidal to make a frontal attack. He thought, cor-
rectly as it turned out, that it would not take much to lure
Audley down into the shallow valley which separated the
two armies. After laagering his supply wagons to protect
his right wing, he feigned a retreat, managing to convey

the impression that he was withdrawing. Audley, mindful of the queen's orders, advanced to take Salisbury by surprise. Instead, as the Lancastrians descended and began to cross the brook, they themselves were attacked by the Yorkists.

Although his cavalry was thrown back in disarray, Audley was now committed to attack. Regrouping, the Lancastrian horse renewed its assault. Finally, the infantry joined in and a bloody mêlée ensued. It is likely that the turning point in the battle came when Audley, who was in the thick of the fighting, met his death. The Lancastrian cavalry would have been the first to withdraw. The infantry, now unsupported, would have followed in disarray.

Some 2,000 Lancastrians perished in the battle and the pursuit launched by the Yorkists. According to tradition, many fled along the banks of the stream until, trapped in a meadow where it joins the River Tern, they were slaughtered.

It was a hollow victory for Salisbury for, although it opened the road to Ludlow, enabling him to join forces with the Duke of York, the combined force was ultimately dispersed by another Lancastrian army led by Henry VI.

The battlefield today

The battlefield lies on the A53, three miles to the east of Market Drayton (OS Landranger 127 7135). Audley's Cross, marking the centre of the battlefield, is on private land, but the surrounding minor road/public footpath network allows for fine views of the battlefield. A good starting point for an exploration of the battlefield is nearby Almington, where there is a little on-road parking and a public footpath leading to the site of the initial Lancastrian position. At Mucklestone, Queen Margaret is said to have watched the battle from the tower of St Mary's Church. She is also depicted in a stained-glass window. Opposite the church is the site of a smithy where 'Queen Margaret had her horse's shoes reversed to aid her escape . . .'

Further reading
Francis Randle Twemlow, *The Battle of Bloreheath 1459* (Leonaur Ltd, 2011).

28. Northampton, 10 July 1460

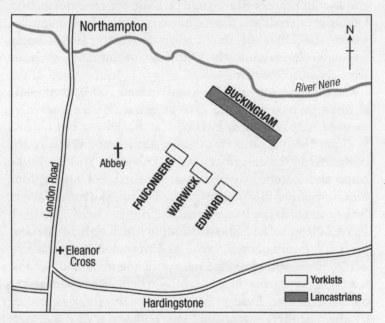

On 12 October 1459, at Ludford Bridge, the morale of the Yorkist armies of the Earls of Salisbury and Warwick and the Duke of York collapsed. The troops dispersed without a fight, handing a bloodless victory to their Lancastrian opponents. The Duke of York fled to Ireland, while the Earls of Salisbury, Warwick and March took refuge in Calais.

York was hoping to recruit an army in Ireland. Perhaps this worried the Lancastrians, for after Henry VI presided over a meeting of Parliament in Coventry in November 1459, he lingered in the midlands. Perhaps he would have been better advised to return to London for, on 26 June 1460, Salisbury, Warwick and March landed at Sandwich with 2,000 followers. By the time they reached London, their numbers had swelled to 20,000.

Henry's arrangements for the defence of the capital were woefully inadequate, and the Yorkists experienced no trouble entering the city. Leaving Salisbury in charge, Warwick and March proceeded north. The Lancastrians, meanwhile, having mustered their forces, moved south to Northampton, where the Duke of Buckingham engineered a strongly entrenched position to the south-east of the town, with the River Nene to his rear.

On the morning of 10 July, the Yorkists approached, marshalling their army at an ancient entrenchment known as Danes Camp. Edward, Earl of March, led the right wing, William Neville, Lord Fauconberg, the left and Warwick the centre. After the customary futile parlay, the Yorkists broke camp and marched by an old drove road to Hardingstone Fields, passing Eleanor's Cross, before skirting Delapre Abbey to reach the Lancastrian camp.

At 2.00 p.m., the Yorkist assault began. The Lancastrians, probably outnumbered, were well provided with artillery while their opponents had none, but the guns had become waterlogged during heavy rain – which continued as the battle developed. Even so, it appeared that ramparts erected by the defenders might hold the Yorkists at bay, for their height rendered them difficult to scale. Treachery often features in Roses battles, though it is not always easy to authenticate, but on this occasion the Lancastrians do seem to have owed their defeat to betrayal. The Lancastrian, Lord Grey of Ruthin, perceived the problem and, instead of repelling boarders, his followers leaned over the ramparts and hauled up the Yorkists. Evidently, this had the effect of creating panic in the loyal Lancastrian ranks, and within a short time all effective resistance had ceased.

The slaughter among the Lancastrian nobility and gentry was not great, but the Duke of Buckingham was among the fallen, allegedly killed while trying to prevent Henry falling into enemy hands. Many of the common soldiers, in attempting to escape, drowned in the River Nene. The king suffered the indignity of being captured by an archer.

In the aftermath, Richard, Duke of York, returned from Ireland and was appointed Protector. Despite the existence of Henry's son, Prince Edward, an agreement was also reached whereby, on Henry's death, York would succeed to the throne.

The battlefield today
The battlefield is on the A508 approach road to Northampton – exit Junction 15 of the M1 (OS Landranger 152 7559). The exact location is uncertain. Traditionally, the site is associated with an area north of Delapre Abbey, close to the River Nene, although an alternative site, between the abbey and Hardingstone, has also been proposed. Car parking (and refreshments) are available at the abbey.

Further reading
Rupert Matthews, *The Wars of the Roses: Northampton 1460* (Bretwalda Books, 2013).

29. Wakefield, 30 December 1460

Richard, Duke of York's recognition as the rightful heir of Henry VI could never be accepted by leading Lancastrians, and within a few months of their defeat at Northampton, they were back in arms – notably Henry, 3rd Earl of Northumberland; Ranulph, Lord Dacre; John, 9th Baron Clifford; John, Lord Neville of Raby; Henry Beaufort, 2nd Duke of Somerset; Henry Holland, 2nd Duke of Exeter; and Thomas Courtenay, 6th Earl of Devon. An army of up to 20,000 was assembled in the north, where Lancastrian support was strongest.

On 2 December 1460, the Duke of York and the Earl of Salisbury marched from London to meet this latest challenge.

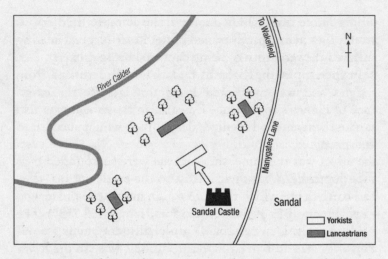

Progress was slow and it was not until 21 December that York reached his own fortress, Sandal Castle, near Wakefield.

Few battles took place during the winter months, for armies generally lived off the land. York knew that he was heavily outnumbered, perhaps by as many as four to one. His eldest son, Edward, Earl of March, was recruiting in Shrewsbury and it was hoped that he could hold out until Edward joined him. The Lancastrian army was camped nine miles away, at Pontefract, and after surprising a Yorkist foraging party, they advanced on Sandal Castle.

The Lancastrians, fielding a large army led by Somerset must have been short of provisions, but the position inside the castle was desperate. No one knows why the Yorkists left the safety of the castle walls – indeed, the Duke's advisers spoke against it – but hunger may have played a part in the decision to do so. It has further been suggested that York was enticed out by Somerset, who concealed half his army in surrounding woodland. And so, on 30 December, when York decided to give battle, he sallied forth under the mistaken impression that Yorkists and Lancastrians were evenly matched.

Somerset's main force was arrayed on Wakefield Green, between castle and town. In the early afternoon, the Yorkists descended to meet it. The Lancastrians left it to their opponents to attack, which the Yorkists did, with great vigour. When they were fully committed, Somerset sprung his trap, horsemen appearing from the woods on both Yorkist flanks.

In an alternative scenario, one of York's supporters, Lord Neville, hove into view but, instead of coming to his aid as York expected, Neville's men joined the Lancastrians and executed the outflanking manoeuvre. In either case, the effect was the same: the Yorkists were surrounded by a superior force. With their retreat to the castle cut off, they had to fight on, which they did for an hour until those who were able to do so began to slip away.

Most of the Duke of York's army, including many senior Yorkists, was destroyed. Richard himself was cut down, as was his youngest son, the Earl of Rutland, apparently put to death on Wakefield Bridge by Clifford, whose act earned him the sobriquet, 'The Butcher'.

Captives, including the Earl of Salisbury, were removed to Pontefract Castle, where the Duke of Exeter was instrumental in having Salisbury beheaded. At length, the Lancastrian army repaired to York, where a paper crown was placed upon the Duke of York's severed head prior to its attachment to the city's Micklegate Bar.

The battlefield today

Sandal Castle lies two miles to the south of Wakefield on the A61 Barnsley road (OS Landranger 110 3318). Look out for the Sandal Castle sign at the junction with Manygates Lane. The castle has a visitor centre and car park. Opposite the recreation ground on Manygates Lane is a memorial supposedly marking the spot where the Duke of York fell.

Further reading
Helen Cox, *The Battle of Wakefield Revisited* (Herstory Writing, 2010).

30. Mortimer's Cross, 2 February 1461

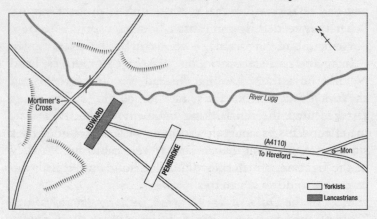

While recruiting in the West Country, Edward, Earl of March, eldest son of Richard, Duke of York, heard of his father's death at the Battle of Wakefield. The victorious Lancastrian army was marching south to London, and Edward set off to intercept it. Another, smaller Lancastrian force, led by Jasper, Earl of Pembroke, and Owen Tudor started off in pursuit of Edward, and he thought it expedient to deal with it first before tackling the main body. The spot he chose was Mortimer's Cross, five miles to the north-west of Leominster.

On the morning of 2 February 1461, Edward deployed his army to the south of the present-day B4362, the River Lugg to his left, high ground to his rear and right, and a plain before him. It is claimed that he was cheered that morning by the appearance in the sky of a most unusual phenomenon: a parhelion or 'sun dog', in which a luminous ring or halo appears on either side of the sun, giving an impression of three suns. Edward later added the rays of the sun to the House of York's White Rose badge, creating *the rose-en-soleil*.

Pembroke approached from Watling Street, deploying his own force on the level ground facing the Yorkists. One can only guess at the size of the respective armies.

Contemporary sources suggest up to 8,000 Lancastrians and 15,000 Yorkists. In reality, the numbers probably would not have exceeded around 3,000 apiece.

No details of the battle have survived, but Pembroke's men – Welsh and some Irish – would have been lightly armed and deficient in archers. Edward lost no time in attacking and the enemy was driven swiftly from the field. Fugitives were pursued towards Hereford, and even into Wales. Pembroke made good his escape, but a number of 'gentlemen of consideration', including Owen Tudor, were captured. Mindful of the Lancastrian excesses at Wakefield, Edward had him executed. Tudor had married Katherine, widow of Henry V, and, as he was about to lose his head, he famously remarked, 'This head must lie on the block which was wont to lie in Queen Katherine's lap.'

The battle was an important one for the Yorkist cause, in part offsetting the disaster at Wakefield and providing the Earl of March with his first victory as a commander in the field. Of course, he had the advantage of familiarity with the local country and the army he faced was inferior to his own. Moreover, he lingered for some days before resuming his march to London, thus depriving the Earl of Warwick of the support that might have turned the tide at the 2nd Battle of St Albans.

The battlefield today

Mortimer's Cross is on the A4110, fifteen miles to the north of Hereford (OS Landranger 149 4262). Car parking is available for patrons of Mortimer's Cross Inn, on the B4362. Mortimer's Cross Mill, also on the B4362, has a modest display dedicated to the battle. A battlefield monument is three-quarters of a mile to the south at the A4110/B4360 junction, adjacent to Kingsland's Monument Inn – lending some credence to the theory that the battle was actually fought here. Other suggestions include the possibility that the action took place on an east-west axis, centring on the present-day B4362.

Further reading
Geoffrey Hodges, *Ludford Bridge and Mortimer's Cross*
(Logaston Press, 2001).

31. 2nd St Albans, 17 February 1461

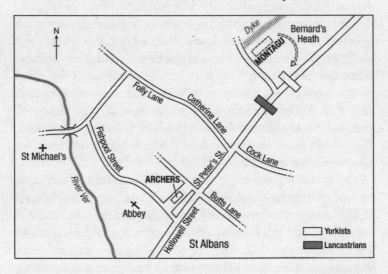

After their great victory at Wakefield, the main Lancastrian
army in the field awaited the return of Queen Margaret,
who had been canvassing for support in Scotland. Edward,
Earl of March's success at Mortimer's Cross on 2 February
had little effect on the Lancastrian master plan, which was
to march on London.

The rag-tag army of Scots that accompanied Margaret
to York must have been received with some disquiet by
the Lancastrian grandees for, as the entire army moved
south, the Scots were allowed to pillage at will, Grantham,
Stamford, Peterborough, Huntingdon and Royston all suffering as a result.

Meanwhile, in London, the Earl of Warwick was preparing to meet the expected onslaught. Taking a captive
Henry VI with him, he marched out to St Albans with his

8,000-strong army on 12 February. He himself camped two and a half miles to the north of the city, at Sandridge. His main defensive position, under the command of his brother, John Neville, Lord Montagu, was nearer to St Albans, on the high ground of Bernard's Heath – drawn up behind Beech Bottom, an Iron Age dyke.

The hardware utilized by the Yorkists is by no means devoid of interest. Caltrops were positioned to impede both cavalry and infantry; pavises, or large shields with holes pierced for arrows, were set up for the use of archers; large nets supported by iron stakes were sited to hamper attackers; Burgundian artillerymen skilled in shooting 'pellets of lead' and 'wildefire' – the medieval equivalent of the incendiary bomb – were also deployed. However, all of these elaborate arrangements were geared to an assault coming from the north-west, the direction from which, naturally enough, an attack was expected to come. Unfortunately, the approaching Lancastrians (perhaps 12,000 of them) were working to a different plan.

At Royston, the Lancastrians left Ermine Street, marching to Dunstable and Watling Street, which enabled them to enter St Albans from the west. On the morning of 17 February, after a night march, they crossed the River Ver by St Michael's Bridge, unopposed, continuing via Fishpool Street, only to run into a party of archers in the market place – the only body of Yorkists stationed within the city itself. Driven back, the Lancastrians (probably commanded by Sir Andrew Trollope) then made their way by Folly Lane into Catherine Lane and St Peter's Street.

Montagu and Warwick may well have decided to sacrifice the archers to give them time to reorganize the Bernard's Heath defences. When the archers had been dealt with, therefore, the Lancastrians advanced on Bernard's Heath to encounter stiff opposition. At first, they were held, even though such artillery and handguns as the Yorkists possessed failed to live up to expectations. Furthermore, Montagu was waiting for Warwick to come to his aid with the Sandridge division.

For some reason, Warwick was slow – too slow – in getting his men on the move. By the time they started, Montagu had finally given way. Trollope had broken through and, as Warwick advanced, he was met by his brother's contingent running towards him. As so often happened, the panic was contagious and many of Warwick's own men turned tail. Somehow, Warwick managed to stem the tide and make a fighting retreat northwards, beyond Sandridge to a location known as No Man's Land. Here, at dusk, the fighting petered out. Despite suffering heavy casualties, Warwick managed to withdraw with some 4,000 men and eventually to join the Earl of March.

The battle had significant repercussions for Warwick: his reputation as a general was irreparably damaged and the Lancastrian Sir John Groby was mortally wounded. The latter issue was important, for Sir John left a widow, Elizabeth Woodville, whose wooing by the future Edward IV would lead to increased tension between king and 'kingmaker'.

The battlefield today
St Albans is twenty-two miles to the north of London (Junction 9 of the M1 or Junction 22 of the M25) (OS Landranger 166 1508). Use the city centre car parks. Fishpool Street survives, as does Folly Lane and Catherine Lane (now Catherine Street). Bernard's Heath is now a built-up area, but stretches of Beech Bottom can still be seen.

Further reading
Peter Burley, Michael Elliott and Harvey Watson, *The Battles of St Albans* (Pen & Sword, 2007).

32. Ferrybridge, 28 March 1461

With the defeat of two Yorkist armies, those of the Duke of York at Wakefield and the Earl of Warwick at St Albans, and while Edward, Earl of March, was isolated in the West

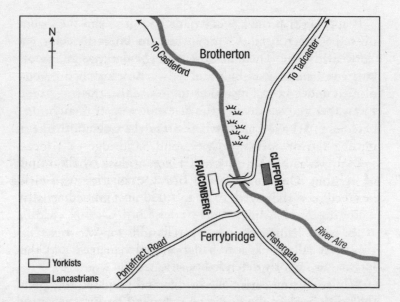

Country, one might have thought that the Lancastrians would consolidate their success by advancing on London. And yet, this they did not do. Their leaders may have been worried that their army would have gone on the rampage, thus sacrificing the much-needed support of the capital's citizens. So, they turned north once more, still plundering as they went.

Meanwhile, the Earl of Warwick had not been idle. With the remnants of his army, he marched westward and joined forces with Edward at Chipping Norton. Together, they marched to London, arriving on 26 February 1461, for Edward to be proclaimed King Edward IV.

Aware that a strong Lancastrian army was still in the field, the new king spent only a short time consolidating his position. By 16 March, he was on the road. By the time he reached Pontefract on 27 March, he had amassed a formidable army of 40,000 men. The Lancastrian army, reportedly over 60,000 strong, left York, passed through Tadcaster and camped two and a half miles south of the town, on Towton Heath.

It appears that the Lancastrians had damaged the bridge over the River Aire at Ferrybridge in order to delay the Yorkist advance. Then, as now, Ferrybridge was an important communications hub and Edward despatched a body of men under Lord Fitzwalter to secure the crossing point. Fitzwalter arrived during the afternoon of 27 March, dispersing a party of Lancastrians arrayed on the north bank of the river, and set up camp.

Early the next day, Fitzwalter was woken by the sound of fighting. Thinking it was a fracas among his own men, he emerged bleary-eyed, to be killed almost immediately by a contingent of Lancastrians under Lord Clifford. Riding at the head of his light cavalry ('The Flower of Craven' as they were called), Clifford had mounted a surprise attack on Fitzwalter's poorly defended position.

While Clifford broke the bridge and prepared to defend the north bank of the Aire, the surviving Yorkists retreated to Pontefract. Rallying their army, Edward and Warwick resolved to march on Ferrybridge. Upon their approach on the afternoon of 28 March, they came under fire from Lancastrian archers. The Yorkist archers replied, while their engineers pondered methods of rendering the bridge serviceable. A makeshift walkway was constructed and a group of Yorkists edged forward to put it in place. Such was the power of the Lancastrian archers that all attempts failed, resulting in heavy casualties, among whom was Warwick, who took an arrow in the leg as he personally led a desperate charge on the bridge.

Edward now devised an alternative plan, which involved flanking Clifford by sending Lord Fauconberg and 1,000 men to cross the river three miles higher up, at Castleford. Fauconberg effected the crossing, but Clifford's scouts got wind of his approach and the Lancastrians began a retreat towards their main army at Towton.

At least the bridge was now open to the Yorkists, and Warwick and Fauconberg pursued the fleeing Lancastrians.

It was Fauconberg who caught up with Clifford. Tantalizingly close to the safety of the Lancastrian camp, at Dintingdale, 'The Flower of Craven' were wiped out. Clifford himself was hit in the throat by a bodkin arrow, the fifteenth-century equivalent of the 'dum dum' bullet, which spread out on impact. The Battle of Ferrybridge was over, and the death, at Clifford's hands, of the young Earl of Rutland at Wakefield three months earlier, avenged. The fight had been a bloody affair, but was as nothing compared to what was yet to come.

The battlefield today

Ferrybridge stands at the multi-junction of the A1, A63, A1M and M62. Exit from Junction 42 of the A1M or Junction 34 of the M62. The bridge of the battle, no longer used by traffic, is off the B6136, adjacent to the A162 (OS Landranger 105 4824).

Further reading

Philip A. Haigh, *From Wakefield to Towton* (Pen & Sword, 2002).

33. Towton, 29 March 1461

The Battle of Towton was the bloodiest encounter of the Wars of the Roses. It followed hard on the heels of the Battle of Ferrybridge, occasioned by the efforts of the Yorkist army of Edward, Duke of York, to secure a passage over the River Aire and so come to grips with the Lancastrian army of Queen Margaret of Anjou.

Following his victory at Ferrybridge, Lord Fauconberg may well have lingered in the vicinity of the village of Saxton to await the arrival of the main body of Yorkists, which straggled in during the evening of 28 March 1461. In contrast to the opposing Lancastrian army, settled in a little to the north, at Towton, the Yorkists must have passed a miserable night. The following morning, the two armies,

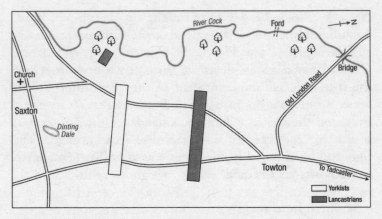

drawn up in lines up to a mile in length, came face to face. Church bells were ringing, for it was a Sunday – Palm Sunday. And it began to snow.

Considering its magnitude, comparatively little is known about the course of the battle. However, it is reasonably certain that the 40,000-strong Lancastrian army was drawn up to the south of Towton. Its leaders included the 2nd Duke of Somerset, the Earl of Northumberland, Lord Dacre and Thomas Courtenay, Earl of Devon. The Yorkist leaders, in addition to Edward, were the Earl of Warwick, William Neville, Lord Fauconberg and the Earl of Norfolk – the latter, lagging behind, would not reach the battlefield until the afternoon. The Yorkist army numbered perhaps 35,000 men.

The battle began in the late morning. Fauconberg ordered the Yorkist archers to advance. After firing a volley into the packed Lancastrian ranks, they withdrew. The Lancastrian bowmen responded, firing repeated volleys of arrows almost blindly into the snow, which was being driven into their faces by an icy wind. Yorkist bowmen stepped forward to retrieve the arrows that had fallen short of their targets.

The Lancastrian front line then advanced. Many were hit by their own wasted arrows as the Yorkist bowmen kept up a continuous fire. At length, the two sides collided, spears and billhooks to the fore, in a trial of strength that lasted for up to two hours. The numbers involved in the battle were so great that as men fell, their places were quickly filled.

It is possible that the Lancastrians had a party of men secreted in the vicinity of Castle Hill Wood, to the extreme left of the Yorkist lines. The ruse had worked at Wakefield a few months earlier, and if an assault from this quarter materialized, then the Yorkists could well have been in trouble. Just when it seemed that their lines must give way, Norfolk finally arrived on the scene with enough weight to redress the balance, but insufficient to turn the tide in a spectacular manner.

The battle-weary troops fought on. During the afternoon, Lord Dacre, pausing to take a drink of water, removed his helmet and was killed by an arrow fired, it was said, by a boy who recognized Dacre as the man who had killed his father. At some point, the Earl of Northumberland was also slain and it could well have been gaps in the leadership which led the Lancastrian rank and file to lose heart. Men in the rear began to steal away. Unchecked, this furtive exodus quickly developed into a steady trickle and, finally, into mass flight.

Much has been written about the likely locations of the greatest slaughter of the retreating hordes. Those on the Lancastrian right fell back towards the River Cock and surrounding treacherous marshland. The area known as 'Bloody Meadow' houses a number of burial pits which contain the bodies of those who were buried where they fell. Many hastened through Towton and along Old London Road where, severely hampered by weight of numbers, they hoped to cross the river by Cock Bridge and make their way to York.

Casualties may have been in the region of 12,000 Lancastrians and 8,000 Yorkists, for the armies had been large and the fighting bloody; the final mortality count included a dozen barons and over forty knights. As some European commentators gleefully noted at the time, it would be long before England could prosecute any overseas wars, owing to the vast numbers slain at Towton. And yet, throughout the Wars of the Roses, the supply of manpower appears to have been inexhaustible, for no sooner had one side suffered a catastrophic defeat than it was back in the field with another substantial army.

Somerset and Exeter escaped, the only Lancastrian commanders to do so. The Earl of Devon was taken prisoner and, in due course, his head replaced what remained of the Duke of York's on Micklegate Bar in York.

On 28 June 1461, Edward was crowned King Edward IV, and the Lancastrians began to plot their revenge.

The battlefield today

The battlefield – complete with battlefield trail and information panels – lies between the villages of Towton and Saxton, off the A162, Ferrybridge to Tadcaster road (OS Landranger 105 4738). The village of Saxton, with on-road car parking by All Saints' Church, is a good starting point for further exploration. Lord Dacre is buried here, his tomb lying on the north side of the churchyard. There is a battlefield monument to the north of Saxton, on the B1217. Castle Hill Wood and Bloody Meadow are still to be seen, to the west of the B1217/Cotchers Lane junction. Old London Road, one of the Lancastrian escape routes, is now a bridleway, but can be followed from Towton's Rockingham Arms down to Cock Beck. At the Saxton end of the B1217, check out the Crooked Billet, occupying the site of an earlier inn which may have served as the Yorkist HQ. In a field opposite is Lead Chapel, sole surviving edifice of the long-gone settlement of Lead. It has no known direct connection with the battle, although it may have acted as a refuge for those taking flight and the wounded. The Richard III Society have reglazed one of the windows, which bears a representation of Richard's crest – a white boar.

Further reading

George Goodwin, *Fatal Colours: Towton, 1461* (Phoenix, 2012).

34. Hedgeley Moor, 25 April 1464

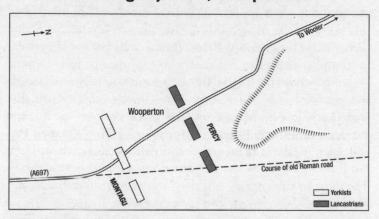

After their wholesale defeat at Towton, the Lancastrians tried to provoke unrest throughout the country, especially in the north of England and in Wales. They had always received encouragement in Scotland, but in the spring of 1464, Edward IV and the Scottish king, James III, entered into negotiations for a closer alliance.

On 10 April 1464, the Yorkist Lord Montagu was sent north with a modest escort to fetch a team of Scottish negotiators from Norham Castle to York, where talks were to take place. En route, the fugitive Duke of Somerset despatched a small force to ambush the Yorkists near Newcastle, but Montagu managed to avoid it, arriving safely in the town, where he received welcome reinforcements.

It was important for Somerset to stop the Yorkists making contact with the Scottish ambassadors, thereby proving to the Scots that the Lancastrian cause was still alive and well. Accordingly, he contrived to scrape together an army a few thousand strong and challenge Montagu on the final leg of his march to Norham. On 25 April, this scratch force, despatched from Alnwick Castle, blocked the Yorkists' path on gently rising open ground at Hedgeley Moor, seven miles south of Wooler.

Although the nature of the Lancastrian deployment is not known, their leaders included Somerset, Thomas, Lord Hungerford, Sir Ralph Grey, Humphrey Neville, Sir Ralph Percy and Henry, Lord Roos. It may well be that they were outnumbered by the Yorkists who deployed to face them.

It is possible that full battle never commenced, for the Lords Hungerford and Roos soon beat a hasty retreat from the centre and left of the Lancastrian ranks. Perhaps the Yorkist advance or an opening salvo from the Yorkist bowmen was sufficient to drive them from the field. Whatever the reason, Sir Ralph Percy was left to fight alone. He and his men took the fight to the enemy, but they were soon surrounded and decimated. Few, if any, can have escaped.

Montagu was now free to continue his journey unmolested. Thanks to his success at Hedgeley Moor, the negotiations between the Yorkists and the Scots went ahead, leaving the House of Lancaster even more isolated.

The battlefield today

The battlefield is off the A697, seven miles to the south of Wooler. Percy's Cross (OS Landranger 81 0419), supposedly marking the spot where Lord Percy expired, is adjacent to a group of farm buildings. Parking is available north of the cross, opposite the woodyard entrance, at Percy's Leap, a copse containing information panels about the battle. At this spot, when Percy made a vain attempt to break out, his horse supposedly made a gigantic leap – hence the name.

Further reading

Philip A. Haigh, *The Military Campaigns of the Wars of the Roses* (Sutton, 1995).

35. Hexham, 15 May 1464

Following Sir Ralph Percy's defeat at Hedgeley Moor, the outlook for Henry Beaufort, 3rd Duke of Somerset, and the

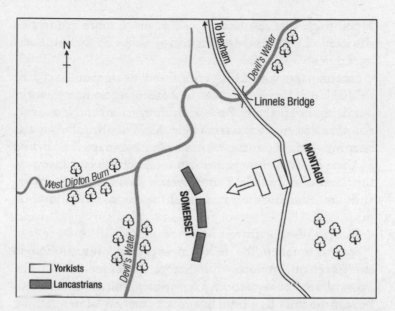

remnants of Lancastrian resistance looked bleak. Largely confined to a few castles within Northumberland, they were helpless. The Yorkist victor of Hedgeley Moor, Lord Montagu, sallied forth again, leaving Newcastle on 14 May 1464. He was bound for Hexham, in the Lancastrian heartland, where he aimed to flush out and destroy the last of the hard-core opposition.

Crossing the River Tyne (probably at Corbridge), Montagu continued south. Somerset, with just a few hundred of his followers, was camped about three miles to the south of Hexham, on the west bank of the Tyne tributary, Devil's Water on Hexham Levels. Ideal as a campsite, it was no place, with his back to the river, for Somerset to give battle.

On 15 May, Montagu approached the location and Somerset probably deployed his men on the gentle slopes in front of his camp. Few details concerning the course of the battle are available, but it is probable that Montagu lost no time in closing with the paltry force facing him. Roos and Hungerford were present and, having fled at Hedgeley

Moor, they were not likely to show much more grit in this situation. Doubtless, the fighting, although bloody, was over quickly.

In company with Hungerford and Roos, Somerset fled the field. All three were taken and executed: Somerset, without delay, in Hexham; Roos and Hungerford in Newcastle. Another leading Lancastrian light, Sir William Talboys, was later found hiding in a coal mine near Newcastle. Executed at York, his head was placed upon one of the city gates. At the time of his capture, a considerable sum of money, apparently intended for the payment of the troops, was found on his person.

Henry VI and Queen Margaret were still at large, but Henry was taken the following year and imprisoned in the Tower of London, while Margaret languished in exile. Edward IV had overcome his enemies, but it remained to be seen whether he would be quite as successful in retaining his friends.

The battlefield today
The battlefield is off the B6306, three miles to the south of Hexham (Landranger 87 9561). The only access to the battlefield is via a track to Linnels Farm. A proposed alternative site for the battle is at the other side of the B6306, on Swallowship Hill (9662). There is a little off-road car parking on the Hexham side of Linnels Bridge. To the west, in West Dipton Wood, is Queen's Cave (9061), where Queen Margaret and Prince Edward allegedly hid after the battle. It was the haunt of bandits, one of whom led the queen and her son to safety – an apocryphal story, but it's still a cracking tale.

Further reading
John Sadler and Alex Spiers, *The Battle of Hexham in its Place* (Ergo Press, 2007).

FRIEND OR FOE?

Today's staunchest friend can be tomorrow's most determined enemy. For example, no one could have prophesied that the most dedicated of Yorkists, the Earl of Warwick, would shift his allegiance to the House of Lancaster, ending his life and career facing his protégé, Edward IV, on the battlefield at Barnet (1470). Similarly, Edward placed implicit trust in his loyal brother, Richard, Duke of Gloucester, only for Gloucester to usurp the throne after his death – Richard, in turn, being betrayed by the Earl of Northumberland and Thomas, Lord Stanley, at Bosworth (1485).

Stanley was a master of the art of keeping his friends close and his enemies closer. Thus, he had failed to join Edward at Blore Heath (1459) and had given armed support to Warwick prior to Barnet, while contriving to remain in Edward's favour. On the other hand, Stanley's contemporary, Lord Wenlock, lacked these skills, openly fighting for Lancaster at 1st St Albans (1455), York at Towton (1461) and Lancaster at Tewkesbury (1471) where, suspected of treachery, he was allegedly despatched by the Duke of Somerset.

Civil wars do tend to test one's loyalties. In January 1642, the Royalist, Sir John Hotham, was appointed Governor of Hull. Three months later, he defected to Parliament and closed the city to the king. In 1643, he and his son, John, entered into negotiations with the Marquis of Newcastle with a view to handing it back again. Their machinations discovered, both Hothams were eventually executed, the son compounding his treachery by turning against his father in the hope of saving himself.

The most prolific turncoat of the Civil Wars is thought to be the Scotsman Sir John Urry. A professional soldier, he fought for Parliament at Edgehill (1642); for the Royalists at Chalgrove (1643); for Parliament at Auldearn (1645) and for the Royalists at Caribsdale (1650), after which he was beheaded. Unlike the Hothams, who resented the power of Lord Fairfax and his son, Sir Thomas, he seems to have harboured no malice, his shifting loyalties merely reflecting mercurial changes in his political views.

Another man of conscience was the Marquis of Montrose, who fought against Charles I in the Bishops' Wars of 1639–40 and then battled valiantly for him in Scotland during 1644–45 – only to be abandoned when it suited Charles to treat with the opposition. Having failed to learn the lesson, Montrose came out again in 1650, fighting at Caribsdale to support the return of the future Charles II. Thrown to the wolves a second time, he paid the supreme penalty.

John Graham of Claverhouse, Viscount Dundee, also served the Stuart dynasty unto death. Having done his duty in the Covenanter Wars of 1679, Dundee remained faithful to James II after his deposition in 1688. Spearheading the '89 Jacobite rebellion in Scotland, Dundee was killed at Killiecrankie, his master having promised support which did not materialize.

The Stuarts would make any promise to anyone who would help them to retain or retrieve power. Some of their supporters did act through self-interest – the Earl of Mar, for example, leader of the 1715 Jacobite rebellion, had changed his allegiance so often that he was known as 'Bobbing John' – but the rank-and-file Highlanders (regarded as a valuable source of cannon fodder) generally displayed unswerving loyalty, for which they would ultimately pay a heavy price with the destruction of their way of life.

C'est la guerre.

36. Battle of Edgcote, 26 July 1469

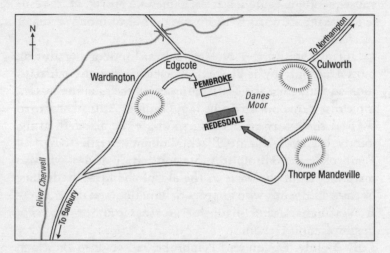

Henry VI had been confined to the Tower of London in 1465, while his queen, Margaret of Anjou, was forced into exile. The problem for the Yorkists was that the young Edward IV wanted to throw off the guiding hand of the Earl of Warwick and stand on his own two feet. Edward wished to create closer links with Burgundy, whereas Warwick wanted to conclude an alliance with France, involving a French marriage for the king. In the end, Edward went ahead and concluded an agreement with Burgundy, and chose his own wife: Elizabeth Woodville, a widow whose husband had died fighting at 2nd St Albans (1461) – on the Lancastrian side.

Aware of the rift in the Yorkist camp, Lancastrian sympathizers were quick to take advantage, inciting riot where once there had only been discontent. Shrewd observers were of the opinion that a disgruntled Warwick was responsible. The most successful risings, based on perennial complaints about taxation, occurred in the north and were led,

ostensibly, by the two 'Robins': Robin of Redesdale (allegedly a name assumed by Sir John Conyers of Hornby) and
Robin of Holderness. The latter was crushed at York and
subsequently executed, but his namesake proved more resil-
ient, leaving Edward with no option but to mount a major
offensive.

During the summer of 1469, Edward moved northward,
mustering an army as he went. Warwick, who was in Calais,
took advantage of the situation to cross the Channel with a
force of his own and marched on London. A third army led
by Redesdale was proceeding south, while a fourth army,
jointly led by William ('Black William') Herbert, Earl of
Pembroke, and Humphrey Stafford, Earl of Devon, was
marching from the west to the aid of the king. Redesdale
bypassed Edward, who appears to have lingered indecisively
at Nottingham, and made for Northampton to intercept
Pembroke and Devon.

By 23 July, Devon and Pembroke had reached Banbury.
Devon, accompanied by Pembroke's brother, Richard
Herbert, led a party of horse to reconnoitre the neighbourhood of Northampton. To their surprise, they encountered
Redesdale's army and, following a sharp engagement, were
forced to retire. Redesdale soon set off in pursuit and took
up a strong position on the hills around Edgcote Lodge, five
and a half miles from Banbury.

In Banbury itself, the outcome of the approaching battle
was already being decided. Pembroke had upset Devon's bil-
leting arrangements and Devon subsequently stormed off in
a huff, setting up camp with his troops – including, crucially,
his archers – some miles away. Despite this blow, which left
him with as few as 6,000 men, Pembroke resolved to challenge Redesdale. On 25 July, therefore, he sent forward his
vanguard, which succeeded in taking the hill at Upper
Wardington, one of those occupied by Redesdale. The morning of 26 July dawned with the Welshmen occupying the hill
in force and, although outnumbered, ready for battle.

The northerners had massed at Thorpe Mandeville and now advanced to Danesmoor, beneath Pembroke's position. From here, they subjected him to volleys of arrows. In the absence of Devon's archers, Pembroke could not respond in kind and was forced to descend to the plain. It is said that a fierce fight ranged for some hours until a force of about 500 men, probably gathered from Northampton and the surrounding villages by John Clapham, a follower of Warwick, appeared on Culworth Hill.

With cries of 'A Warwick! A Warwick!' ringing in their ears, it was too much for the Welsh. Perhaps fearing that Warwick himself had arrived, they broke and fled. The northerners (in the absence of Redesdale *alias* Conyers, who was killed during the battle) set off in pursuit, slaying and capturing them in large numbers. Pembroke and his brother survived, only to be executed in Northampton the next day on Warwick's orders. Devon, who, according to some accounts, had arrived belatedly to join the fight, was eventually run to ground and executed in Bridgwater.

Edward was in the midlands when the news of Edgcote reached him. His army promptly deserted and he was reduced to going cap in hand to Warwick. Eventually, a public reconciliation took place, but Edward must have been aware that as long as Warwick lived, he could never be master in his own kingdom.

The battlefield today

The battlefield is off the A361, five and a half miles to the north-east of Banbury – exit from Junction 11 of the M40. There is no monument, but the site (Landranger 151 5047) can be explored easily via the public footpath system from either Upper Wardington (4946) or Chipping Warden (4948). On-road parking is available in both villages.

Further reading
Philip A. Haigh, *The Military Campaigns of the Wars of the Roses*
    (Sutton, 1995).

37. Empingham, 12 March 1470

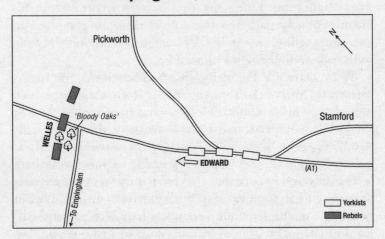

The mutual distrust between Edward IV and the Earl of
Warwick continued to simmer throughout the early months
of 1470. Edward's problems were compounded by a number
of local risings; some revolved around general discontent,
while others were family feuds seasoned with a dash of
Yorkist–Lancastrian rivalry.

In Lincolnshire, unrest was fomented by a Lancastrian,
Richard, Lord Welles, and his son, Sir Robert, assisted
by Lord Welles' brother-in-law, Sir Thomas Dimmock.
Supposedly, the focus was on a dispute between Lord Welles
and Sir Thomas Burgh of Gainsborough, a member of the
king's household. When Burgh's house was destroyed,
Edward summoned Lord Welles and Dimmock to the capital but, fearing his wrath, both sought the sanctuary of
Westminster Abbey.

On 6 March, determined to nip any trouble in the bud,
Edward set out for Lincolnshire with the nucleus of an

army, having given instructions for more troops to assemble at Grantham, and for Warwick and the Duke of Clarence to raise as many men as they could in the midlands. En route to Grantham, news reached him that Sir Robert Welles was raising an army to oppose him. On promise of safe conduct, Lord Welles and Dimmock were hurriedly brought up to Huntingdon, where they admitted their involvement in encouraging discontent. Welles was made to write to his son with instructions to give himself up.

By 11 March, Edward had reached Stamford, his scouts informing him of the approach of Sir Robert's army, which halted five miles short of the town. It was there, along the ridge of high ground slightly to the north of present-day Tickencote Warren, that Sir Robert deployed his men. Edward promptly had Lord Welles and Dimmock executed.

The total strength of the rebel force is difficult to estimate. Stamford was strongly Yorkist and all available manpower had been mobilized before the rebels' arrival, with leading local families such as the Mackworths of Empingham throwing their weight behind the king. The highest contemporary estimate of rebel numbers is 30,000, but the total is more likely to have been fewer than half that number, especially when allowance is made for the probability of the disaffected slipping away as the prospect of battle loomed.

Edward's army may not have been substantially larger. Sir Robert's arrival had stopped him from reaching Grantham and had also forestalled a planned rendezvous with Warwick and Clarence. However, he must have been aware of the relatively poor quality of the opposition, for he chose to take the fight to them, marching out of Stamford on the morning of 12 March to attack the strong defensive position Sir Robert had selected.

Edward had a number of cannon, which were dragged laboriously up the Casterton road towards Tickencote, and progress must have been slow as the rebels, drawn up squarely across the present-day A1, watched them coming on. As soon as the enemy was within range, the cannon were made ready and several salvos were fired into their lines. Apparently, the damage wreaked by the guns was sufficient to strike terror into the hearts of the rebels. The firing was probably inaccurate and may not have caused much by way of death and destruction, but it did give the impression of superior strength. Edward then ordered an assault on the enemy position.

That there was some resistance is borne out by reported cries within the rebel ranks of 'A Clarence! A Warwick!', designed to rally the troops, but as Edward's cavalry reached the ridge, all opposition, real or feigned, collapsed. It is said that, in their haste to escape, the panic-stricken rebels cast away their tunics, thus giving the confrontation its alternative title: 'The Battle of Losecoat Field'. In the hope of avoiding identification, it is probable that some men – for example, Sir Robert's own retainers, who would have worn his livery – did throw away their coats. Others may have worn emblems that would have been torn from jackets and headgear. Sir Robert himself was captured, but the slaughter among the fleeing rebels must have been great.

Soon after the battle, on 19 March 1470, Sir Robert was executed, having provided a confession implicating Warwick and Clarence in the Lincolnshire rising. Edward denounced both men as traitors and posted rewards for their capture, but they slipped through his net. Accompanied by a substantial retinue, they sailed for the continent, acquiring sanctuary in Honfleur, courtesy of Louis XI.

There were some who believed that Edward had concocted the idea of a Warwick/Clarence-led conspiracy; the Lincolnshire rising, it was claimed, presented a convenient scenario for the implementation of his own plans to dispose of the pair. Whatever the truth of the matter, for the time being at least, Edward's position was secure.

The battlefield today

The battlefield is five miles to the north of Stamford, between the Empingham and Pickworth junctions of the A1

(OS Landranger 130 9711). The wood bordering the north-bound carriageway is still known as 'Bloody Oaks' and was allegedly an area in which many rebels were killed. Roadside parking is available in Empingham.

Further reading
Rupert Matthews, *The Battle of Losecoat Field 1470* (Bretwalda Books, 2013).

38. Barnet, 14 April 1471

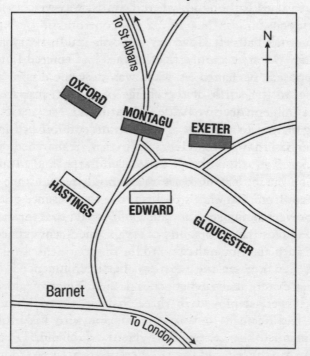

When the Earl of Warwick fled to France after the Battle of Empingham, he forged an alliance with his old enemy, Queen Margaret of Anjou, against Edward IV. On 13 September 1470, Warwick returned to England with an invasion force, and the unprepared Edward was forced to flee abroad. He repaired to

Burgundy, where he found sufficient backing to enable him to return on 14 March 1471 – to find Warwick and the Duke of Clarence installed as joint protectors of the realm.

At the end of March, Warwick was recruiting in the west midlands when he learned that the recently arrived Edward, with an increasing number of supporters, was advancing towards him. He retreated within the walls of Coventry to await the arrival of his collaborator, Clarence. When Clarence did arrive, Edward held out the olive branch and the two brothers joined forces. Together, they left Warwick and marched to London, where Edward was welcomed by the citizens.

Warwick had left Coventry and was only twenty miles behind. When he learned that Edward had entered London unopposed, he halted at what was described as a 'faire plaine' to the north of the village of Barnet, prepared to risk all on one decisive battle. Edward, too, was anxious to bring matters to a speedy conclusion and, on 13 April 1471 – Easter Saturday – with Henry VI in tow, he marched out of London. Towards nightfall, he reached Barnet and advanced beyond the settlement to set up camp. There was some harassment from Warwick's artillery, but the presence of thick fog prevented any serious damage. It is said that the armies were so close that the sound of men's voices was carried on the leaden air from one camp to the other.

At 5.00 a.m. on the next day, battle commenced, both armies evenly matched at around 15,000 men. Warwick's troops were deployed in three 'battles'. Lord Montagu, who had decided to throw in his lot with his brother, commanded the centre, with Henry Holland, Duke of Exeter, on the left and John de Vere, Earl of Oxford, on the right. Warwick may have been in the rear, commanding a reserve. For Edward, William, Lord Hastings, commanded the left wing, Richard, Duke of Gloucester (later King Richard III), took command of the right, with Edward in the centre.

In the slowly clearing mist, a preliminary exchange of arrows and artillery fire had limited effect, and the two sides advanced on each other at a comparatively early stage. However, poor visibility had led to an overlapping of the opposing lines. Edward's division overlapped that of Montagu, and Gloucester found himself advancing on a vacant position. Similarly, Hastings was out of alignment with Oxford's division and the latter's advance over reasonably level ground developed into an outflanking manoeuvre which discomfited the Yorkist left wing, putting it to flight.

Oxford experienced some difficulty in controlling the ensuing pursuit, and the cut-throat element embarked on a rampage which saw many within Hastings' division chased halfway to London. Survivors who reached the city brought stories of a wholesale Yorkist collapse, throwing the citizens into a panic.

Meanwhile, on the Yorkist right wing, Gloucester also advanced upon a vacant position, and so he turned to outflank Exeter, a movement lacking the punch of Oxford's because he was marching uphill. Exeter held his ground. In the centre, Edward was pushed back by Montagu. The overall result, with the men of Oxford and Hastings absent from the field, and with Gloucester's pressure on Exeter, was to shift the axis of the fighting from north-south to east-west. At this stage, Warwick must have felt that victory was within his grasp. If so, then his hopes were to be dashed by the return of Oxford, who had managed to partially regroup.

In the lingering mist, Oxford was unaware of the new battle lines and advanced upon what he thought was the Yorkist rear but what was, in fact, Montagu's right flank. Montagu's men, similarly confused, bombarded Oxford with a hail of arrows. Convinced that Montagu had changed his colours, Oxford's men abandoned the field for the second and last time. Hard upon the heels of this disaster there occurred the death of Montagu himself. With Exeter also seriously wounded, Warwick was left in sole command of his confused and now rapidly disintegrating army.

At this juncture, any reserves at Edward's disposal would have been thrown into the conflict. Warwick, on the other hand, may well have been compelled to call on men already exhausted and confused. The day was lost and by 10.00 a.m. or noon at the latest, victory lay with Edward. The dead may have numbered as many as 3,000 or as few as 1,500. Edward instructed his men to give no quarter, and many wounded Lancastrians must have been despatched.

The appearance of Edward in London put the citizens' minds at rest. Warwick's body was brought to the capital and placed on show so that his demise could not be doubted. So ended the life of the man called 'the kingmaker' and 'the last of the barons'.

As for Edward, there were still pressing matters to which he must attend, for, on the day of his victory at Barnet, Queen Margaret of Anjou landed at Weymouth and the Countess of Warwick at Portsmouth.

The battlefield today

The battle took place to the north of Barnet at Hadley (OS Landranger 166 2497). Exit from Junction 1 of the A1M/ Junction 23 of the M25 and follow the A1081 into Monken Hadley and Barnet, where there are a number of public car parks, e.g. Stapylton Road and Moxon Street. Alternatively, if using public transport, make for High Barnet station on the Northern Line. A battlefield monument, allegedly marking the site of Warwick's death, stands at the junction of Kitts End Road and Hadley Highstone. Barnet Museum, in Wood Street, houses a model of the battle and is an essential first port of call prior to any exploration of the battlefield via the public footpath system.

Further reading
David Clark, *Barnet 1471* (Pen & Sword, 2007).

39. Tewkesbury, 4 May 1471

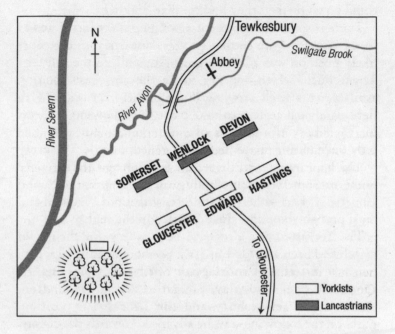

Had the Earl of Warwick awaited the arrival of Queen Margaret of Anjou and her supporters from France before engaging Edward IV at Barnet, that battle may have had a different outcome. As it was, when the queen learned of Warwick's defeat, Lancastrians the Earl of Devon and Edmund Beaufort, 4th Duke of Somerset, had to persuade her to remain in England.

While Margaret proceeded through the West Country, slowly gathering support, Edward rode out of Windsor at the head of an army of Barnet veterans and new recruits. On 2 May, the Lancastrians were advancing on Gloucester, with a view to crossing the River Severn and linking up with Jasper Tudor in Wales. Much to their consternation, the gates of the town were closed to them, and they turned for Tewkesbury, ten miles upstream. When they arrived, in the late afternoon

of 3 May, the queen and Somerset realized that the tired army
could go no further: they had to stand and fight.

There is some disagreement among military historians as
to the defensive site chosen by the Lancastrians. The most
likely position was a low ridge at Gupshill, to the south of
Tewkesbury, which appears to be the strongest position
available to a tired army with its back to the wall. With
fighting almost certain to take place the following day, rest
for the weary troops was of paramount importance, the
only outstanding matter being the order of battle. The army
would be drawn up in three divisions along the ridge, the
Duke of Somerset commanding the right wing and John
Courtenay, Earl of Devon the left, with Lord Wenlock and
most probably young Prince Edward in the centre.

The Yorkists must also have been weary, for their own
march had been attended by its own share of hardship, particularly in terms of shortage of water and provisions. At
about 4.00 p.m. on 3 May, Edward rested at Tredlington,
just short of Tewkesbury and the Lancastrian position.
Early on the following day, he advanced towards the enemy.
Lord Hastings was on the right, the Duke of Gloucester on
the left, and Edward and the Duke of Clarence in the centre.
Some 200 spearmen were deployed in woodland on the far
left. In all, Edward had about 5,000 men opposed to the
Lancastrians' 6,000.

Edward began by subjecting the Lancastrians to an arrow
and artillery barrage, the brunt of which appears to have been
borne by Somerset. Perhaps as part of a set-piece manoeuvre
or maybe simply to relieve the pressure, Somerset advanced
to meet Gloucester. Veering to the left, his men ended up
nearer to the Yorkist centre. Despite the suddenness of the
attack, the Yorkist centre held. Somerset, however, remained
unsupported and, when Gloucester attacked his right flank,
his position quickly became untenable. When the Yorkist
spearmen were called to action, the Lancastrian right wing
collapsed. As in many such instances, well-led disciplined

troops fighting a rearguard action might have regained their original position, but Somerset's men took flight. The Duke survived to berate Wenlock – some said, he shattered his skull with a battle-axe – for his failure to support him.

The pursuit of Somerset's survivors was left to Gloucester, while Edward and Hastings now advanced to engage the enemy centre and left. Demoralized, the Lancastrians seem to have offered little resistance and were rolled back until they, too, turned tail. Both Devon and Wenlock were killed, together with Prince Edward and some 2,000 additional Lancastrians, a good many in the field still known as Bloody Meadow, as against 500 Yorkists. Somerset and others sought refuge in the abbey, and were either dragged or enticed out, to be executed two days later.

As a result of his victory at Tewkesbury, all Edward's Lancastrian enemies were either dead or in custody. Queen Margaret was taken and remained in captivity until 1476, when she was permitted to return to France, where she lived in straitened circumstances until her death in 1492. Henry VI died in the Tower of London, supposedly of natural causes, although he may have been murdered on Edward's orders.

Following his unsuccessful attempt to link up with Margaret's army before Tewkesbury, Jasper Tudor and his nephew, Henry, Earl of Richmond, fled to Brittany where they lived in poverty for the next fourteen years. Edward kept a wary eye on them, but he was not unduly worried. After all, what sort of a challenge to Yorkist supremacy could ever be made by an impoverished exiled Tudor?

The battlefield today

Tewkesbury is off Junction 9 of the M5/Junction 1 of the M50. The battlefield is to the south of the town, off Gloucester Road (OS Landranger 150 8931). Allow a full summer's day for a visit. Best car parking can be found by the abbey in Gander Lane, looking out over The Vineyards.

Tewkesbury Museum in Barton Street houses a model of the battle. There is a battlefield monument in The Vineyards and the battlefield can be explored via a waymarked battlefield trail. An interpretation panel is located in Bloody Meadows.

Further reading
Christopher Gravett and Graham Turner, *Tewkesbury 1471: The Last Yorkist Victory* **(Osprey, 2003).**

FINAL PHASE

40. Bosworth, 22 August 1485

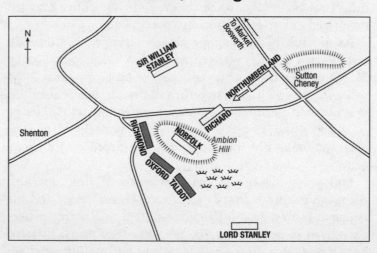

On 7 August 1484, Henry Tudor, Earl of Richmond (the future Henry VII) landed at Milford Haven with a view to ousting King Richard III. Two years earlier, Richard had usurped the crown by denouncing as illegitimate Edward V, young son of the newly deceased Edward IV. Richmond's ancestral claims to the throne were distinctly Lancastrian, as a result of which he had been forced into exile.

Richard knew that an invasion was imminent and had chosen Nottingham as a central location for his base, from where his efforts to raise an army were coordinated. Richmond had started out with only 2,000 second-rate mercenaries but attracted much support as he progressed through his native Wales. By 15 August, he was at Shrewsbury and then moved on to Lichfield, Tamworth and Atherstone where, on 20 August, he met the brothers Thomas, Lord Stanley and Sir William Stanley, who promised their support.

It was not until 20 August that Richard felt sufficiently confident to march on to Leicester, which he reached on the same day. Within twenty-four hours, his force had mushroomed into an army numbering around 12,000 men. Turning out in support of their king were the Lords Zouche and Ferrers, the Duke of Norfolk and the Earls of Northumberland, Lincoln, Surrey and Shrewsbury – and, he thought, Lord Stanley, commanding an additional 7,000 men. To guarantee Stanley's loyalty, Richard was holding his son, George, Lord Strange.

On 21 August, Richmond reached White Moors, to the north of Stoke Golding, where he camped. Arriving from Leicester, Richard camped three miles to the west of White Moors, near the village of Stapleton.

Early on the morning of 22 August 1485, Richard advanced to occupy Ambion Hill, which overlooked White Moors. In the van was the Duke of Norfolk, his lines resplendent with archers; Richard moved in behind with the main battle; the Earl of Northumberland brought up the rear, somewhat apart. Lord Stanley's forces stood to the south and Sir William Stanley's to the north at a distance, despite orders from Richard to join him without delay.

Richmond, slower to start the day, advanced on Ambion Hill when Norfolk was already in place. He skirted to the left in order to avoid marshland, a move which caused some confusion within his ranks. Perhaps Richard should have chosen this moment to attack but, erring on the side of caution, he decided to allow Richmond to deploy. In the van was the Earl of Oxford with archers; Sir Gilbert Talbot led the right wing, with Richmond and Sir John Savage on the left – in total, about 5,000 men.

The battle began with an exchange of arrows and cannon fire. Then the two armies advanced upon each other, clashing halfway up the hillside. Richmond may have been outnumbered, but his men held their ground while Northumberland remained immobile. For an hour or so, the two sides remained deadlocked until the Stanleys approached. Instead of throwing their weight in behind Richard, they attacked both his left and right flanks. Northumberland was still doing nothing.

It was all too clear to Richard that the game was up. Ordering the immediate execution of the captive Lord Strange (an order which was never carried out), he rushed into the thick of the fighting in a frenzied search for Richmond or, some said, the treacherous Lord Stanley. His horse became bogged down and he fought on, on foot. He may well have called for a horse, although, in reality, he no longer had a kingdom to give in exchange. Finally, he fell. It is said that Lord Stanley placed the crown on Richmond's head.

Yorkist casualties probably numbered about 1,000 while Richmond's losses may have amounted to as little as 250. With Richard's death, the fighting appears to have drawn to a close and there does not seem to have been a very vigorous pursuit of the losers – factors which kept the casualty figures down to a minimum.

To his credit, Richmond saw no justification for punitive measures against the rank and file. As far as the Yorkist leaders were concerned, seven, including Norfolk, Lord Ferrers and Sir Robert Percy, had conveniently fallen in battle. Of the remainder, the new king appreciated the expediency of placating his erstwhile enemies. Had he been too severe, then Bosworth might have become just another battle in the Roses series. As it turned out, two years were to elapse before the Yorkists were able to mount a final, much-weakened challenge.

The battlefield today

The battlefield is on the A447, five miles north of Hinckley and nine miles from Junction 1 of the M69 (OS Landranger 140 4000). A battlefield heritage centre includes an extensive interactive exhibition area (and fee-payable car parking) and is an essential starting point for any exploration. There is also a waymarked battlefield trail, featuring King Richard's Field, site of Richard's death. St James's Church in nearby Sutton Cheney has a memorial plaque to Richard and those who died in the battle.

Proposed alternative sites for the battle include Atherstone, to the west, and Stoke Golding, to the south, but the fact remains that the current site provides an excellent starting point for the study of British battlefields.

Further reading

Peter Hammond, *Richard III and the Bosworth Campaign* (Pen & Sword, 2010).

41. Stoke Field, 16 June 1487

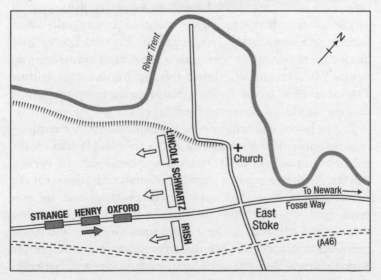

The Yorkist cause did not die with Richard III at Bosworth. Its adherents hoped to regain the ascendancy and, to this end, sponsored a claimant to the throne – someone who could be presented to the public as Edward, Earl of Warwick, son of the Duke of Clarence, last of the Plantagenets, who was known to be held captive in the Tower of London. The wretch chosen for this imposture was Lambert Simnel, the ten-year-old son of an Oxford tradesman, whose claim was effectively stage-managed by Richard Simons, a priest with an eye for the main chance. According to Simons, Simnel was none other than Edward V's brother, Richard, who had escaped from the Tower. Simons took his protégé across the sea to Ireland, always a hotbed of Yorkist activity.

The military side of the project was run by John de la Pole, 1st Earl of Lincoln, with Francis, Viscount Lovel, and a group of Yorkists exiled to continental Europe. In company with 2,000 German mercenaries commanded by Colonel Martin Schwartz, they sailed for Ireland, where they acquired a further 4,500 Irish mercenaries.

On 4 June 1487, Lincoln and his party, including Simnel (who had been proclaimed Edward VI in Dublin), arrived on the Lancashire coast. They were subsequently joined by a number of sympathizers, including Sir Thomas Broughton, but not so many as the mercenaries had been led to believe. About 9,000 strong, the army reached Masham on 8 June. The initial objective was York but, learning that the gates of the city would be closed to them, they turned south, pressing on to Boroughbridge, to join the Great North Road.

Meanwhile, Henry VII had not been idle. He had established headquarters in the midlands to await developments. As the Yorkists moved south, he marched his army to Leicester and from there to Nottingham, where he was reinforced by George Stanley, Lord Strange, giving him a total force of some 12,000 men. When Henry left Nottingham, the two armies were on a collision course which seemed likely to lead to a head-on clash at Newark.

On 15 June, the Yorkists crossed the River Trent at Fiskerton, pitching their tents around the village of East Stoke. Henry camped six miles to the south, at Radcliffe. Early the next morning, he marched on in battle formation to the Yorkist position.

Lincoln had deployed his army along a ridge, the right flank – probably occupied by Lincoln himself – stretching towards the River Trent, with the Irish on the left and Schwartz in the centre. As Henry approached, his column became strung out with the 6,000-strong vanguard, commanded by the Earl of Oxford, well out in front. Henry followed, with Lord Strange in the rear.

The German mercenaries included crossbowmen and hand gunners, who probably commenced hostilities by directing their fire at Oxford's approaching division. Oxford's archers replied, causing far more damage. Perceiving that there was little likelihood of Oxford trying to take the ridge when he could decimate the defenders at long range, Lincoln decided, as Richard III had done at Bosworth, to take the fight to the enemy. Gathering momentum, the Yorkists charged down the slope into Oxford's front lines.

Oxford's men were still forming up when the Yorkists struck, sending a shock wave throughout their ranks. Some, easily discouraged, turned and ran but the majority, under Oxford's leadership, held their ground. Both sides resolved to slug it out in a brutal hand-to-hand battle that lasted for three hours. The longer the contest went on, the better were Henry's chances. The gaps which appeared in Oxford's lines were easily filled as fresh troops arrived to press forward from the rear. The same did not happen on the Yorkist side for, outnumbered as they were, they possessed no reserves. As Lincoln's effort stalled, Henry's numerical advantage began to tell. Slowly but surely, the Yorkists were pushed back up the slope.

It is thought that the poorly armed Irish were the first to cave in, taking flight towards the river. Lincoln's right wing followed suit, leaving Schwartz to fight on and, eventually, to be overwhelmed. As was often the case in 'Roses' battles, one location in particular was the scene of the greatest slaughter – in this instance the 'Red Gutter', a gulley to the rear of the Yorkist right wing. Others drowned while trying to cross the Trent.

Overall, casualties were high. Henry probably lost around a thousand men, while the Yorkist dead may have amounted to four times that number. With the exception of Viscount Lovel, who disappeared, the Yorkist campaign leaders all chose a soldier's death. Lambert Simnel was captured and put to work as a scullion in the royal kitchens. His mentor, Simons, was imprisoned for life.

In theory, Stoke Field brought the Wars of the Roses to an end. There would be no more battles, yet the Yorkist threat remained. All of ten years later, another pretender, Perkin Warbeck appeared on the scene. His challenge failed to gain momentum – he and Edward, Earl of Warwick, were both executed – but the Tudors continued to cast uneasy glances over their shoulders for many years to come.

The battlefield today

The battlefield is immediately to the south of East Stoke on the B6166 (Fosse Road), off the A46, four and a half miles to the south of Newark (OS Landranger 129 7449). Car parking is available by St Oswald's Church, on Church Lane. A memorial stone near the church porch commemorates the dead of the battle. A small display relating to the battle is to be found within the entrance to the church tower. The 'Red Gutter' can be found by following Church Lane around to the point at which the road becomes a bridleway. A battlefield trail, established to mark the quincentenary of the battle in 1987, has not survived, although the public footpath system permits some exploration of the area.

Further reading
David Baldwin, *Stoke Field* (Pen & Sword, 2006).

PART FOUR:
THE SIXTEENTH CENTURY

Part 4

42 Flodden
43 Solway Moss
44 Ancrum Moor
45 Pinkie Cleugh
46 Langside

WARFARE IN THE SIXTEENTH CENTURY

The sixteenth century was a period of transition for the military. Armies that existed at its end were very different to those seen on the battlefield at the beginning. Oddly enough, a time of relative peace was needed in which to achieve this transformation, although the century was not without its troubles. There were sporadic expeditions to France. In 1513, for example, Henry VIII personally led an army of 35,000 men across the Channel to win the Battle of the Spurs – and war with France often meant war with Scotland.

By and large, English armies were weaker than those of the leading European nations. The age of the archer was passing, but the English still clung to the longbow and to the golden age of Crécy and Agincourt which it represented. They were far more comfortable fighting in the style of yesteryear against the Scots than they were at adapting to the requirements of modern warfare in the wider world.

There was still no standing army, but the system of

'Trained Bands' was developed, whereby paid volunteers would undergo military training in their spare time, fulfilling a role not dissimilar to that of today's Territorial Army. Instead of constituting a reserve, however, the Trained Bands were the first line of defence. In a national emergency, they would be responsible for training conscripted 'Untrained Bands'. Organized on a county basis, the more affluent administrations would furnish their bands with a livery to distinguish them as a unit. The quality of the troops trained in this manner left much to be desired, while they were often armed with several different types of weapon.

Certainly, for much of the period, British weaponry owed more to the Early Middle Ages than to contemporary innovation. The Scots tended to be more adventurous than the English, but it did not always work out to their advantage. At Flodden (1513), for instance, they tried to use heavy siege guns, but their size made it impossible to manoeuvre them into position.

English foundries were established comparatively late in the day, but eventually they made up for lost time, producing a wide range of artillery. Indeed, the sheer variety in itself was something of a problem. With experimentation being the order of the day, there was initially no attempt at standardization and the result was a bewildering array of guns, each with its own unique design and individual requirements for shot. The basic division was between the culverin and the cannon, the former having a long barrel, the latter a shorter one. The larger pieces, in addition to requiring many teams of horses or oxen to transport them, could be used only sparingly because they needed long periods between shots in which to cool down.

Perhaps the most significant military development of the sixteenth century, as far as England was concerned, was the establishment of a permanent navy. Henry VIII did have the sense to appreciate the importance of having a fleet of warships to counter the threat of invasion, and by 1547 over fifty vessels (of which the *Mary Rose* was a prime example) were under sail. The ships accompanying the Duke of Somerset's Scottish expedition, culminating at Pinkie (1547), made a major contribution to the success of the campaign.

The Tudors and Scotland

42. Flodden, 9 September 1513

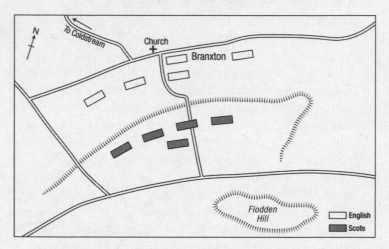

In 1511, England's new king, Henry VIII, was persuaded to join the Holy League against France. After initial setbacks, he decided to take personal command of operations, arriving at Calais on 30 June 1513. Louis XII of France countered by providing King James IV of Scotland with men, munitions and money to launch a diversionary invasion of England.

In Henry's absence, responsibility for the defence of the kingdom rested with the septuagenarian Lieutenant-General of the North, Thomas Howard, Earl of Surrey, who lost no time in making preparations. By 21 July, he was ready to march north, amid rumours that James was amassing a vast army, perhaps 30,000 strong. Well armed, and with an experienced French contingent and a formidable artillery train, James must have considered his force to be unsinkable.

Henry's army had been drawn from the southern counties, leaving Surrey heavily dependent upon successful recruitment en route to the border country. He did not reach Alnwick until 3 September, by which time he had in the region of 20,000 men under his command. The Scots had actually crossed the border on 22 August, at Coldstream, reducing Norham Castle and the smaller fortresses of Wark, Etal and Ford. As Surrey approached, there took place an exchange of heralds, both sides agreeing to a pitched battle by 9 September at the latest.

When Surrey arrived at Wooler, he discovered that James had occupied a seemingly impregnable position on Flodden Hill. Indignant at what he regarded as a breach of professional etiquette, he demanded that the Scots descend to level ground to ensure a fair fight. James refused to budge and Surrey decided to outflank him by moving north. On the morning of 9 September, therefore, Surrey, with half his army, forded the River Till at Milford while his son, Thomas Howard, recrossed the river at Twizel Bridge. James appeared to be unconcerned, merely turning his army about to advance to Branxton Hill, a position not much less formidable and from which Surrey's laborious approach could be observed.

As it approached the new Scottish position, the English army found it way blocked by Pallin's Burn and the marshland surrounding this tributary of the River Till. Thomas struggled across on a causeway running through the centre, with Surrey effecting a crossing further east.

At length, the two armies faced one another, each adopting what was an unusual formation. As opposed to the customary three 'battles', both armies were deployed into four divisions and a reserve unit. On the Scottish left were the Earls of Huntley and Home, facing Lord Edmund Howard, younger brother of the Lord High Admiral. The second Scottish division under the Earls of Crawford and Montrose, opposed the Admiral. Fittingly, perhaps, King James faced Surrey, while the Earls of Lennox and Argyle opposed Sir Edward Stanley, who arrived late. The Earl of Bothwell with the French Count D'Aussi commanded the Scottish reserve, and Lord Dacre the English reserve.

In the late afternoon, with rain blowing into the faces of

the English, an exchange of artillery fire began. Little damage appears to have been inflicted but, having taken immense pains to get them into the field, both sides must have been determined to make use of their heavy guns. Perhaps the English guns were more accurate, for the Scots suddenly decided to take the initiative, Huntley and Home advancing on the English right wing. The younger Howard's men, outnumbered, crumbled under the ferocity of the Scottish assault, and it fell to Lord Dacre, with a timely intervention, to stabilize the English defence.

Encouraged by this initial success, the two Scottish centre columns, supported by Bothwell's reserves, hurled themselves against their English counterparts, whose front lines held firm – bolstered by the rump of Edmund Howard's division. The men of Home and Huntley, meanwhile, had stopped fighting so that they might strip the dead and wounded.

The action that turned the tide of battle in Surrey's favour took place on the Scottish right. Argyle and Lennox were the last to engage the enemy, their inactivity, it has been argued, being due to Stanley's late arrival on the scene, owing to problems encountered in crossing Pallin's Burn. When he appeared, Stanley ordered a portion of his division to make a frontal attack while the remainder, with Stanley at their head, contrived to approach the Scottish right flank unobserved.

The strategy was devastatingly successful. As soon as they realized that they had been outflanked, the Scottish right wing disintegrated, enabling Stanley to penetrate the centre. The divisions of James and Crawford and Montrose were already struggling, the English billhooks proving more than a match for the long pikes, of little value in close combat, wielded by the Scots. Count D'Aussi was unable to relieve the pressure, and an attack by Lord Dacre on their centre-left ended resistance. The battle had been fought to a conclusion in a little over two hours.

The English sustained as few as 2,000 casualties. Up to 10,000 Scots may have perished including, it has often been remarked, the flower of Scotland's nobility. As they retreated towards the border, the survivors engaged in as much plundering as their weakened condition allowed, robbing their own dead and dying countrymen and turning on their French allies, who they blamed for their defeat. The remains of King James, identified by the victors, were taken to Sheen Priory, near Richmond, and laid to rest.

The invasion had been a complete failure. Instead of diverting Henry's attention, the Scottish defeat had, if anything, strengthened his hand.

The battlefield today

Flodden is reached via the Branxton turning on the A697 Wooler–Coldstream road, six miles south of Coldstream (OS Landranger 74 8837). Car parking is at the battlefield monument, where there is an interpretation panel and the starting point of a battlefield trail. The Church of St Paul in Branxton, where the body of James IV initially rested, is a place of pilgrimage for all visitors and usually contains a stock of leaflets about the battle. The King's Stone, marking the spot where James fell, is at Crookham Westfield (8838). Possibilities for further exploration are almost endless. English Heritage property, Etal Castle (9239) has a display about the battle, which is also commemorated in a stained glass window in the parish church in Coldstream's High Street.

Further reading

John Sadler and Rose Serdiville, *The Battle of Flodden 1513* (History Press, 2012).

43. Solway Moss, 24 November 1542

The Battle of Solway Moss resulted from friction between Henry VIII, who wanted Scotland to break with the Catholic Church, and James V of Scotland, who was determined not to do so.

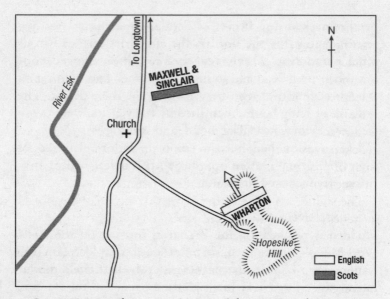

On 24 November 1542, a Scottish army, at least 10,000 strong, crossed the border in the west and began ravaging the countryside. In response, Sir Thomas Wharton, Deputy Warden of the West Marches, mustered some 300 men and marched out of Carlisle to meet them.

Wharton was able to establish the position of the enemy by the smoke from the fires they had started. They were laying waste to land in the Oakshawhill district, to the north-west of Longtown. Wharton sent forward 'prickers' (riders armed with lances) to harry them and provide him with intelligence. At length, the Scots moved down, beyond Longtown and towards Arthuret, driving the prickers before them. In response, Wharton marched on to Hopesike Hill, from where he despatched an advance party with six standards by way of a show of strength, despite having increased his numbers to no more than 1,200.

The ruse appeared to work. Wharton was considering how best to meet the impending assault when the Scots, who were moving towards the advance party, drew to a halt 'as in a maze'. The rearmost ranks then began to retreat, followed by those in the van. The English horse set out in pursuit, coming upon them as they tried to ford the River Esk at a point not too far from the present-day Longtown Bridge. A few of the Scots may have offered resistance, but Wharton's prickers had the majority at their mercy. Few combatants were actually cut down, probably owing to Wharton's tardiness in joining the horse, but it is said that many panic-stricken Scots drowned in the Esk as they sought to gain the tract of peat bog known as Solway Moss on the west bank. In excess of 1,000 Scots were taken prisoner.

The sudden collapse of the Scottish army may have been hastened by friction among its leaders. The truth of the matter may never be known, but it appears that Robert, Lord Maxwell was in command and that his leadership was challenged (to the consternation of the rank and file) by Oliver Sinclair, a favourite of James V.

Within weeks of the battle, James V died and was succeeded by his newly born daughter, Mary I (Queen of Scots). For a time, Henry followed a more conciliatory policy towards Scotland, aiming for a betrothal of Mary and his own infant son, Prince Edward. This was agreed to by the nobles captured at Solway Moss, but getting the agreement of the Scottish Parliament was another matter.

The battlefield today
The battlefield is ten miles to the north of Carlisle, immediately to the south of Longtown (OS Landranger 85 3867). There is no monument, but a battlefield information panel (with car parking) can be found at the northern end of Hopesike Woods. The nearby Church of St Michael & All Angels on Arthuret Road lay in ruins for many years, the victim of frequent border raids.

Further reading
George MacDonald, *The Steel Bonnets: Story of the Anglo-Scottish Reivers* (HarperCollins, 1989).

44. Ancrum Moor, 27 February 1545

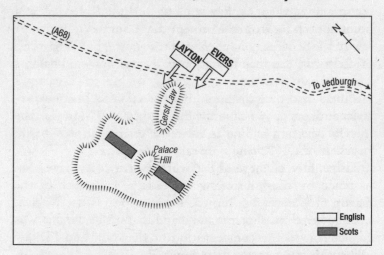

When the Scots failed to embrace Henry VIII's suggestion of the betrothal of Prince Edward and Mary I, he introduced his policy of 'Rough Wooing'. It was rough indeed, with English armies burning and pillaging many border towns and monasteries during 1544.

Early in 1545, Sir Ralph Evers, Warden of the Middle Marches, led another expedition – a mongrel force consisting of 3,000 German and Spanish mercenaries, 1,500 English borderers and 700 Scottish borderers. Having plundered Melrose, Evers marched south to Jedburgh, camping at Ancrum, three and a half miles to the north-west of the town on 27 February.

As the English army settled in, their scouts reported the presence of a Scottish force on nearby Gersit Law. With the scouts looking on, the Scots began to move back. Evers decided to go on to the offensive. His troops were tired but, if they moved quickly, the Scots could be wiped out. The mounted men-at-arms, followed by the infantry, rushed to the top of Gersit Law. The Scots had retreated to the east, in the direction of Palace Hill, but there were far more of them than Evers thought – about 2,500 – and included horse and infantry led by Archibald Douglas, Earl of Angus, and James Hamilton, Earl of Arran.

Instead of taking flight, the Scots had dug in. While it is unlikely that they had time to prepare defensive ditches, as is occasionally reported, the foot soldiers would have been able to assume defensive schiltron formations. The English heavy horse charged down the rear slopes of Gersit Law, only for their front line to come to grief on the Scottish spears. In the resulting confusion, the Scots went on the offensive, driving forward and forcing the English to recoil on their own men. An attempt was made to regroup towards the top of Gersit Law, but the momentum of the Scottish assault proved too much.

Evers commanded a number of hackbutters. They had the opportunity to operate their unwieldy firearms but, apart from creating smoke which added to the English confusion, they seem to have made little impression. The border Scots within the English army also failed to live up to expectations. Perceiving that they had backed the wrong side, they decided to go over to the enemy and turned on their comrades-in-arms. In addition, it is claimed that border womenfolk joined in the fighting. One such amazon, according to popular mythology, was 'Maid Lilliard' who died on the battlefield. At the very least, when the English were in full flight, local women would have emerged to finish off the dead and wounded.

It was during the pursuit that the light Scottish ponies came into their own. The English and their allies, nimbly run to earth, died in their hundreds. Evers was killed, along with his co-commander, Sir Brian Layton, governor of Norham Castle. About 1,000 prisoners were taken. The outcome demonstrated that the Scots were not going to take their medicine laying down, convincing Henry VIII that what they really needed was a larger dose.

The battlefield today

The battlefield is off the A68 (with speed cameras every couple of miles), three miles to the north-west of Jedburgh (OS Landranger 74 6025). A good place to start is Harastanes Visitor Centre (6424), off the B6400, with car parking. During the season, the centre has a number of walks open, including one to the top of Paniel Heugh. You can also walk up the Roman Road, Dere Street, to Ancrum Moor, where you will find an information panel and Lilliard's Stone, commemorating Maid Lilliard. The battle is open to several interpretations, in some of which Paniel Heugh is substituted for Palace Hill.

Further reading

James Robson, *Border Battles and Battlefields* (British Library, 2010).

PHANTOM FORCES

Most, if not all, British battlefields have ghost stories attached to them: the shambling figure of a solitary clansman on Culloden Moor; riderless horses galloping wildly over Roundway Down; ragged, battle-weary figures haunting the rural lanes bordering Marston Moor; phantom armies re-enacting the Battle of Edgehill. The latter tale is worth consideration, for it was investigated by a Royal Commission.

Some two months after the Battle of Edgehill, shortly before Christmas 1642, the local population reported seeing and hearing the battle being refought in the skies above the field of conflict. Witnesses included Justice of the Peace, William Wood, and Minister of St Peter's, Kineton, Samuel Marshall. The phenomenon, repeated on several nights in succession, lasted for between three and four hours at a time, 'the adverse armies fighting with as much spite and spleen as formerly'.

Some folk were so affected that they fled their homes,

and Marshall reported the matter to Charles I. The king responded by sending Colonel Lewis Kirke and five other potential 'witnesses of credit' to investigate. They, too, experienced the phenomenon, recognizing a number of the battle's participants – but, of explanation, there was none, the official conclusion being that the ghastly vision was 'a sign of God's wrath against this land, for these civil wars'.

Since that time, other, more prosaic, explanations have been proposed. According to one theory, ergot poisoning may have been responsible. In its mildest form, ergot, a fungal disease of grain (particularly rye), acts as an hallucinogen, similar to LSD. Thus, locally produced bread and ale, if infected with the ergot fungus, would have acted on residents and investigating commissioners alike, triggering mass hallucination – perhaps making the story a little easier to swallow.

During the Civil Wars, popular belief in supernatural forces was exploited by both sides. For example, there was the curious incident of Prince Rupert's dog. 'Boye', a white poodle, accompanied Rupert everywhere. According to Puritan propaganda, the animal was Rupert's 'familiar' (a demon taking the form of an animal assigned to protect a witch). Boye, it was argued, could become invisible at will and was observed protecting his master by catching bullets intended for him between his teeth. Boye met his end at Marston Moor (1644) when he was allegedly shot by a Parliamentarian skilled in the magical arts.

Puritanical zeal did not stop the Parliamentarians from employing a soothsayer, the celebrated William Lilley. Once a favourite of the king, Lilley was supposedly offered an annual income of £50 to change sides. In August 1644, he produced a pamphlet entitled 'A Prophesy of the White King', in which he predicted that a battle would take place 'at an ancient seate near a running River' where 'assaulted before and behind . . . the White and noble King [Charles] shall dye'. Although Marston Moor was fought while the pamphlet was still at the printer's, the prophecy was

promoted as an accurate prediction of the battle and its outcome. Of course, no river was involved and Charles had not
even been present, but such minor details were not permitted to obscure the big picture.

Provided its practitioners were not working against you,
the 'black arts' were always quite acceptable. Thus, the fog
which settled over the battlefield at Barnet (1471) was said
to have been conjured up by one Friar Bungay, specifically
to aid the Yorkists, even though Bungay had lived and died
two centuries before the battle took place. Had Warwick
been victorious, doubtless the fog would have been created
to help the Lancastrian cause.

45. Pinkie Cleugh, 10 September 1547

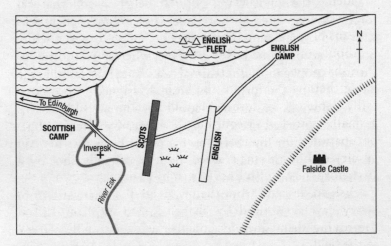

When Henry VIII died in January 1547, Edward Seymour,
Duke of Somerset, secured the job of Lord Protector for the
duration of the minority of the nine-year-old Edward VI.
Keen to continue his late master's policy of 'Rough Wooing'
in respect of the Scots, Somerset was ready to mount an
invasion of Scotland by the autumn.

On 4 September 1547, the English army was preparing to leave Berwick. By 7 September, having bypassed a heavily defended Dunbar, it reached Longniddry. Its progress had been shadowed by the English fleet, sailing up the Firth of Forth in support, and Somerset now ordered the admiral, Lord Clinton, to drop anchor at the mouth of the River Esk, at Musselburgh. Somerset proceeded as far as Prestonpans, where he set up camp on 8 September.

On the west bank of the River Esk, about three miles from the English encampment, was the Earl of Arran's Scottish army, amassed to protect the homeland. At a maximum strength of 25,000 men, it was superior numerically to the English army, which was probably around 19,000 strong. Somerset's advantage lay in his cavalry, of which he had 4,000 against Arran's 1,500. In addition, the English commander had eighty pieces of ordnance, and he could count on the support of his fleet both in terms of firepower and as a means of evacuation if necessary.

About a mile inland from Somerset's campsite, the ground rose sharply to Falside Hill and Carberry Hill, and it was along the lower slopes of the high land that Somerset initially deployed his forces. (Falside Castle was manned by a small Scottish garrison, but it constituted only a token occupation.) On the morning of 9 September, the Scottish cavalry of Lord Home crossed the Esk and cantered to and fro before the English lines in a show of defiance, daring the English to descend from their vantage point. Lord Grey's heavy cavalry obliged by charging into their midst and destroying them, thereby compromising Arran's mobility in the field.

The next day, after rejecting a suggestion from Arran to settle the matter by pitting select groups of knights against each other, Somerset moved against the Scottish positions. Somerset, with his second-in-command, John Dudley, 2nd Earl of Warwick, occupied the centre with the cavalry of Lord Grey and Sir Francis Bryan occupying the right and left wings respectively. With the Scots entrenched behind the Esk, it was a bold move, and Somerset's surprise must have been great when he perceived the Earl of Argyll's Highlanders crossing the river to face him.

Perhaps Arran was worried about the English taking the high ground around St Michael's Church, or the Scottish ranks may have been taking a pounding from the English fleet. Nevertheless, Somerset remained immobile while the Scots filed across the Esk via a narrow bridge. Once on the west bank, they formed three dense schiltrons. The final deployment is uncertain, but Arran and Argyll may have taken the centre, with the Earl of Angus on the right and the Earl of Huntly on the left.

Lord Grey's cavalry moved forward to attack. The impetus of his cavalry charge was dented by a tract of boggy ground and the Scottish pikes held firm. After suffering heavy losses, Grey was compelled to retreat. However, the Scottish rear was still being pummelled by the guns of the English fleet – and with his artillery, harquebusiers and archers now in position, Somerset was able to wear down resistance. When he perceived that the Scots were attempting to retreat, he unleashed his cavalry once more. This time, the charge was driven home successfully, resulting in a rout. Many Scots were caught crowding on to the bridge while others threw themselves into the Esk. Several thousand were killed during a pursuit in which the taking of prisoners for ransom was not a top priority. The following day, Falside Castle was burned along with its garrison.

Somerset's victory earned him a little fleeting popularity at home. The Scots invited over 7,000 French troops to deter any further incursions, while Mary I went to live in France and, ultimately, marry the Dauphin.

The battlefield today
The battlefield lies immediately to the south-east of Musselburgh – exit the Musselburgh Junction of the A1 (OS

Landranger 66 3571). Car parking can be found in the town. A monument to the battle is situated off Crookstone Road, above the A1 slip-road (362712). The old bridge is sandwiched between two modern road bridges at the end of Market Street. St Michael's Church was rebuilt in 1806, and Falside Castle (3770) is also a modern restoration. Musselburgh Museum in High Street houses a few relics of the battle.

Further reading
Jonathan Cooper, *Scottish Renaissance Armies 1513–1550* **(Osprey, 2008).**

46. Langside, 13 May 1568

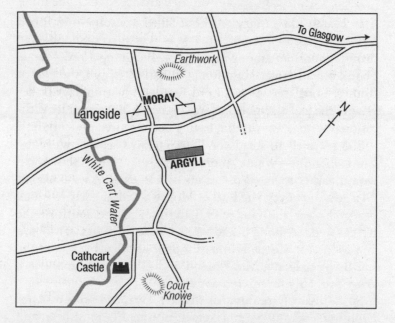

Mary, Queen of Scots had arrived in Scotland in 1561, following the death of her first husband, Francis II, King of France. A devout Roman Catholic, she was distrusted by the new Protestant Church of Scotland. Neither was her choice of suitors to the taste of the Kirk. She was almost certainly implicated in the murder of her second husband, the unsavoury Lord Darnley in February 1567, before marrying the equally unpleasant Earl of Bothwell.

This was too much for the country's powerful Protestant lords. On 15 June 1567, they took to the field against Mary and Bothwell, at Carberry Hill, near Musselburgh. Mary backed down, promising to surrender on condition that Bothwell was given his freedom. He went into exile and she was imprisoned in Loch Leven Castle, situated on an island in the loch of the same name. On 24 July, she was made to abdicate in favour of her (and Darnley's) son, James, who became James VI, with the Earl of Moray, Mary's half-brother, acting as Regent.

In March 1568, Mary tried but failed to escape from Loch Leven. A second attempt, on 2 May was successful. She had many supporters among the gentry, including Lord Claude Hamilton, Sir James Hamilton, the Earl of Argyll, the Earl of Rothes, Lord Herries and Lord Ross and, within days of her escape, she had assembled a force of over 6,000 men. Her abdication, she said, was invalid, having been secured under duress.

She planned to head for Dumbarton Castle, owned by Lord Fleming, where more supporters from the north would gather to swell the ranks of her army. As she neared Glasgow, however, the Earl of Moray acted quickly to block her path near the village of Langside, to the south of the River Clyde. Among his adherents were the Earls of Morton and Menteith, Lords Home, Lindsay and Ruthven, and the Lairds of Balgany, MacFarland and Glengarnock. Moray's army probably numbered about 4,000.

Sir William Kirkaldy, for Moray, advanced with cavalry. Each horseman had a musketeer mounted behind him, and when they reached Langside, the musketeers took cover by the road along which Mary's army, commanded by the Earl of Argyll, would pass. The main body deployed in two divisions, the right wing in the village and the left stretching out northwards, to Pathhead Farm. The approaching queen's men occupied Clincart Hill.

Hostilities appear to have begun with an exchange of artillery fire, but Argyll had little choice but to attack and attempt to dislodge Moray. With Mary watching from nearby Cathcart Castle, her vanguard, led by Lord Claude Hamilton, advanced to find itself running the gauntlet of Moray's musketeers. Pressing on, Hamilton was met by the Earl of Morton's pikemen. In what was a very confined area, the press of men swayed back and forth with the push of the pike. Moray's right wing began to give ground, but was reinforced before Hamilton could press home his advantage. Then Moray's cavalry charged and the enemy line wavered, to give way at last when the Laird of MacFarland's Highlanders were unleashed. It was all over in just three-quarters of an hour. Casualties were comparatively light – around 400 – owing largely to Moray's decision not to allow a pursuit.

With her defeat at Langside, Mary's cause was lost and she fled to England, to throw herself on the mercy of Queen Elizabeth I. She would languish under house arrest for eighteen years, prior to her trial and execution at Fotheringhay Castle. In Scotland, Protestantism was now firmly in the ascendant.

The battlefield today

The battlefield is within urban Glasgow, in the 'Battlefield' district (OS Landranger 64 5861). A battlefield monument stands in Battle Place. The spot where Mary watched the defeat of her army, Court Knowe, is marked by a memorial stone. Roadside parking can be found on Old Castle Road. A battlefield display is housed in Kelvingrove Art Gallery and Museum.

Further reading

Alexander Scott, *The Battle of Langside 1568* (British Library Historical Print Editions, 2011).

PART FIVE: THE SEVENTEENTH CENTURY

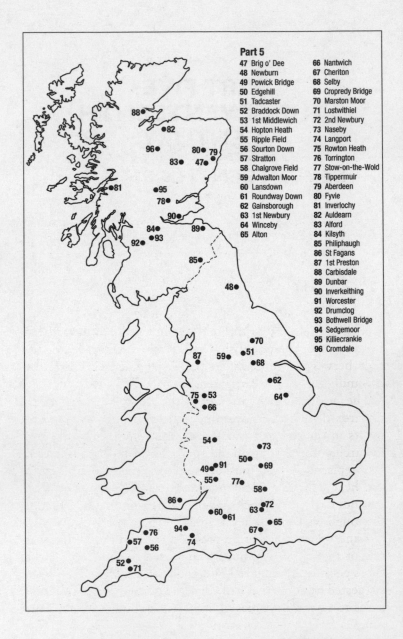

Part 5

47 Brig o' Dee
48 Newburn
49 Powick Bridge
50 Edgehill
51 Tadcaster
52 Braddock Down
53 1st Middlewich
54 Hopton Heath
55 Ripple Field
56 Sourton Down
57 Stratton
58 Chalgrove Field
59 Adwalton Moor
60 Lansdown
61 Roundway Down
62 Gainsborough
63 1st Newbury
64 Winceby
65 Alton

66 Nantwich
67 Cheriton
68 Selby
69 Cropredy Bridge
70 Marston Moor
71 Lostwithiel
72 2nd Newbury
73 Naseby
74 Langport
75 Rowton Heath
76 Torrington
77 Stow-on-the-Wold
78 Tippermuir
79 Aberdeen
80 Fyvie
81 Inverlochy
82 Auldearn
83 Alford
84 Kilsyth
85 Philiphaugh
86 St Fagans
87 1st Preston
88 Carbisdale
89 Dunbar
90 Inverkeithing
91 Worcester
92 Drumclog
93 Bothwell Bridge
94 Sedgemoor
95 Killiecrankie
96 Cromdale

WARFARE IN THE SEVENTEENTH CENTURY

British battlefields of the mid-seventeenth century are an expression of the English Civil Wars, the ten-year conflict between the 'Cavaliers' of King Charles I and the 'Roundheads' of his Parliament.

The uncertainties attending the first faltering steps towards democratic government are reflected in developments in the tools of warfare. In the seventeenth century, the archer, for so long an indispensable arm of the military, was replaced by the musketeer. Nearly five feet in length and heavy, the matchlock musket had to be supported with a stand. Early matchlocks seemed to be a poor substitute for the longbow. Often, they would fail to go off, especially in wet and windy weather. In practice, the best rate of fire was one or two shots a minute, as opposed to the ten or more shots per minute achieved by a good archer. It has even been suggested by some that had Charles I gone ahead with initial plans to raise companies of archers, he could have won the war.

Artillery had been developing over previous centuries, the process of continuous refinement leading to the muzzle-loading brass and iron cannon which remained in use until the introduction of breech-loaders. The heaviest pieces required a team of half-a-dozen oxen to transport them, and lighter brass-barrelled guns bound with leather, mounted on a slender carriage and capable of being drawn by a single horse, proved more popular.

Despite developments in firearms, the pike was still the mainstay of the infantry regiment. Pikes were supposed to be eighteen feet in length, but they were often much shorter, pikemen preferring a less unwieldy shorter shaft. Many a Civil War battle was ultimately decided by 'push of pike'. The head, unlike its predecessors, was of a simple design, tapering to a single point. Indeed, the general trend in both arms and armour was towards minimalism. Armour was reduced to the breastplate and the heavy sword of previous centuries was replaced by much lighter weapons.

Cavalry assumed an unprecedented importance in the seventeenth century. Initially, the Royalists held the upper hand, Prince Rupert's cavalry charges having entered into folklore. However, while a well-coordinated charge could scatter one's opponents, the trick was to control your men in its wake. At Naseby (1645), Rupert's cavalry charged through the hole punched in the opposing ranks, and kept going. By the time they regrouped, the battle was lost. Cromwell's cavalry, on the other hand, was sufficiently disciplined to remain on the battlefield for further deployment.

'Text-book' deployment of troops became accepted practice, thanks to the involvement in European wars of leaders on both sides. Everyone was anxious to put into practice on home turf lessons learned abroad, and there were often differences of opinion between commanders over the best model to use, whether it be Dutch or Swedish.

There was no professional army until the formation of Parliament's New Model Army, quite late in the day, in 1645.

Made up of full-time troops, its first commander-in-chief was Sir Thomas Fairfax and, with promotion based on ability, a man could rise through the ranks. Clad in the famous buff leather coat, breastplate and 'lobster-tailed pot' helmet, the New Model soldier is instantly recognizable to us. The disadvantage of using professional soldiers is that they have to be paid, and dissatisfaction caused by non-payment led to the battle of St Fagans (1648).

Allowing for all these developments, one might still catch a glimpse of times past on seventeenth-century battlefields. Archers popped up occasionally, making what was probably their final appearance at Tippermuir (1644). And Sir Arthur Hesilrige's mounted cuirassier regiment, charging into battle in full plate armour, must have been a magnificent sight. To his contemporaries, however, Hesilrige and his 'lobsters' were simply eccentric (Charles I once remarking that if Sir Arthur was as well victualled as fortified, he might endure a siege of seven years). The Age of Chivalry was being eclipsed by the Age of Reason – and both the conduct of warfare and the motives for going to war were growing increasingly complex.

The Bishops' Wars

47. Brig o' Dee, 18 June 1639

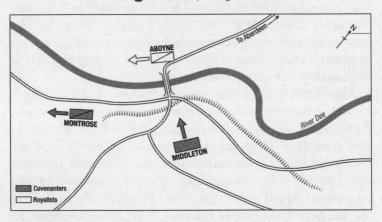

The First Bishops' War came about as a result of the determination of King Charles I to replace Presbyterianism with an Episcopalian system of worship in Scotland. Opposition to this proposal was formulated in the National Covenant of 1638, decrying the king's interference in religious affairs north of the border.

The resulting war was an untidy affair, with hostilities largely confined to minor actions between Covenanter forces and Charles's Scottish supporters. However, in early June, James Gordon, Viscount Aboyne, sailed into Aberdeen harbour to claim the city for the king. His attempts to push inland were thwarted by the Covenanters and he was soon pushed back to his starting point. With a force much reduced from the 2,500 with which he had begun, Aboyne set up a defensive position at Brig o' Dee, the bridge crossing the River Dee to the south of Aberdeen, which was seen as the gateway to the city. At the very least, he hoped to hold the position until he could be reinforced.

The bridge itself looked much as it does today, with its seven stone arches and standing well above the broiling of the Dee. At the southern end, there was a turreted gate-house, where Aboyne stationed a handful of musketeers. A barricade of turf and stone blocked the passage across.

For the Covenanters, James Graham, 5th Earl of Montrose, reached the Brig o' Dee on 18 June. He lost no time in setting up artillery, which included two huge demi-cannon, on high ground on the southern approaches. His 2,000 infantry and 200 cavalry were placed well to the rear, out of range of the muskets and light artillery of the Royalists.

Both sides spent the day pounding each other with shot, large and small, but to little effect. It is recorded that sightsc-ers gathered to watch the proceedings – a ghoulish pastime which would grow in popularity in the years to come – while the women of Aberdeen put themselves in harm's way to provide the defenders with refreshments. A single attempt was made to storm the bridge, but the Covenanter infantry were easily driven back.

Nightfall brought an end to the duel, but Montrose did use the darkness to move his heavy guns closer to the bridge. Luck was with him, for the defences were weakened when many Aberdonians withdrew to attend the funeral of one of their number who had been killed. The attackers' fire was now more accurate, but although the bridge suf-fered much damage, the Royalists managed to hold out. As a last resort, Montrose resorted to subterfuge. Assembling a portion of his cavalry, he led them upstream, in clear view of the enemy, in an attempt to create the impression that he was going to outflank the defenders by fording the river at another spot.

That he would have been able to do this was very unlikely, given that the Dee was in flood, but Aboyne nevertheless despatched 180 of his own precious horse along the north bank to monitor Montrose's progress. Aboyne did this on the advice of Colonel William Gunn, who had been seconded to his command by the Marquis of Hamilton, commander of the king's expeditionary force in Scotland. During the campaign, Gunn's advice was so poor that he would later be accused of treachery.

When Montrose saw that his ruse had been successful, he sent back the greater part of his cavalry, under Captain John Middleton, to make a vigorous attack on the bridge, which was still being pounded by the heavy cannon. The remaining defenders abandoned their positions and retreated, leaving Aberdeen to its fate. Montrose did stop his men from burning the town, but he could not prevent the inevitable looting and damage to property, the cost of which was put at £133,000.

The battle is of interest, in part because it marks the debut of Montrose, who would rise to prominence – as a leading Royalist – during the Civil War. The result was important because it confirmed that the king would find it difficult to enforce his will on the Covenanters. He had only an ill-trained, poorly equipped army waiting to march and decided that, under the circumstances, it would be preferable to negotiate.

In fact, a peace treaty was signed on 19 June, while the Battle of Brig o' Dee was still being fought. The Pacification of Berwick did allow for church issues to be resolved by a General Assembly, but several other matters were fudged and both sides were dissatisfied with the terms.

The battlefield today
The Bridge of Dee is now part of the A90 (Stonehaven Road) on the southern approach to Aberdeen (OS Landranger 38 9203). The surrounding area is well on the way to becoming almost completely urbanized – car parking is available in the retail park on Garthdee Road on the north bank. Surprisingly, there is no memorial, but a visit can be conveniently combined with a site visit to the battlefield of Aberdeen (see pp. 246-8).

Further reading
Mark Charles Fissell, *The Bishops' Wars* **(Cambridge University Press, 1994).**

48. Newburn, 28 August 1640

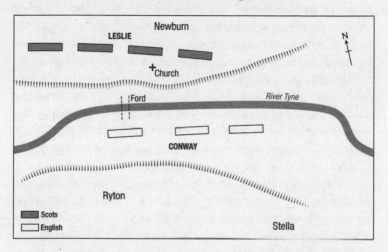

The Pacification of Berwick, which had terminated what is called the First Bishops' War of 1639, succeeded only in deepening the distrust that existed between Charles I and the Scottish Covenanters. It was only a matter of time before the conflict was renewed, as the Second Bishops' War.

The Covenanters were in the stronger position militarily, having only partially disbanded their army. Charles had discharged his army straight away, and was reduced to going cap in hand to his closest friends and supporters for the money to raise a new one. In this manner, he acquired £300,000, sufficient to cobble together a large but ill-equipped and poorly trained force.

By late August 1640, 20,000 Scots, led by Sir Alexander Leslie, were on the march to Newcastle. In order to hold them until the English army arrived, Edward, Viscount Conway, was sent forward with a woefully inadequate force of 1,500 cavalry and 2,000 infantry (later reinforced to 3,000). Leslie planned to attack Newcastle from the north and the south by dividing his army at Newburn, where part of it would cross the River Tyne.

On 27 August, Leslie arrived at Newburn to find that Conway had deployed his army on the south bank facing two fording points which the Scots could use to cross the river at low water. His preparations included hastily constructed breastworks shielding musketeers and artillery. Leslie sent part of his army, probably under the Earl of Montrose, on to Newcastle. Then, under cover of darkness, he concealed his own musketeers and artillery on wooded slopes, and in lanes and houses on the north bank. A few improvised guns were even hoisted on to the tower of the Church of St Michael and All Saints.

Throughout the following morning, the two armies watched each other, neither anxious to make the first move. Conway thought his position too weak to give battle, but he received a message from the Earl of Strafford ordering him to fight. While he was still pondering the question, shots were heard.

Apparently, a Scottish horseman, watering his horse on the riverbank, had unsportingly been shot dead, and Leslie's artillery opened up. The fire was accurate, doing considerable damage to the earthworks and the men sheltering within, forcing them to retreat. The English guns, on the other hand, were not so successful owing to the lack of clear targets, and Scottish horse and infantry began to cross the river.

A portion of the English cavalry – led by a young Henry Wilmot, at the beginning of a distinguished career – put up a fight, forcing the Scots to retreat, but the Scottish guns eventually pushed them back, together with the infantry which should have advanced in support. A good number of the English simply fled to save their lives, but there was no pursuit, which allowed others to make a more dignified retreat with the artillery intact. Thus, casualties were comparatively light. Wilmot, marooned on level ground between the river and the advancing Scots, was captured.

To Leslie's surprise, Conway abandoned Newcastle,

enabling the Scots to march in two days later. Accused of cowardice, Conway threw the blame on his recruits whom he described as 'the meanest sort of men about London', which was probably true. Faced with this situation, the king had to sue for peace.

Pending a permanent settlement, the Treaty of Ripon, signed on 14 October 1640, allowed for a Scottish army to occupy Northumberland and Durham, at a cost to the English government of £850 per day. A final agreement, the Treaty of London, signed on 10 August 1641, decreed that episcopacy would not be introduced into the Kirk of Scotland and, by way of a final humiliation, that the Scots would receive £300,000 to cover their expenses for the war.

The battlefield today

Newburn is situated off the A69, four miles from Newcastle. Follow the signposts through the town to the Tyne Riverside Country Park (with car parking) and the battlefield (OS Landranger 88 1665). Interest in the battle has increased in line with improvements in the battlefield's accessibility. Prior to the 1980s, the area was largely an industrial waste-land of old mine workings, scrap yards and rubbish tips. One's visits were necessarily focused on the fine church and the bridge – the latter lying in proximity to the Tyne's seventeenth-century fording points. With the creation of the country park, the area was transformed and, latterly, enhanced further by the introduction of a battlefield monument and interpretation panels.

Further reading

Mark Charles Fissel, *The Bishops' Wars* (Cambridge University Press, 1994).

The English Civil Wars

First Civil War

49. Powick Bridge, 23 September 1642

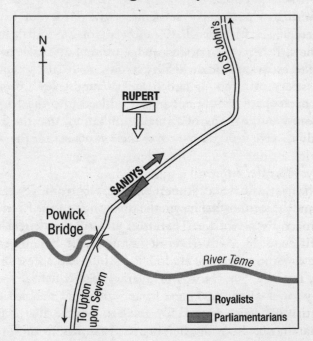

On 22 August 1642, King Charles I raised the Royal Standard at Nottingham, signalling the beginning of the First Civil War. From Nottingham, Charles moved west to Shrewsbury, where he planned to recruit. In addition, a mint established at Aberystwyth was transferred to Shrewsbury so that the Royalists could transform donated gold and silver plate into hard currency.

In Oxford, the university colleges had collected a substantial quantity of silver plate and, on 12 September, Sir John Byron left the city to deliver it to the king. Hearing of the plan, the Earl of Essex, commander-in-chief of Parliament's army, attempted to intercept Byron's convoy, which was escorted by only 150 dragoons. Essex was already on the march west, but he sent ahead a force of 1,000 cavalry and dragoons to do the job.

On 16 September, Byron reached Worcester. It was clear to him that he lacked the strength to hold it, and yet he lingered here for a week, awaiting the arrival of Charles' nephew, Prince Rupert, despatched with 1,000 men by the king to escort the treasure into Shrewsbury.

Essex's advance guard under Nathaniel Fiennes, approached on 22 September, but pulled back six miles, to Upton, to await the arrival of the main body. Colonel Edwin Sandys, in the van, thought it made sense to take control of Powick Bridge on the River Teme, advancing to it accordingly. His men sat up all night guarding it.

The next day, Prince Rupert arrived. He had the same idea as Sandys, considering it prudent to cover the Powick Bridge approach to Worcester. Therefore, he deployed his men in the fields to the north of Powick Bridge while arrangements were made to evacuate the town. Oddly enough, it seems that, initially, Sandys was unaware of the Royalists' proximity for, at about 4.00 p.m., he and Colonel John Brown, a Scottish officer employed in an advisory capacity, decided to march over the bridge before being adequately reinforced.

Rupert, in turn, is sometimes presented as being surprised by Sandys' advance. He and his men may have been resting, and yet he had been sufficiently wary to deploy a party of dragoons close to the bridge. When they opened fire on the approaching Parliamentarians, the prince was alerted and sprang into action.

The speed of Sandys' advance was hampered by the narrowness of the bridge and the presence of a gate further along the track. All the same, many Parliamentarians were able to draw up in proper order in the fields of Lower Wick.

Undoubtedly, given time, Sandys' troops would have charged, but Rupert did not provide them with the

opportunity. Instead, the Royalists hurled themselves forward along the whole length of the Parliamentarian front
line. The right wing, which included Sandys, was hit particularly hard, Sandys himself being mortally wounded by
carbine fire. The left wing also gave way and Royalist interpretations of the fight depict the Parliamentarians retreating
in panic. According to Parliamentarian accounts, however,
the surrounded centre held until, in the absence of support,
they were forced to break out, retreating back through the
gate and over the bridge – gallantly held by Colonel Brown
and a handful of dragoons. In fact, the Royalists were in no
shape to engage in a pursuit, all their senior officers, with
the exception of Rupert, having received wounds.

This was of little moment, for Byron was already trun-
dling on towards Shrewsbury, and Rupert was able to
regroup to cover his progress. The wagon train got through
and the treasure was saved. The beaten Parliamentarians
made haste to report to a chagrined Essex, who contented
himself with occupying Worcester.

Powick Bridge was a minor action. Only a few hundred
troops were involved and casualties were light, but it was
the first concentrated fighting of the Civil War. Also, apart
from proving the superiority of the Royalist cavalry, it high-
lighted Prince Rupert's bravery and impetuosity – traits
which would be demonstrated time and again in the trou-
bled years to come.

The battlefield today

Powick Bridge lies at the junction of the A649 and A422 two
miles to the south-west of Worcester (OS Landranger 150
8352). The land to the north of the old bridge, occupied by
Lower Wick, is now built-up, but the bridge itself, a little to
the west of the new road bridge, is much the same as it was
at the time of the battle. There is a car parking area off the
adjacent roundabout. You will find two small stone monuments – one relating to the action at Powick Bridge and

The Battle of Hastings in 1066 by Francois Hippolyte Debon (1807–72). A distinctly mid-Victorian treatment of the action. (Musee des Beaux-Arts, Caen, France/Bridgeman Images)

An Illustration of the Battle of Barnet (1471) from the Ghent manuscript. The action, purely symbolic, shows Edward IV despatching the Earl of Warwick with a lance. (Centrale Bibliotheek van de Universiteit, Ghent, Belgium/Bridgeman Images)

With All Their Banners Bravely Spread, Sir John Gilbert's oil painting depicting the Battle of Flodden (1513). (Leeds Museums and Galleries (Leeds Museums and Galleries (Leeds Art Gallery) U.K./ Bridgeman Images)

Giovanni Fattori's romanticised portrayal of Mary Stuart a the Battle of Langside (1568). Mary is believed to have watched the battle from nearby Cathcart Castle.
(Galleria d'Arte Moderna, Florence, Italy/Bridgeman Images)

The Battle of Edgehill 1642 by the Flemish engraver, Michael van der Gucht (1660–1725). (National Army Museum, London/Bridgeman Images)

Vol. I. P. 44.

The Battle at Edge-hill. 1642:

M. V^r Gucht Sculp.

Prince Rupert's cavalry charge at the Battle of Edgehill (1642). An illustration by Henry A. Payne (1868–1940) for Hutchinson's *The Story of the British Nation* (c.1920). (Private Collection/Bridgeman Images)

The Battle of Marston Moor (1644) by John Joseph Barker (1824–1904). The defeat of the Royalists destroyed their power in the North of England. (Cheltenham Art Gallery & Museums, Gloucestershire, UK/Bridgeman Images)

The victorious New Model Army in *After the Battle of Naseby* (1645), an illustration by William Barnes Wollen for Sir Evelyn Wood's *British Battles on Land and Sea*, published in 1915. (Private Collection/Bridgeman Images)

Cromwell at Dunbar (1650) by Andrew Carrick Gow (1848–1920). (Imperial Defence College, Camberley, Surrey, UK/Bridgeman Images)

The Battle of Drumclog (1679). A lithograph by George Harvey taken from an 1879 edition of John Howie's *The Scots Worthies*. (Private Collection/ Ken Welsh/ Bridgeman Images)

The Battle of Sedgemoor (1685) resulted from the Duke of Monmouth's attempt to seize the crown from King James II. A contemporary engraving. (Universal History Archive/UIG/ Bridgeman Images)

The Battle of Glenshiel (1719) as depicted by the Flemmish artist Peter Tillemans (c.1684–1734). (Scottish National Portrait Gallery, Edinburgh, Scotland/Bridgeman Images)

Sir William Allan's depiction of the death of Colonel James Gardiner at the Battle of Prestonpans (1745). Gardiner was felled by an axe blow to the head as he tried to rally the Hanoverian troops.
(Private Collection/ Bridgeman Images)

Bonne Prince Charlie by G. Dupre (1689–1770). Prince Charles Edward Stuart, the 'young pretender', was the focus of the 1745 Jacobite Rebellion. (Private Collection/ Bridgeman Images)

The Battle of Culloden April 16 1746, an engraving published by Laurie & Whittle in 1797. (British Library, London, UK/British Library Board. All Rights Reserved/Bridgeman Images)

another commemorating the Scots who fell at the Battle of Worcester in 1651.

Further reading
Stuart Peachey, *The Battle of Powick Bridge 1642* (Stuart Press, 1994).

50. Edgehill, 23 October 1642

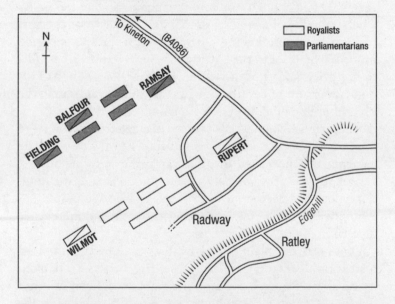

On 12 October 1642, after assembling an army at Shrewsbury, Charles I started out for London. By 21 October, he had reached Southam, to the east of Warwick. The following day, he moved on to Edgcote House, although his army was strung out along the road for miles.

The Earl of Essex was also hot on his trail, having left Worcester in an effort to stop him reaching London. Essex had already reached the Warwickshire village of Kineton, and the Royalists knew that they must stand and fight. Otherwise, they could be caught between two armies: that of Essex and the army raised to defend London, under the command of the Earl of Warwick. Therefore, on the morning of 23 October, Charles followed Prince Rupert's suggestion to occupy the heights of Edgehill, above Kineton. The Parliamentarians deployed to the south-east of Kineton, to await the king's pleasure.

It took Charles most of the morning to gather together his scattered troops, up to 14,000 in all. The Royalists certainly may have had enough 'indians', but they also had too many chiefs. Initially, the king's commander-in-chief was the Earl of Lindsay but, following a disagreement, he was replaced immediately prior to the battle by the Earl of Forth. In addition, Prince Rupert of the Rhine, the king's nephew, had his own command of cavalry. Finally, as time would show, the king himself could rarely refrain from interfering.

At about 2.00 p.m., the Royalists decided to descend from their vantage point. Essex was not likely to try to scale the escarpment; moreover, he was awaiting reinforcements. Originally, his army heavily outnumbered that of the king, but troops had been siphoned off to garrison Worcester and a number of other towns, leaving the armies quite evenly matched.

Down on the plain, the Royalists assumed a standard formation of infantry (in this case, five brigades), flanked by cavalry – Prince Rupert on the right and Henry Wilmot on the left. On the Parliamentarian side, the infantry in the centre was flanked by Lord Fielding's cavalry on the right, with Sir James Ramsay's cavalry on the left. Dragoons were positioned on the extremes of each flank.

After a short exchange of artillery fire and skirmishes involving the dragoons of both sides, Prince Rupert led his cavalry forward. As at Powick Bridge, the Parliamentarian cavalry was unable to deal with the impetus of his charge. Possibly aided by treachery within the Parliamentarian ranks, Rupert carried all before him, sweeping Ramsay from the field. As the Parliamentarian cavalry retreated, they were accompanied by some of their own untried infantry. Rupert followed them into Kineton, where his men set to plundering.

In like manner, Wilmot drove back Fielding's cavalry, most of the remaining Royalist cavalry joining in the pursuit. With the advance of the Royalist infantry, Charles must have thought that a resounding victory was within his grasp, but he was to be sorely disappointed, for two Parliamentarian cavalry units – those of Sir Philip Stapleton and Sir William Balfour, which had been posted to the rear of the infantry on the right – remained in situ.

The Parliamentarian infantry was holding its centre ground as Stapleton and Balfour began to pick off and scatter the Royalist infantry brigades one by one. In response, the king rode among his troops, exhorting them to stand fast, even though the battlefield was descending into chaos and confusion. Eventually, elements of the Royalist cavalry returned and began harrying the Parliamentarian rear. In truth, both sides were exhausted and, as the light began to fade, the fighting died down, Royalists and Parliamentarians retreating to pass a miserable night within earshot of one another. The next day, neither side was anxious to renew the fighting and the armies withdrew to lick their wounds.

Reliable estimates of casualties have been lost in the propaganda war waged by both sides. Parliamentarian pamphleteers, for example, publicized losses of 3,000 Royalists as against 300 Parliamentarians. Most probably, the number of dead would have totalled around 1,500 per side, with many more wounded.

For the Royalists, the road to London was still open but, instead of pressing on, Charles spent precious time in occupying Banbury and then Oxford. Essex, meanwhile, pushed on to the capital. When, eventually, the Royalists did move on London, they were stopped at Turnham Green. Reluctantly, Charles retreated to Oxford, which became his base for the next four years.

The battlefield today

Exit the M40 at Junction 12, taking the road to Kineton.
From Kineton, take the B4086 Banbury Road. Half a mile
beyond the village, on the left, is a battlefield monument (OS
Landranger 151 3550). From here on, the area to the right,
as far as the escarpment ahead, is the battlefield. Much of it
is Ministry of Defence land and, as such, is out of bounds
– meaning that a second, earlier monument, in Graveyard
Coppice (OS Landranger 151 3549) is inaccessible. Not to
worry: follow the road round to Ratley. Continue past the
village turn-off to the Castle Inn, marking the point from
which Charles I studied the ground prior to the battle – as
you can do yourself with your sketch-map to hand.

Until about twenty years ago, there was a battlefield
museum, based at Farnborough Hall, on the other side of
the M40, but although the hall (an English Heritage property) is still open, the museum facility no longer exists,
making Edgehill the only battlefield in the country which
has witnessed a decline, as opposed to an expansion, in visitor facilities.

Further reading

Keith Roberts and John Tincey, *Edgehill 1642: The First Battle of
the English Civil War* (Osprey, 2001).

51. Tadcaster, 7 December 1642

During the First Civil War, the contest in the north
of England was essentially between the Royalist
William Cavendish, Earl of Newcastle, and the team of
Ferdinando, Lord Fairfax and his son, Sir Thomas, acting
for Parliament.

Initially, owing in part to his enormous personal
wealth, Newcastle had the upper hand. At the beginning
of December 1642, he received the keys of York and the
city became a Royalist stronghold. Before Newcastle's

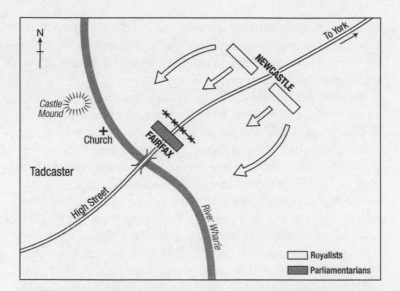

arrival, Lord Fairfax, intent on maintaining the integrity of the strongly Parliamentarian cloth towns of the West Riding, had secured the bridges over the River Wharfe at Wetherby and Tadcaster. Unfortunately, Fairfax had only 900 men under his command, as opposed to the 4,000 which Newcastle could put into the field. Accordingly, he abandoned Wetherby and concentrated his forces at Tadcaster.

Without delay, Newcastle launched an attack. He concentrated his main force on Tadcaster, while a second group under the Earl of Newport made for Wetherby. The plan was for Newcastle to attack from the east, while Newport would sweep down from the west, thus catching the Parliamentarians in a pincer movement.

Fairfax wanted to march out of the town to face Newcastle – probably to the present-day Gallows Hill – but the latter's advance early on the morning of 7 December caught him unawares, necessitating a hurried withdrawal to breastworks beyond the north end of the bridge. It was now about 11.00 a.m. and the Royalists attempted to storm the

defences, but were driven back by the Parliamentarian musketeers, who held their fire until the last moment. With the
support of two demi-culverins, the assaults continued, but
were repulsed every time.

Seventeenth-century Tadcaster consisted of one main
street, leading up to the bridge, although there was a row
of dwellings lining the north bank of the river. Newcastle
tried to outflank the defenders by sending forward parties
to occupy them. Twice they succeeded in occupying buildings, only to be driven out with heavy losses.

The fight raged throughout the day with such unrelenting
ferocity that both sides ran out of ammunition, but Fairfax
held on. By 4.00 p.m., Newcastle was a worried man; the
light was fading and Newport had still not arrived. Had
Newcastle retained the cavalry and dragoons he had sent
with Newport, he could have overrun the Parliamentarian
positions. As it was, they had been wasted. Perhaps
Newport, encumbered with artillery, had moved too slowly.
Others accused him of treachery. It was also claimed that
he was duped into halting by a runner who arrived with a
note bearing Newcastle's forged signature, cancelling the
operation. Whatever the reason, Newcastle decided to withdraw for the night, having sustained casualties (according to
Fairfax) of 200 dead and wounded.

Under cover of darkness, Fairfax evacuated the town and
marched to Selby so that, on the morrow, the Royalists were
able to enter Tadcaster unchallenged. It was something of a
hollow victory, for although the town was now in Royalist
hands, the offensive had failed to destroy Fairfax's army,
which remained intact and ready for further action.

The battlefield today

Tadcaster is off the A64 between York and Leeds, ten miles
to the west of York. There is a car park by the bridge (OS
Landranger 105 4843). The seventeenth-century bridge,
although narrower, was also a stone structure. The oldest

building in the town, and one probably utilized by the occupying forces, is the timber-framed 'Ark' in Kirkgate which, until the 1980s, housed a museum. Defensive entrenchments seem to have run along a line defined by St Joseph's Street, stretching to the present-day brewery buildings to the south and on to Castle Hill to the north. The motte and bailey of the Norman Tadcaster Castle, originally a possession of the Percy family, can be viewed from the riverside walk (Ebor Way). Although neglected by the time of the Civil Wars, it was incorporated into Fairfax's defences, with the addition of artillery emplacements. St Mary's Church is essentially nineteenth century, an earlier structure having been destroyed by the Scots in 1319, during their incursion which culminated in the Battle of Myton.

Tadcaster was a minor battle and there is no memorial. However, the Civil Wars included a great many such actions and it is occasionally refreshing to exchange the beaten track of the major battlefields for little gems like this one.

Further reading
David Cooke, *The Civil War in Yorkshire* (Leo Cooper, 2004).

52. Braddock Down, 19 January 1643

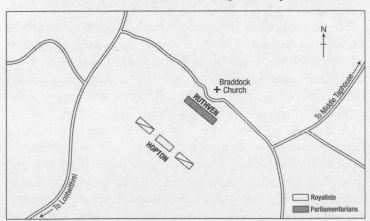

At the start of the Civil Wars, the county of Cornwall was a Royalist bastion, and it remained so to the very end. In charge of the Royalist war effort was Sir Ralph Hopton, who depended upon the support of local gentry such as Sir Bevil Grenville, to raise armed support.

Hopton faced a number of adversaries throughout his military career in the West Country. At the outset, the Earl of Stamford, based at Plymouth, constituted the main Parliamentarian opposition. He considered that Hopton's poorly armed scratch force could be brought to heel without too much difficulty and despatched an army of 4,000 men, commanded by Colonel William Ruthven, to prove his point.

The Royalists were rather better placed than Stamford had thought. Hopton could call upon 5,000 men who were now well supplied and armed, thanks to the seizure of three Parliamentarian supply ships which a storm had driven into Royalist Falmouth. On 18 January, the Royalists set up camp at Boconnoc Park, near Liskeard. The following morning, they marched towards Liskeard, where it was thought Ruthven was ensconced. However, Ruthven had also been on the move, having taken up a position in front of Braddock's parish church, St Mary's, just one mile shy of Boconnoc.

Hopton speedily deployed his troops, Grenville with the infantry in the centre, flanked by cavalry and dragoons. The Parliamentarians drew up in battle order, but they may not have been expecting Hopton, for their artillery was not yet in position. Later, Ruthven would make a face-saving claim to the effect that he had been ambushed.

According to Grenville, both sides settled down to a lengthy exchange of musket fire until Hopton broke the deadlock by ordering an attack, possibly because Ruthven's guns had arrived. In any event, the Parliamentarians gave ground almost straight away. Ruthven had taken the precaution of lining the hedgerows to his rear with musketeers, and it was hoped that they would provide cover to make for an orderly retreat, but they were swept along by their retreating comrades, Grenville remarking that the advance of his infantry 'struck a terror in them'.

Neither side sustained serious casualties, but some 600 Parliamentarian prisoners were taken. Hopton and his Cornishmen had shown Parliament that the war in the west would not be easily won.

The battlefield today

St Mary's Church stands in splendid isolation off the A390, four miles to the east of Lostwithiel (OS Landranger 201 16623). Rumour has it that there is a battlefield monument. I paid a single visit thirty-five years ago and was unable to find one. If it exists, then it must lie in the vicinity of map reference 201 160618, where a battle marker appeared on old ordnance survey maps. Car parking is available by the church. An alternative site suggested for the battle itself is Middle Taphouse, a little to the north-east.

Further reading

Stuart Peachey, *The Battle of Braddock Down 1643* (**Stuart Press, 1993**).

53. 1st Middlewich, 13 March 1643

The 1st Battle of Middlewich was a contest between the Parliamentarian, Sir William Brereton, and the king's man in Cheshire, Sir Thomas Aston. Both sides were anxious to secure the county, not least because they wanted control of the port of Chester.

On 11 March 1643, Aston was in Middlewich (about ten miles to the north of Nantwich) with some 1,500 men. It was not a walled town and he was in hostile territory, with Brereton recruiting in Northwich, just eight miles to the north-west. Although he wanted to move on, Aston had

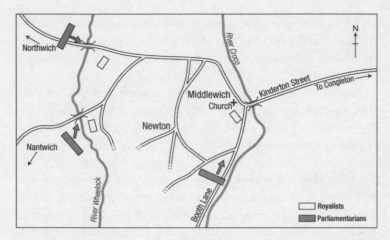

been promised some Royalist recruits, to be provided by Lord Brereton (a relative of Sir William who had chosen the opposite side), and so he tarried. The next day, the Royalists were harassed by Sir William and two companies of dragoons. The Parliamentarians retired to Northwich in the evening, intending to make a direct assault on Middlewich the following morning.

Sir William had been expecting reinforcements from Nantwich and, although they had not arrived, he still decided to attack. Both bridges spanning the River Wheelock were covered, but Aston focused his defences on the western perimeter of the town, on Sheathe Heath. Until mid-morning, the fight 'was equal' and Aston's defences held. Then, Sir William's reinforcements arrived – some 800 foot and 300 horse – advancing along Booth Lane, to enter the town where Aston had positioned another gun. The Nantwich men were forced off the road and into the fields, but gradually worked their way forward until the Royalist master gunner fled.

Aston's forces were now overstretched and, with Parliamentarians now flooding into the town from Booth Lane, he ordered a retreat to High Town and St Michael's churchyard. Instead of establishing a defensive position in the churchyard, however, his infantry took shelter inside the church. As a last resort, Aston ordered his cavalry to regroup and launch a flank attack, but they were unable to reform until they were beyond Kinderton Hall. Now virtually alone, Aston succeeded in making his own escape through the maze of the town's narrow lanes.

Casualties were by no means high, but over 400 Royalists were taken prisoner. Brereton was delighted, and he had every right to be, for his victory consolidated the Parliamentarian hold on the county. (Ironically, nine months later, at Middlewich, Brereton would suffer what would be his only defeat in an encounter with Lord Byron.)

The battlefield today

Middlewich is on the A54, ten miles to the north of Nantwich (OS Landranger 118 7066). Exit at Junction 18 of the M6. The old town has suffered from the need to keep traffic flowing, but the bridges are still there, as is Booth Lane and the church. The town is keen on promoting its heritage, and much could be done to highlight its role in the First Civil War. Use the town centre car parks.

Further reading

Thomas Malbon, *Memorials of the Civil War in Cheshire and the Adjacent Counties* (Ulan Press, 2012).

54. Hopton Heath, 19 March 1643

Throughout the Civil War years, one of the most important garrisoned towns of the west midlands was Lichfield. Like many another town in the land, it changed hands on a number of occasions, making life doubly difficult for the inhabitants.

Initially held by the Royalists, it was taken for Parliament by Sir John Gell in early March 1643. Gell also hoped to occupy Royalist Stafford and, to this end, arranged to link up with Sir William Brereton's Cheshire Parliamentarians.

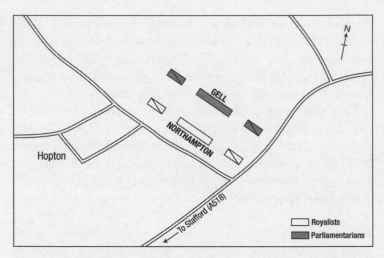

The two armies would meet three miles from Stafford, on Hopton Heath. Gell duly arrived on Hopton Heath early on 19 March, Brereton arriving on the scene at about 2.00 p.m.

Meanwhile, the Royalists had not been idle. Keen to secure Stafford and take back control of Lichfield, they also had two armies in the field – those of the Earl of Northampton and of Henry Hastings, which joined forces to enter Stafford on the evening of 18 March. The next morning, Northampton and Hastings were in church (as it was a Sunday) when they received news of the Parliamentarian presence on Hopton Heath. The Royalist troops were billeted everywhere and it took time to assemble them. In the end, the leaders galloped out with their cavalry while the infantry laboured in the rear.

Gell had selected a good defensive position, on high ground, his infantry in the centre, with dragoons on both flanks, in total about 1,500 men. The Royalist force, 1,200 strong, comprised mainly cavalry, and their comparatively few infantry were deployed in the centre to the rear. An attack was launched on the Parliamentarian right flank, occupied by Brereton's dragoons, who were slowly driven back. A Royalist assault on the other flank also bore fruit, the Parliamentarian dragoons again being forced to give ground.

Northampton had a huge cannon, nicknamed 'Roaring Meg'. After firing a few broadsides, he led a charge at the enemy centre, but was repulsed, Gell fighting with his men in the front line. A second charge was also driven off, but Northampton's horse stumbled in a rabbit hole, throwing its rider. The earl was surrounded by Parliamentarians and killed. The fighting continued but, try as they might, the Royalists could not break the Parliamentarian infantry and, as it grew dark, they fell back. During the night, Gell withdrew, leaving the Royalists in possession of the field.

The Royalists had suffered heavy casualties losing, in addition to the Earl of Northampton, perhaps 500 men including a good number of officers, but Stafford was saved and the victory served as a springboard for the retaking of Lichfield. Gell consoled himself with taking possession of Northampton's body, which he offered to return to the Royalists in exchange for some pieces of ordnance that they had managed to capture during the battle. When they refused, he paraded the embalmed corpse through the streets of Derby.

The battlefield today
The battlefield is off the A518, three miles to the north-east of Stafford, close to the village of Hopton (OS Landranger 127 9526). Exit from Junction 14 of the M6. The area is partially covered by a Ministry of Defence storage facility, but the public footpath network facilitates exploration. There are two memorials: a plaque by the village hall in Hopton and a monument on the battlefield itself.

Further reading
Roy Sherwood, *The Civil War in the Midlands 1643–51* (Sutton Publishing, 1992).

55. Ripple Field, 13 April 1643

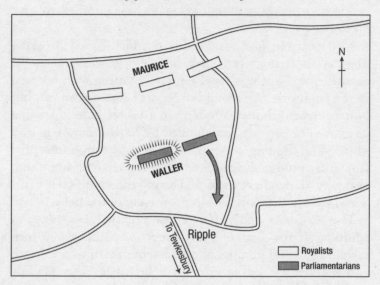

This relatively minor battle is of interest owing to the lead-ing role played by Prince Maurice. The younger brother of Prince Rupert, Maurice lived in Rupert's shadow, his opportunities to shine not being helped by the fact that for much of the First Civil War he was tucked away in the West Country. The tussle at Ripple Field between Maurice and the Parliamentarian commander, Sir William Waller, devel-oped out of Royalist attempts to stem a string of successes enjoyed by Waller in the west.

On 24 March 1643, Waller captured 2,000 Welsh Royalists at Highnam, two miles from Parliamentarian-held Gloucester. Engaged in a poorly organized, half-hearted venture to take the city, the Royalists surrendered without

a shot being fired. Waller tried to build on this success by extending his theatre of operations into South Wales, marching against Monmouth on 4 April, before moving on to Usk and Chepstow. Two days later, he learned that Prince

Maurice, despatched from Oxford, had crossed the River Severn by a bridge of boats near Royalist-held Tewkesbury.

On 10 April, Waller marched from Chepstow in the hope of surprising the prince in the Forest of Dean, but Maurice was alerted and, after a sharp skirmish, Waller was forced to seek the safety of Gloucester. Still hoping to retain the initiative, Waller sent Colonel Edward Massey, Governor of Gloucester, to take Tewkesbury. Massey completed the task on 12 April, also destroying the ill-guarded pontoon bridge that Maurice had used to cross the Severn.

Arriving too late to secure the crossing, Maurice now made for the permanent bridge at Upton-on-Severn, six miles to the north. This time, his advance guard beat Waller's advance guard to the objective, and the bridge was held by the former until Maurice and his main force arrived early on 13 April. Waller was marching from Tewkesbury and halted three miles short of Upton, just beyond the village of Ripple, drawing up his army on 'Old Nan's Hill'. Maurice advanced from the bridge to deploy on the open ground below.

Waller was short of infantry and was also outnumbered, with around 1,400 men to oppose Maurice's 2,000 or so. Both sides possessed artillery and, during a preliminary exchange of fire, Waller discovered that he did not have the right ammunition for his guns. He tried to take the initiative by sending forward a party of horse, but they were easily repulsed by Royalist musketeers deployed behind the field hedges. At this point, Waller appears to have lost his nerve and decided to retire to the safety of Tewkesbury. He tried to cover his retreat by blocking the lane leading from Old Nan's Hill to the village with dragoons, supported by musketeers positioned in the hedges on either side.

Emboldened by Waller's retreat, the Royalists advanced. As his brother had scattered the opposition at Powick Bridge (1642), so Maurice now dispersed Waller's dragoons, who disordered the musketeers in their hasty retreat. Sir Arthur

Hesilrige's horse galloped back down the lane to try to stall the attack, but he, too, was forced to give ground, and the Parliamentarians were pursued until met by reinforcements despatched from Tewkesbury to see them home.

Only a handful of casualties resulted from the fight and Maurice was unable to capitalize on his advantage but, to the keen observer, Waller's weaknesses had been exposed.

The battlefield today
Ripple is off the A38, three miles to the north of Tewkesbury. Exit from Junction 1 of the M50 (OS Landranger 150 8738). On-road parking can be found in the village. The battle took place in a field (known locally as 'Dead Man's Field', by Astalleigh House. Minor, unspoilt battlefields with good public footpath networks, such as this one, are a treat for the visitor.

Further reading
John Adair, *Roundhead General: A Military Biography of Sir William Waller* **(MacDonald & Co., 1969).**

56. Sourton Down, 25 April 1643

One of the main difficulties faced by Charles I and Parliament during the First Civil War was the average soldier's lack of appetite for fighting away from home. Yorkshiremen were always reluctant to wage war outside Yorkshire and, similarly, Cornishmen showed little interest in extending their theatre of operations beyond Cornwall or, at a pinch, Devon. The Royalist commander in the south-west, Sir Ralph Hopton, had his work cut out to maintain his position and yet, in the spring of 1643, the king expected him to march to Bristol and take the city, then in Parliamentarian hands.

To attain this objective, Hopton first had to fight his way out of Cornwall. On 23 April 1643, at Launceston, he

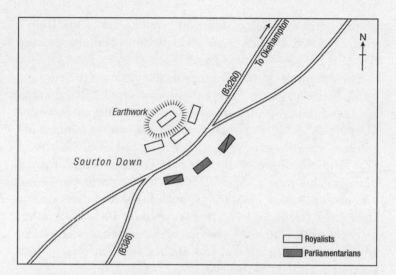

trounced a Parliamentarian force of 3,500 men, commanded by Major-General James Chudleigh, but the affair did not end there. The onset of darkness, coupled with injuries caused by an explosion of gunpowder, meant that Hopton was unable to pursue the Parliamentarians, who were retreating towards Okehampton.

Hopton was on the move eastwards, and by the evening of 25 April had reached Bridestowe, where he intended to camp. Then he received information from Okehampton, four miles away, to the effect that Chudleigh was still there, 'in great disquiet and fear'. It was too great a temptation for Hopton, and he resolved to make an overnight march to Okehampton, to surprise the Parliamentarians at dawn.

Hopton had, under his command, 3,000 foot, 300 dragoons and 300 cavalry. He began his march over Sourton Down with half of the foot, dragoons and infantry in the van, followed by four pieces of ordnance, followed, in turn, by the remaining half of his men. Scouts were deployed but given the nature of the intelligence they had received, no trouble was expected. Suddenly, at about 11.00 p.m., Chudleigh and 200 Parliamentarian cavalry loomed up out of the darkness. Before Hopton could react, Chudleigh's men unloosed a volley from their carbines and charged the Royalist dragoons in the van.

The dragoons, new and untried, fell back on the cavalry, and Chudleigh got in among them, routing the Royalists as far as the ordnance that divided the two columns. Sir Bevil Grenville's infantry gathered about the cannon and made a stand, repulsing the attack, with the aid of Sir Nicholas Stanning who brought up the rear column. Hopton then deployed his men as best he could in the darkness, lining an old trench with musketeers, with horse and dragoons to their right, the position further secured by what was known as a 'Swedish feather' – a series of long stakes with pieces of iron nailed to each end and pushed into the ground as a defence against a cavalry charge.

Chudleigh, flushed with success, brought all his men from Okehampton, but a cavalry assault came to a premature halt by the palisade, while the Parliamentarian infantry were stopped by fire from their own artillery, captured at Launceston. They drew off, leaving Hopton to pass a miserable, wet night. At daybreak, he retreated to Bridestowe.

Thus ended Hopton's first attempt to break out of the south-west. He had lost about sixty men and weapons and supplies. His papers were also taken, giving details of the grand plan regarding Bristol.

The battlefield today

Sourton Down is three miles to the south-west of Okehampton, off the A30 (OS Landranger 191 5491). The coming of the railway coupled with 'improvements' to the A30 have resulted in blots on the local landscape, but the earthwork used by the Royalists for their stand has survived, to the south of the Travelodge. A car parking area is also available on this section of road. Historian Rupert Matthews has provided an excellent exploratory guide to the site in his book mentioned below.

Further reading
Rupert Matthews, *Battlefield Walks: Devon* **(Frances Lincoln Ltd, 2008).**

57. Stratton, 16 May 1643

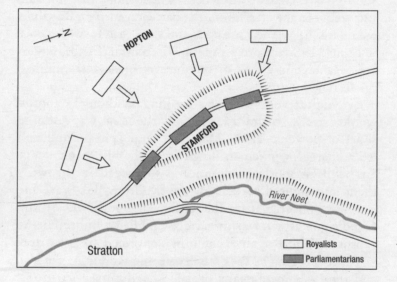

Anxious to prevent Sir Ralph Hopton marching west to link up with Prince Maurice, the Earl of Stamford, commanding Parliament's army in Devon, sought to block Hopton's path at Stratton. By 15 May 1643, the Parliamentarians had occupied an escarpment half a mile to the north of the village. Culminating in an Iron Age earthwork, the land to the east was thickly wooded and fells away sharply. To the west – the direction from which Hopton would be advancing – the slope was more gentle.

Hopton spent the night of 15 May camped about one mile from Stratton, convinced that Stamford would attack, but the hours passed by without incident. In fact, Stamford had sent most of his cavalry to Bodmin and although he still had 6,000 men to Hopton's 3,000, Hopton decided to attack at daybreak. The plan was a simple one: the Royalist infantry would assault the Parliamentarian position in four columns while their cavalry waited in reserve.

At 5.00 a.m. on 16 May, Hopton put his plan into action, the Royalist infantry advancing up the hill towards Stamford's entrenched defences. Throughout the morning and well into the afternoon, the battle raged. The Royalists would discharge their muskets and then rush forward, only to be held by Stamford's superior firepower. (In addition to his advantage in terms of numbers of musketeers, he had thirteen heavy guns.)

By mid-afternoon, it was looking as though Hopton would have to withdraw, particularly as he was running short of powder. Then, Major-General James Chudleigh led a charge of pikemen down from the hill to challenge Sir Bevil Grenville's column and succeeded in throwing them into some disorder. However, Grenville's wavering line was bolstered from the left by Sir John Berkeley and Chudleigh's attack was thwarted, Chudleigh himself being captured. The Royalist columns continued to press forward, converging as they finally neared the top of the hill, and the Parliamentarians broke. Abandoning their guns, they fled, as best they could, down the steep slopes to their rear.

That night, in Stratton, Hopton took stock of his gains: thirteen pieces of artillery, seventy barrels of powder, much-needed food and additional supplies, and 1,700 prisoners. While Hopton claimed that about 300 Parliamentarians were killed, he made no mention of his own losses which, given the nature of the battle, must have been heavy. All the same, it was a great victory.

Stamford's defeat effectively ended his career. He retreated to Barnstaple and then to Exeter, which he later surrendered to the Royalists. Chudleigh was encouraged to change sides, which he did, only to be killed in action later in the year.

The battlefield today

Stratton is on the A3072, one and three-quarter miles to the east of Bude. The battlefield is to the north of the village, on Stamford Hill (OS Landranger 190 2207), named after the Parliamentarian commander. An imposing battlefield memorial arch leads to the earthwork, and a little further up the hill there is a battlefield information panel. In Stratton itself The Tree Inn in Fore Street has a commemorative plaque originally displayed at the battle site. The inn was also the birthplace of Anthony Payne, the seven-foot, two-inches (2.2 metres) tall servant to Royalist Sir Bevil Grenville, who fought at Stratton. Many casualties of the battle were buried in Stratton's St Lawrence Church, where the visitor can view some battlefield artefacts. Car parking can be found in the main village car park near The Tree Inn.

Further reading

John Barratt, *The Civil War in South-West England 1642–1646* (Pen & Sword, 2005).

58. Chalgrove Field, 18 June 1643

In June 1643, Prince Rupert, then in Oxford, heard from Colonel John Urry, a turncoat, that Parliament was to move a sum of £21,000 in gold from London to Thame for the payment of the Earl of Essex's army. It would be easy, Urry insisted, to intercept the convoy. And so began one of Rupert's most celebrated adventures.

On the afternoon of 17 June 1643, the prince left the Royalist capital accompanied by 1,700 men. He crossed the River Thames at Chislehampton, reaching Chinnor at about 5.00 a.m. the following day – surprising the Parliamentarian garrison and taking 120 prisoners. The exercise, although an excellent example of cut-and-thrust guerrilla warfare, failed in its aim, for the paymaster's convoy, then in the locality,

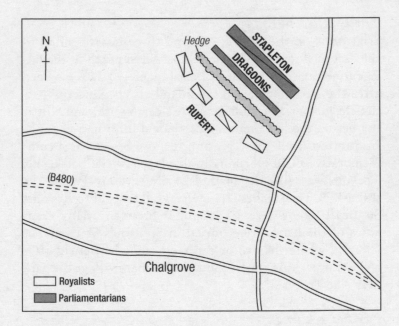

responded to these alarums and excursions by taking refuge in woodland.

Rupert now had to engineer a retreat to Oxford. The enemy, aware of his position, harassed him at every turn as he retired towards Chislehampton. When he reached Chalgrove, about four miles from the bridge across the Thames, he halted in a cornfield, deploying his cavalry to face the growing number of Parliamentarian troops who were following. He sent his infantry on to secure the bridge and lined the road leading to it with dragoons.

Instead of meekly following into the trap which had been laid for them, the Parliamentarians – about 1,000 of them, commanded by Sir Philip Stapleton – held back a party of dragoons lining the field's boundary hedges. Turning his horse's head, the prince spurred on his mount and cleared the hedge immediately to his rear to land in the midst of the amazed dragoons. He was followed in this fool-hardy venture by several of his lifeguard. The dragoons hurriedly withdrew to where their own cavalry waited. Rupert ordered his men to charge. The Parliamentarian horse stood their ground until Rupert personally led a second charge to come in on their left flank. It was enough to scatter them and they galloped off to seek refuge in the surrounding settlements. The Royalists were able to cross the bridge to the east bank where, after fourteen hours in the saddle, they camped for the night before proceeding on their way.

About forty-five Parliamentarians had been killed, for the loss of twelve Royalists. The most serious immediate consequence for Parliament, however, was the loss of one of their elder statesmen, John Hampden, whose refusal to pay the 'ship money' tax had been an important contributory factor in the outbreak of war. He had also been one of five Members of Parliament whom the king had attempted to arrest in January 1642. Riding with Stapleton as a gentleman volunteer during the battle, he was wounded in the shoulder. A week later, despite the king's gallant offer to send his personal physician to attend him, he died.

For the Royalists, the victory confirmed Rupert's daring, and the prince was able to enter Oxford with prisoners and a selection of pennants and colours. These were good times for the king, but could he capitalize on them?

The battlefield today

The battlefield is on the B4840, ten miles to the south-east of Oxford, near the village of Chalgrove (OS Landranger 165 6497). Exit from Junction 6 of the M40. Car parking is available by the Hampden Monument, where there is an adjacent battlefield information panel. (In 1943, an airfield to accommodate the 9th USAAF was constructed on the site. It is not unusual to find the remains of Second World War airfields adjacent to historic battlefield locations.)

Further reading

John Adair, *A Life of John Hampden: The Patriot 1594–1643* (MacDonald, 1976).

59. Adwalton Moor, 30 June 1643

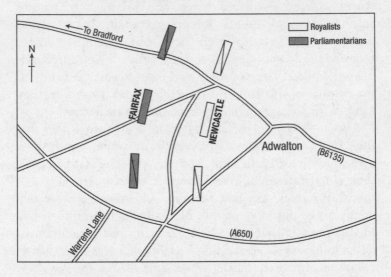

During the first six months of 1643, the army of the Earl of
Newcastle held sway in Yorkshire. By June, Newcastle was
ready to lay siege to Bradford, the HQ of Parliamentarian
Lord Fairfax.

On 22 June 1643, Newcastle attacked Howley Hall, occupied for the Parliamentarians by Sir John Savile. It fell after
three days, and on 30 June some 9,000 Royalist troops set
out for Bradford. Having few provisions, Fairfax and his
son, Sir Thomas, thought it would be impossible to defend
the town and decided to march out to meet the Royalists in
the hope of surprising them.

They had intended to start out no later than 4.00 a.m. on
30 June, but did not get under way much before 8.00 a.m.
Indeed, they had marched just four miles when they came
upon the enemy. Sir Thomas reports that the Royalists
were ready and waiting for them, deployed in formation
on a plain by the village of Adwalton. According to the
Royalists, however, it was Lord Fairfax who was ready and
waiting, Parliamentarian musketeers subjecting them to a

withering fire as they tried to form up. The latter account may be more accurate, for the cavalry on Newcastle's left wing was hampered by open-cast coal mines, a position he would scarcely have chosen. (In addition, there was a ditch fronting the Parliamentarian lines, further restricting cavalry movement, while a preponderance of hedges favoured musketeers, of which Fairfax had the greater number.)

Both sides were drawn up in three divisions. For the Parliamentarians, Sir Thomas Fairfax commanded the cavalry on the right wing with Major-General John Gifford on the left. Lord Fairfax, in overall command of a total of 4,000 men, occupied the centre with the infantry. Newcastle's army eventually assumed a similar deployment.

As soon as the Royalists had organized themselves, they went on to the offensive, yet owing to the difficulties they experienced in using their cavalry to the best advantage, their attacks were beaten back. Even though they did succeed in getting in among the Parliamentarians, Sir Thomas Fairfax managed to rally and pursue them back to their own lines.

Within as little as half an hour, Newcastle was on the verge of ordering a retreat when a final assault of Royalist pikemen on Gifford's wing bore fruit. Led by a Colonel Skirton, described by Sir Thomas Fairfax as 'a wild and desperate man', the attack sent Gifford's men reeling. Thus encouraged, Newcastle brought on his reserves and the Parliamentarians began to flee. Owing to the ground, which was uneven, Sir Thomas did not have a clear picture of what was happening off to his left and by the time he received orders to retreat, he had been outflanked. His father fell back on Bradford, while he took the only road open to him, a lane (Warrens Lane) leading to Halifax.

According to Newcastle, 500 Parliamentarians were killed at Adwalton Moor and 1,400 taken prisoner, while his own casualties (if he is to be believed) were remarkably light, standing at only twenty-two dead. Despite the unequal nature of the battle, it was recognized as an important

Royalist victory and Newcastle was created Marquis of Newcastle soon afterwards. Now, nearly all of Yorkshire (with the very significant exception of Hull) lay at the king's feet.

The battlefield today

The battlefield, partially urbanized by the village of Drighlington, is off the A650 – exit Junction 27 of the M62 – five miles east of Bradford (OS Landranger 104 2228). A battlefield monument is situated on the western side of Station Road, while an interpretation panel can be found at the library on Moorland Road. Roadside parking is available. A preferable base is Oakwell Hall Country Park (OS Landranger 104 2127) from where the battlefield can be approached on foot via Warrens Lane, Sir Thomas Fairfax's escape route.

Further reading

David Johnson, *Adwalton Moor 1643: The Battle that Changed a War* **(Blackthorn Press, 2003).**

60. Lansdown, 5 July 1643

In February 1643, Sir William Waller was appointed Parliament's Major-General in the West, thereby putting him on a collision course with his old friend, Sir Ralph Hopton, Lieutenant-General of the Royalist Western Army.

By the early summer of 1643, Hopton's army had increased in size to 2,500 cavalry and 4,000 infantry. While Waller's combined cavalry and dragoons could match the enemy cavalry, he had only 1,500 infantry, his main problem being a lack of funds to pay his men. He was soon on the back foot and, on 3 July, Royalists and Parliamentarians clashed to the east of Bath, at Claverton Down. Waller was forced to retreat into Bath itself, with the Royalists on his heels.

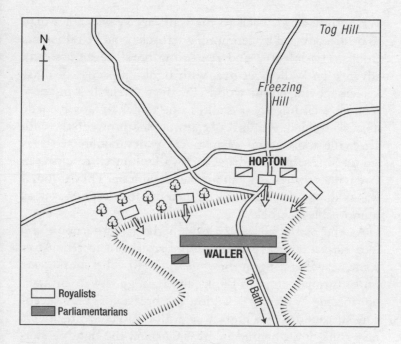

Hopton would have preferred to occupy high ground – the Lansdown plateau – above the city, but his men were spread out and he decided to make camp at Batheaston. The next morning (4 July), Hopton made an early start with a view to occupying Lansdown, only to discover that Waller had beaten him to it. The Royalists retreated to Marshfield, four miles to the north-west.

Twenty-four hours later, Waller moved up to the other end of Lansdown and his men began to construct breastworks for cover. Musketeers were also deployed in woodland on both flanks. Hopton, meanwhile, was assembling his troops on Tog Hill, one and a half miles to the north-east. During the morning, there were skirmishes between opposing parties of dragoons, notably in the locality of Freezing Hill. By the afternoon, the Royalists were on the defensive, their dragoons having been repulsed. Hopton was pushed back to the foot of Tog Hill.

Hopton had his back to the wall, but he was not a man to be discouraged by temporary setbacks, and he rallied his troops. His infantry and remaining horse began a steady advance on Waller's centre, with flanking parties of musketeers moving on the woods. Sir Bevil Grenville's infantry regiment, leading the assault, came under fire, as it made its way resolutely uphill. Attaining the brow of the hill, Grenville took heavy casualties, cavalry counter-charges led by Sir Arthur Hesilrige and Waller himself resulting in Grenville's own death, but his men fought on. They stood, it was said, 'as upon the eaves of an house for steepness, but as unmoveable as a rock'.

As the battle wore on through the late afternoon and into early evening, Royalist numbers began to tell. After some heavy fighting in the woods, the Royalist musketeers broke through on both flanks and light guns were brought up, forcing Waller to abandon his breastworks. A sheepcote surrounded by a high stone wall lay to the rear, and his men took cover behind it. By 8.00 p.m., the fighting subsided into a long-range musket duel in which the Royalists, struggling to consolidate their bridgehead on the brow of the hill, were at a disadvantage. The onset of darkness saved them from taking severe punishment. Pinned down as they were in the hollows where they had sought shelter, they did not know that Waller had chosen the early hours to make a withdrawal to Bath. His men had lit slowmatches (used for firing muskets) along the top of the stone wall and had left pikes standing upright to give the impression that the defences were still manned.

At first light, the Royalists occupied Waller's abandoned positions, enabling them to claim victory, despite having lost at least 200 men killed with many more injured compared to a handful of Parliamentarian casualties. At length, Hopton retired to Tog Hill, where some Parliamentarian prisoners had been placed in an ammunition cart containing several barrels of gunpowder. As Hopton approached, one of the captives lit a pipe, accidentally dropping a slowmatch among the barrels. The resulting explosion, which was heard in Bath, killed or injured many who were in proximity to the wagon. Hopton was left temporarily blinded and paralysed. While Waller stocked up with fresh supplies (including sixty barrels of gunpowder) in Bath, the Royalists made their way disconsolately to Marshfield.

The battlefield today

The battlefield lies two miles to the north-east of Bath, on the road to Wick (OS Landranger 172 7270). The Grenville Monument, commemorating Sir Bevil Grenville, can be seen from the road. Innovations include a little off-road parking near the monument, interpretation panels and a battlefield trail.

Further reading

John Wroughton, *The Battle of Lansdown, 1643: An Explorer's Guide* (Lansdown Press, 2008).

61. Roundway Down, 13 July 1643

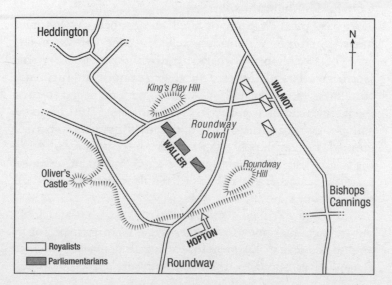

The Battle of Roundway Down followed hard on the heels of Lansdown. Sir Ralph Hopton's Royalists had retreated to Devizes, and on 11 July 1643, Sir William Waller laid siege to the town. However, the cavalry of Prince Maurice and the Earl of Hertford had already left for Oxford, where they sought aid. On 12 July, at Marlborough, the pair linked up with Lord Wilmot, bringing their total strength to 1,800 horse, as opposed to Waller's 2,000 horse and 2,500 infantry.

Waller learned of the reinforced Royalist cavalry's approach on the morning of 13 July. He was now sandwiched between them and Hopton's 2,000 foot within Devizes. Abandoning his siege, he moved out to Roundway Down, a plateau three miles to the north of the town to meet this new threat.

The Royalists arrived to find the Parliamentarians drawn up in good order, Waller's cavalry on the left, Sir Arthur Hesilrige's cuirassiers on the right, with the infantry in the centre. The Royalists also deployed in three 'battles': Sir John Byron on the right, Wilmot on the left and the Earl of Crawford in the rear.

At 3.00 p.m., Wilmot ordered an advance. As his men moved forward, Waller despatched a party of skirmishers. They were thrown back by Royalist skirmishers and Hesilrige charged forward in their support. In turn, the cuirassiers were engaged by Wilmot, who managed to turn them. Hesilrige's attempts to regroup failed and his men galloped off in confusion. Although the Royalists were outgunned, the Parliamentarian artillery were unable to fire as the fleeing cuirassiers were in the way. (Sir Arthur escaped unscathed, neither sword nor bullet able to penetrate his full plate armour.)

Waller now moved forward with his cavalry and foot, but he met the same fate as Hesilrige. Byron's men got in among the enemy horse before using their pistols at close range. After standing their ground for 'a pretty space', the Parliamentarian left wing eventually gave ground and were swept from the field. Many fell to their deaths from the steep eastern face of Roundway Hill into what became known as 'Bloody Ditch' at the bottom. Waller stayed, trying to steady his now unprotected infantry, but the Royalists were able to capture and use his artillery against him. When Hopton's infantry was perceived to be advancing from Devizes, the remaining Parliamentarian resistance collapsed.

The number of Royalist casualties is unknown, but Parliamentarian casualties were in the hundreds, killed, wounded or captured. In what Waller called 'my dismal defeat', owing to Royalist audacity and resolve, his army had been destroyed, his artillery and supply train lost into the bargain. The triumphant Royalists could now move on Bristol unhampered.

The battlefield today

Roundway Down is three miles from the centre of Devizes (OS Landranger 173 0264). Take the A36 eastbound carriageway from the town centre and then Folly Road to Roundway. Keep going north and at the T-Junction, turn left, following the track up to the small car parking area at Oliver's Castle. The latter is an Iron Age hill fort ('Bloody Ditch' is beneath its steep descent to the west) and, like many another monument named after the great man, has no known connection with Oliver Cromwell. However, it provides a good starting point, with a battle interpretation panel. The public footpath system facilitates a circular walk of the battlefield. The present-day Devizes Castle is nineteenth century in origin, the original having been slighted by Parliament in 1648.

Further reading

John Adair, *Roundhead General: Campaigns of Sir William Waller* (Sutton, 1997).

62. Gainsborough, 28 July 1643

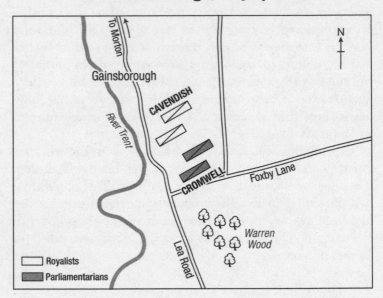

During the First Civil War, the North Lincolnshire town of Gainsborough was of interest to both Royalists and Parliamentarians. A crossing point of the River Trent, it also constituted an important part of the east midlands' road network.

Gainsborough (whose inhabitants naively hoped to remain neutral) was first taken by the Royalists in March 1643. It proved to be a useful base for mounting raids into Parliamentarian country to the east, and Parliament's commander-in-chief in Lincolnshire, Francis, Lord Willoughby, resolved to occupy it. No sooner was Willoughby installed, however, than he himself was besieged by Royalists led by Sir Charles Cavendish, young cousin of the Earl of Newcastle.

Parliament, in its turn, organized a relief mission and on 26 July, at Grantham, Sir John Meldrum joined forces with Colonel Oliver Cromwell. An additional contingent of men from Lincoln was collected the next day, at North Scarle, bringing the total to around 1,200. After marching throughout the early hours of 28 July, the small army reached the village of Lea, a mile and a half to the south of Gainsborough, where they encountered an advance party of Royalists.

After a skirmish, the Royalists retreated up Foxby Hill, followed closely by the Lincolnshire Parliamentarians. It was a difficult ascent, for the ground was pitted with rabbit holes and then, as they neared the summit, the pursuers came upon Cavendish and his main force. Cromwell remarks that the Royalists were 'well set', in two bodies, and that they charged downhill to try to take the attackers off balance. The Parliamentarians held firm, Cromwell occupying the right wing. The ground was disputed, in Cromwell's words, for 'a pretty time', until the Royalists began to falter. Driving home their perceived advantage, the Parliamentarian horse drove them from the field, pursuing them for five or six miles.

Thinking to turn the situation to his advantage, Cavendish led his reserves in an attack on the 'Lincolneers' who remained. However, Cromwell had also held back three troops of horse and promptly took Cavendish in the flank as the Lincolnshire troops scattered. The Royalists were chased downhill into a quagmire. Cavendish either fell or was knocked from his horse and was despatched by a sword thrust.

Gainsborough was hurriedly re-provisioned, but more Royalist troops were already reported as approaching from the north. Some horse, accompanied by Willoughby's infantry, marched out to confront them, only to fall back in confusion when they came upon the Earl of Newcastle's main army. The infantry, not without loss, retired into the town, while Cromwell made a fighting withdrawal to Lincoln.

Newcastle retook Gainsborough after three days, but it continued to change hands for the rest of the war. This particular battle is reckoned to be of importance because it marked the emergence of Cromwell as a cavalry commander of note. He might have been censured for abandoning Gainsborough to its fate when his brief had been to secure it for Parliament, but he argued that there was little point in bottling up his cavalry inside the town.

The battlefield today

Gainsborough lies on the A631, eighteen miles to the north-west of Lincoln. The battle was fought to the east of the town on the slopes of Foxby Hill, above Sandsfield Lane (OS Landranger 112 8388). A monument is situated along Foxby Hill. Use town centre car parks.

Further reading

John West, *Oliver Cromwell and the Battle of Gainsborough* **(Richard West Publications, 1992).**

63. 1st Newbury, 20 September 1643

Following the defeat of Sir William Waller's Parliamentarian army at Roundway Down (1643), Charles I might have been expected to challenge the Earl of Essex, whose own army was ailing, through sickness, lack of supplies and depleted numbers. Instead, the king tied down his forces in a siege of enemy-held Gloucester. Essex was given more men and told to march to the relief of the town.

Charles had begun the siege on 10 August 1643. He thought it would fall quickly, but it held out until Essex arrived on 8 September, the Royalists having withdrawn four days previously. Having raised the siege, Essex had to march back to London, and it was now that the king decided to take him on. For a while, it looked as though Essex would make it home, for it was only after much jockeying for position that the Royalists managed to block the path of the Parliamentarians on 20 September at Newbury.

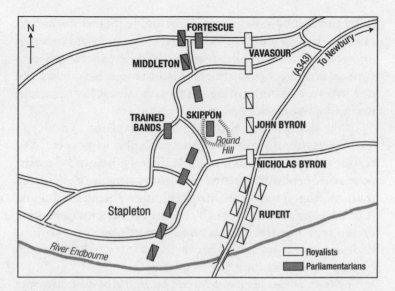

Charles drew up his army on a north-south axis to the south-west of the town, below the River Kennett. Most of the cavalry, under Prince Rupert, were deployed to the south, on the open ground of Wash Common. An infantry brigade separated Rupert from Sir John Byron's cavalry, with further infantry brigades under Sir William Vavasour deployed to hold enclosed ground to the north.

Despite having arrived first, the Royalists had failed to occupy Round Hill, the high ground in front of the centre of their lines. Approaching on the morning of 20 September, the Parliamentarian infantry of Sir Philip Skippon took it for themselves, adding their artillery for good measure. The cavalry of Sir Philip Stapleton opposed Prince Rupert, while Colonel John Middleton's cavalry, supported by Major Richard Fortescue's musketeers, deployed to the north. The London Trained Bands, with which Essex had been reinforced, were held in reserve – and were to prove very valuable. With up to 15,000 men apiece, the sides were evenly matched. The battle began at 7.00 a.m. and went on, in some parts of the field, until 10.00 p.m.

To the north, Vavasour and Fortescue locked horns and reserves had to be despatched to Fortescue's aid when it looked as if he would be overrun. Middleton's cavalry was wasted as there was little room to manoeuvre among the hedgerows, and the fighting in this area, although fierce, was never likely to be decisive.

To the south, Prince Rupert charged Stapleton's cavalry as it advanced on to Wash Common. If Rupert had expected to scatter the Parliamentarian horse, then he was to be disappointed, for the line held and Stapleton was able to deploy all his men. Rupert tried a second time, only to be repelled again. A third assault broke through and the Parliamentarians were driven from the field. Even now, Rupert's success was limited, for he was unable to break an infantry brigade which had moved up in support of Stapleton.

The fight in the centre revolved around Royalist attempts to take Round Hill. An initial advance by Royalist musketeers was beaten back, but came close to gaining a foothold when Sir Nicholas Byron's infantry brigade advanced to support them. When they were finally beaten back, the cavalry of Sir John Byron and Sir Thomas Aston were thrown in. Skippon's infantry began to fall back, but Trained Band regiments were introduced to redress the balance and it was the Royalists' turn to retire.

For much of the day, the fighting was accompanied by artillery fire – the Parliamentarian guns on Round Hill and the Royalist guns beneath them, on Wash Common. In this too, despite the elevated Parliamentarian position, the two sides appear to have been evenly matched. By the time darkness fell, they had fought to a standstill. Essex thought that the battle would continue on the morrow, but the Royalists withdrew during the night. They had run out of gunpowder.

Even the casualties of the battle had been fairly evenly divided, at around 1,700 dead on each side. However, the Parliamentarians chalked up a victory, for they had secured their passage to London. Prince Rupert harried them along the way, but on 28 September Essex arrived to a hero's welcome.

The battlefield today

The battlefield is one and a half miles to the south-west of Newbury town centre (OS Landranger 174 4565). Construction of the A34 Newbury Bypass did not encroach on the battlefield as much as had been feared, although the area occupied by the Royalists has been thoroughly urbanized. The public footpath system facilitates exploration of the Parliamentarian positions. The Falkland Memorial, commemorating the Royalist, Viscount Falkland, who lost his life in the battle, is at the corner of the A343 Andover Road and Essex Street, on the fringe of Wash Common, where there is also an information panel. There is some makeshift lay-by car parking on Enborne Road (4566) although town centre car parking is much improved. Bigg's Cottage, where the Earl of Essex allegedly slept the night before the battle, is at Bigg's Hill (4363).

Further reading

Christopher L. Scott, *The Battles of Newbury* (Pen & Sword, 2008).

64. Winceby, 11 October 1643

By the autumn of 1643, the Yorkshire Royalists were losing the initiative. Instead of marching south, the Earl of Newcastle became bogged down in a siege of Hull. It was not the tightest of sieges, for Parliamentarians are recorded as popping in and out almost at will. On 22 September, Colonel Cromwell was in the city and Lord Willoughby looked in the following day.

The Earl of Manchester and his army of the Eastern Association were able to exploit Newcastle's predicament by advancing into Lincolnshire and laying siege to Bolingbroke

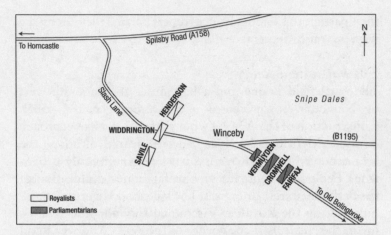

Castle on 11 October 1643. Learning of the approach of the Lincolnshire Royalist, Sir William Widdrington, who was marching from Lincoln to Bolingbroke's aid, Manchester abandoned the siege in order to confront him. They met at Winceby, a hamlet four miles to the east of Horncastle.

The two sides were evenly matched, each with about 3,000 men, although Manchester's infantry had not yet arrived and he hurried back to chase them up. Both armies occupied ridges half a mile apart, the land sloping gently towards open ground in the middle. For the Parliamentarians, Colonel Vermuyden led off with a 'forlorn hope', or advance guard, with Colonel Oliver Cromwell following and Sir Thomas Fairfax in the rear. For the Royalists, Sir John Henderson was on the left, Sir William Savile on the right and Widdrington in the centre.

Battle commenced with a preliminary clash of Vermuyden's dragoons and a forlorn hope of Royalist dragoons. The horse moved in, and as Cromwell charged forward, his horse was shot from under him. Scrambling to his feet, he was knocked down by Sir Ingram Hopton, a prominent Yorkshire Royalist. Probably acting from a sense of honour, Hopton chose to make Cromwell his prisoner but, in the confusion following the clash of the cavalry, Hopton was killed.

A Parliamentarian trooper provided Cromwell with a replacement mount, upon which Cromwell rallied the troops and led his men on to force the Royalist van back upon their rear lines. There was fierce hand-to-hand fighting for half an hour, but Fairfax was able to make a flank charge on the enemy which routed them. Driven back off the road and into the fields, Savile's men were halted in their flight by a high hedge, broken by a gate which opened inwards, towards the mass of riders converging upon it. Unable to get through, the would-be fugitives were cut to pieces, the spot acquiring the graphic title 'Slash Hollow'.

The line of retreat for Henderson and Widdrington was more open, but they still fared badly, many Royalists falling to the east of Winceby in the marshland of Snipe Dale. The battle was actually over before the arrival of Manchester's infantry, which was sufficiently fresh to join in the pursuit. Some 200–300 Royalists were killed, the survivors falling back on Lincoln, while the victorious Parliamentarians settled for a well-earned night's rest in Horncastle.

The Parliamentarians' victory at Winceby marked the turning of the tide for them in Lincolnshire. On the following morning, the Earl of Newcastle raised his siege of Hull and retreated to York, bringing the fighting season to a far from satisfactory end. On 27 October, in recognition of his sterling services to the Crown, he was created Marquis of Newcastle.

The battlefield today

Little remains of the medieval settlement of Winceby, which stands on the B1195, off the A158, four miles east of Horncastle (OS Landranger 122 3268). The battle has never quite 'caught on' although, within the past twenty years, a small monument has appeared in the front garden of Winceby House Farm. Snipe Dales Country Park is a good base for further exploration of the area, but an additional car parking spot has become available nearer to the scene of action, at the adjacent nature reserve. An information panel is located on the B1195, to the west of the hamlet.

Further reading
Betty Brammer, *Winceby and the Battle* **(Richard Kay, 1994).**

65. Alton, 13 December 1643

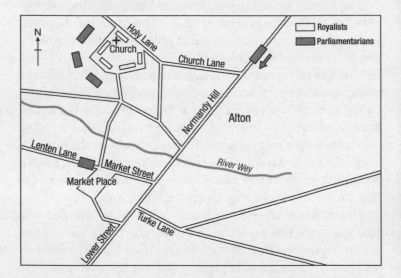

While Parliament was keen to advance into the West Country, the king was over-anxious for Lord Hopton (Sir Ralph had been given a peerage) to break out into Hampshire. On 9 December 1643, Hopton did succeed in securing Arundel, but his forces were now spread very thinly. He proposed to go into winter quarters, a plan which involved installing the Earl of Crawford in Alton. The town was fortified and Crawford settled in.

Parliament was concerned about the Royalist advance and Sir William Waller, stationed at Farnham, resolved to subject

Alton to a surprise attack. Waller was famous for his night marches, which earned him the name 'The Night Owl', and, late on the evening of 12 December, he set off from Farnham with 5,000 men. Initially, to throw any Royalists scouting parties off the scent, he marched north-west for two miles, towards Royalist-held Basing House, before striking south for Alton. Making use of woodland to mask his approach, he surprised Royalist sentries to the west of the town on his arrival at about 9.00 a.m. on 13 December.

The Earl of Crawford got wind of Waller's approach and quickly fled with 500 horse. After assuring the Royalist infantry that he would bring back reinforcements, he tried to make his exit to the east but, being halted by Parliamentarian horse approaching from that direction, took the road south. After engaging in a short pursuit, Sir Arthur Hesilrige's cuirassiers returned to block all entrances to the town.

The Royalist foot, commanded by Colonel Richard Boles, was about 1,300 strong. Boles had thought that any threat would come from the east, directly from Farnham, and it must have come as a shock to find Waller's infantry attacking from the north and north-west.

The main action took place around St Lawrence's Church, where Boles concentrated his strength. A half-moon redoubt and trenches on the north side of the church, together with an adjacent barn, were the chief strong points. Scaffolding had been erected within the church itself to enable Royalist musketeers to fire from the elevated windows, while 'divers houses' were also manned.

It was two hours before the Parliamentarians, gradually drawing a cordon around the churchyard and using hedgerows for cover, could make any headway. Boles was eventually driven from the south-east corner of the churchyard by a pounding from the light leather guns which Waller had brought along. Parliamentarian musketeers flooded in and the churchyard became the scene of furious hand-to-hand fighting, the Royalists finally being pushed back inside the church. A last effort to retrieve the situation was made by the defenders of the trenches to the north, who rushed in to help, but their musketeers were driven back upon their own pikemen following in their rear.

Most of the defenders now surrendered, leaving a hard core of about eighty Royalists, with Boles at their head, inside the church. There had been no time to barricade the doors, and so the Parliamentarians soon gained entry. Boles and a handful of his men refused to ask for quarter and were cut down, Boles, according to some accounts, being shot down in the pulpit.

Royalist dead numbered about eighty, while Waller may have lost only a handful killed. Most of the 900 or so Royalist prisoners were held in the church before being marched off to Farnham. Waller's reputation was enhanced by his victory and the way was now open for him to advance upon Arundel. Hopton, who took the defeat 'with extraordinary trouble of mind', could only write to his friend, Waller, asking him to forward Boles's corpse together with a list of prisoners.

The battlefield today

Alton is on the A31, nine miles to the south-west of Farnham (OS Landranger 186 7139). The seventeenth-century street pattern is readily discernible. The Parliamentarian infantry would have entered the town via Lenten Lane (now Lenton Street), Market Lane (now Market Street) and Holy Lane (now Odiham Road). The Earl of Crawford made good his escape via Lower Street (now Turk Lane). The exterior of the Church of St Lawrence bears the scars of musket balls and the interior has some artefacts from the battle on display, as well as a memorial to Colonel Boles. More artefacts are on show in the Curtis Museum, off the High Street. Use the town centre car parks.

Further reading
Robert Morris, *The Storming of Alton and Arundel* **(Stuart Press, 1993).**

66. Nantwich, 25 January 1644

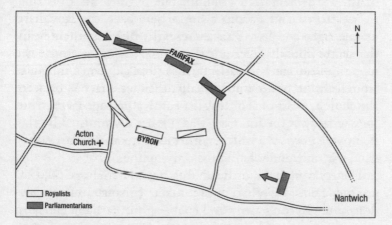

In March 1643, after the Battle of Middlewich, the Parliamentarians had Cheshire at their feet. By the end of the year, the situation was reversed, with Nantwich the only remaining Parliamentarian stronghold in the county. Lord Byron's attempt to storm the town on 18 January 1644 proved an expensive failure and he learned that Sir Thomas Fairfax was marching from Lincolnshire to the relief of the garrison. Fairfax, commanding 4,500 troops, arrived on 24 January, having swept aside a small Royalist force at Barbridge.

Byron had drawn out to Acton, a mile or so to the west of Nantwich, deploying his force of 3,500 men in front of the village. The Parliamentarians decided to press on to Nantwich, relieve the garrison and return with the additional manpower. This suited Byron, for flooding of the River Weaver had led to a portion of his cavalry being cut off, and he needed the time to allow them to come up. When they did so, he attempted to launch an assault on Fairfax's right flank.

Caught on the move, Fairfax had to wheel to his right to meet the attack. He was probably saved by the nature of the terrain, the narrow lanes and hedgerows which broke up the landscape hampering the movement of cavalry. The Royalists made simultaneous contact with the van and rear of the Parliamentarian column, but Byron's lines became overstretched and Fairfax's horse beat back the Royalists on the right and left. Fairfax remarks that his infantry in the centre initially 'gave a little ground' before getting into its stride and methodically pushing back Byron's infantry from hedge to hedge until, finally, they were forced back to the church. Most of the Royalist cavalry managed to retreat to Chester, but the infantry was further discomfited by the Nantwich garrison, which sallied forth to add to its confusion, with surrender being the only option.

The total number of dead was not much above 50, but around 1,800 Royalists were taken prisoner, effectively destroying Byron's army and enabling the Parliamentarians to begin to re-establish their hold on Cheshire.

The battlefield today
Acton is on the A534, one mile to the north-west of Nantwich (OS Landranger 118 6353). The Shropshire Union Canal has cut the battlefield in half, but a track with a bridge enables the visitor to explore the area. On-road parking can be found in the village. Much of the interior of St Mary's Church was destroyed by the Parliamentarians. Nantwich Museum houses a display about the battle.

Further reading
John Barratt, *The Battle of Nantwich 1644* (Stuart Press, 1994).

67. Cheriton, 29 March 1644

Parliamentarian Sir William Waller and Royalist Lord Hopton spent the winter of 1643/44 revitalizing their armies

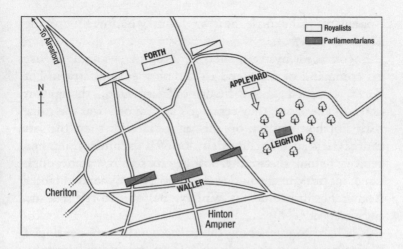

in the south. As it turned out, at the beginning of the 1644 campaigning season, neither had a free hand to prosecute the war. Parliament decided to despatch more troops to the north and told Waller to be wary about giving battle. Hopton, in dire need of reinforcements, had to accept help from the septuagenarian Earl of Forth, who assumed command of Hopton's army.

Towards the end of March 1644, a confrontation became inevitable. Waller commanded 3,500 cavalry and 6,500 infantry, while Forth and Hopton could muster only 2,500 cavalry and 3,500 infantry. Despite his instructions, Waller considered that he would be justified in forcing an issue. On 28 March, after much manoeuvring and counter-manoeuvring, the two armies faced each other on opposing ridges to the east of Winchester, at Cheriton.

Very early the following morning, Waller sent a strong party of musketeers under Colonel Walter Leighton to occupy Cheriton Wood, which flanked the western edge of the projected battleground. It was misty and Leighton reached the wood unobserved. Hopton sent 1,000 musketeers under Colonel Appleyard to take the wood while the Earl of Forth marshalled his forces on the northern ridge.

Appleyard made little headway until reinforced, forcing Leighton to retreat.

Encouraged by this success, Hopton wanted to use his command of the wood to launch a general attack, but Forth, worried about being outnumbered, thought it unwise. Therefore, they remained strung out over the ridge with Forth's infantry on the right, Hopton's on the left and cavalry covering both flanks. Waller, meanwhile, had deployed along the southern ridge crossed by Lamborough Lane, infantry in the middle with horse commanded by Sir Arthur Hesilrige and Sir William Balfour, to the left and right respectively.

It is hard to guess how the battle would have developed if commands had been obeyed. There might have been no battle at all. However, during the late morning, a Royalist officer on the right flank, Sir Henry Bard, led his cavalry regiment forward down the slope. Hesilrige was quick to react, advancing to block his retreat. The impetuous Bard was captured, his command routed.

A general engagement ensued. Waller sent in his infantry, which was soon inching its way up the northern slope. Hesilrige and Balfour supported their progress on the left and the cautious Forth was finally compelled to send in cavalry to oppose them. The Royalists could only descend to the level in piecemeal fashion, owing to the narrow lanes, while Waller, leading his own cavalry, was harassed by Royalist musketeers with which Hopton had had the foresight to line the hedges.

Eventually, the Royalists were pushed back all along the line. It was a fighting retreat which disordered the Parliamentarians to such an extent that they had to pause and regroup. This gave Hopton the chance to engineer an orderly withdrawal from the field. By using two different routes, he was able to bring the army safely to Reading.

Parliamentarian casualties of the battle were in the region of 60 dead and wounded; Royalist casualties were higher, at about 300. As always, one should spare a thought for the wounded: Captain Euble Floyd, 'wounded in ye very midst of his backe'; Captain Raoul Fleury, whose foot was shot off by a cannonball; Colonel Thompson, whose leg was amputated; Sir Henry Bard, who lost an arm; Major Bovill, 'wounded in the belly that he cannot live'. Was it all worth it? Cheriton had the makings of a decisive battle, but ended in anti-climax. Forth's army survived, but the Royalists were being squeezed; their future strategy in the south would become far more circumspect than had hitherto been the case.

The battlefield today

The battlefield is on the B3046, off the A272, nine miles to the east of Winchester (OS Landranger 185 5929). On-road car parking can be found in Cheriton village. A monument (with information panel) is situated at the junction of Badshear Lane and Scrubbs Lane (6030). The public footpath network facilitates exploration, and an excellent battlefield trail leaflet can be downloaded from the Visit Winchester website.

Further reading

Laurence Spring, *The Battle of Cheriton 1644* (Stuart Press, 1997).

68. Selby, 11 April 1644

On 28 January 1644, the Marquis of Newcastle led the bulk of his Royalist army out of Yorkshire, marching north to oppose the Earl of Leven's Scottish army. The Scots had joined the Civil War on the side of Parliament and it was imperative to check their advance into England. Colonel John Belasyse was appointed Governor of York with the impossible brief of consolidating the Royalist position in the county.

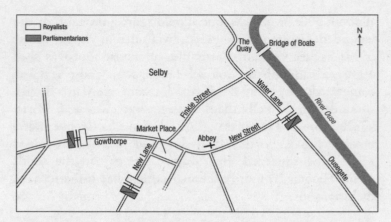

Following an unsuccessful foray into the West Riding, Belasyse fell back on Selby – a town on the River Ouse which occupied a pivotal position between the East and West Ridings and which was also the gateway to York. Taking advantage of Newcastle's absence, the Parliamentarian Lord Fairfax emerged from Hull, determined to take Selby.

On 10 April 1644, at Ferrybridge, Fairfax joined forces with his son, Sir Thomas, who had returned from active service in Cheshire and Lancashire. They spent the night camped immediately to the west of Selby, at Thorpe Willoughby. Their combined strength was in the region of 3,000 troops, the foot slightly outnumbering the horse. To defend the town, Belasyse had around 2,000 men. Barricades were erected, but the Royalist cavalry remained penned in.

The Fairfaxes were well acquainted with Selby, and the capture of a few careless members of the garrison doubtless proved valuable. It was decided to make a three-pronged infantry assault. Lieutenant-Colonel Needham would attack a barricade in Gowthorpe while Sir John Meldrum advanced via Brayton Lane to the market place and Lord Fairfax marched along the riverbank to take the barricaded Ousegate. The cavalry of Sir Thomas would support all three.

On the morning of 11 April, the Parliamentarians put their

plan into action. Belasyse was ready for them, Sir Thomas reporting that, following the initial attack, the Royalists 'defended themselves stoutly a good while'. Finally, Lord Fairfax dislodged the defenders from the Ousegate barricade, although he could not advance owing to a dense column of Royalist cavalry blocking the narrow thoroughfare. His son managed to force a passage through the barricade and charged the enemy horse, putting them to flight across the river via a bridge of boats.

Sir Thomas had an unfortunate knack of getting ahead of his troops. It was a habit which nearly brought him to grief on a number of occasions, of which this was one. Here, he was caught alone when the remaining Royalist horse made an unexpected counter-attack. Thrown from his own mount, he had to be rescued by his men. In the process, they forced the enemy to retreat up the Cawood road and on towards York. During this latter action, Belasyse was captured. Disheartened, the defenders of the other barricades also gave ground and, before long, the Parliamentarians were in possession of the town. Some 1,600 Royalists were taken, along with artillery and supplies.

The action at Selby was one of the most significant of the Civil Wars, for Fairfax's victory exposed York to attack. It led directly to the Earl of Newcastle's retreat to York, the siege of the city and, ultimately, the Battle of Marston Moor.

The battlefield today

Selby is off the A63, fourteen miles south of York (OS Landranger 105 6132). Parking is available in town car parks. The course of the fighting can be followed, for the old town street pattern is not very much changed. The Market Place, Ousegate, Micklegate, Gowthorpe and Finkle Street are still there; Brayton Lane has developed into the A1041 (Park Street), while the Cawood road is now the B1223. The abbey was allegedly used by the Parliamentarians to stable their horses – a tale adapted to suit many a religious establishment.

Further reading
David Cooke, *The Civil War in Yorkshire* **(Leo Cooper, 2004).**

69. Cropredy Bridge, 29 June 1644

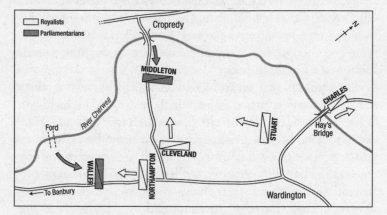

While momentous events were happening in the north of England, Charles I started to worry about the security of Oxford. By abandoning Reading, he added 2,500 troops to the Oxford garrison, but he remained concerned about being overrun by a concentrated Parliamentarian assault. Accordingly, he marched his army out of the Royalist capital, to lead his adversaries, the Earl of Essex and Sir William Waller, on a wild goose chase through the Cotswolds.

Eventually, Essex went south to relieve the Siege of Lyme, leaving Waller to continue alone. The king now sought an opportunity to take the initiative, and on 28 June 1644, preliminary skirmishing between the armies took place in the vicinity of Banbury.

In the early hours of 29 June, Waller occupied a commanding position to the south-west of Banbury, on Crouch Hill. To entice him down, Charles marched off northwards towards Daventry. While taking the bait, Waller chose to shadow the Royalists by taking the Southam road, meaning that the armies were marching almost parallel, separated only by the River Cherwell – Royalists on the east bank and Parliamentarians on the west.

The Royalist column became invitingly strung out over a distance of one and half miles, Charles having crossed the Cherwell at Hay's Bridge, while Lord Wilmot's rearguard was still at Williamscot. Waller saw an opportunity to split it into two, trapping the rearguard in a pincer movement. Lieutenant-General John Middleton was sent across the bridge at Cropredy, while Waller crossed the river at Slat's Mill. (It was now about 1.00 p.m.)

Unfortunately for Waller's bold plan, the Royalists were not going to take it lying down, and Waller came under attack from the Earl of Northampton. Middleton, meanwhile, was challenged by the Earl of Cleveland, both Royalist cavalry forces being supported by the infantry of Sir Bernard Astley. Cleveland held Middleton until the king sent Lord Bernard Stuart back from Hay's Bridge to lend support. Despite his best efforts, Middleton was pushed back across Cropredy Bridge. Cleveland even succeeded in taking several pieces of Parliamentarian artillery. To compound the Royalist success, Northampton forced Waller to retreat over the ford.

Waller retired to high ground near Bourton, leaving detachments to hold the bridge and the ford at Slat Mill. Charles drew up his forces at Williamscot. The Royalists assaulted the ford, which was quickly taken, but the Parliamentarians at the bridge held out. As the day wore on, both sides contented themselves with firing ineffectual artillery broadsides. The day certainly belonged to the king, who sent a message to Waller, offering an amnesty to all who would lay down their arms – terms with which Waller said he had no authority to comply.

Throughout the following day, neither side moved, but during the night of 30 June/1 July, the Royalists pulled out. Royalist casualties probably amounted to at least 50 dead, with Parliamentarian casualties certainly much higher – probably in the region of 200. Oxford was now secure and the king eventually marched west, to take on the Earl of Essex. Waller, beset by desertions and mutiny among his men, was in no position to do anything about it.

The battlefield today

Cropredy is off the A361, four miles to the north-east of Banbury. Exit the M40 at Junction 11 (OS Landranger 151 4746). There is a commemorative plaque and information panel on the bridge (rebuilt in the 1930s). Slat Mill can be reached via School Lane or the Oxford Canal Walk. The Church of St Mary the Virgin used to house a collection of artefacts, and there is still some armour on display. On-road car parking in Cropredy and a good public footpath network facilitates exploration.

Further reading

Robert Morris, *The Battle of Cropredy Bridge 1644* (Stuart Press, 1994).

70. Marston Moor, 2 July 1644

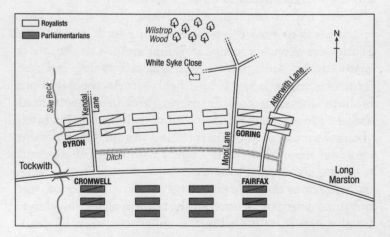

Between 2 February and 13 April 1644, the Marquis of Newcastle was tied down at Newcastle, engaged in a stand-off with a 20,000-strong Scottish army led by the Earl of Leven. Through the agreement known as 'The Solemn League and Covenant', the Scots had joined forces with Parliament, and the marquis had hurried north to meet this new challenge. When he heard that York was being threatened by Lord Fairfax, however, he marched south, arriving at York on 16 April. He soon found himself besieged by three armies: that of the Scots, which had followed in his wake, and those of Lord Fairfax and the Earl of Manchester.

The task of relieving the siege fell to Prince Rupert. On 30 June, after an epic march, he reached Knaresborough, fourteen miles to the west of York. Persuaded that he intended to launch an assault on their positions from that direction, the allies effectively raised the siege by marching out to meet him on Marston Moor, an expanse of heath about seven miles from the city. Instead of advancing on cue, however, Rupert swung north, crossing the River Ure at Boroughbridge and the River Swale at Thornton Bridge, before turning south. Upon arriving in the vicinity of York on the evening of 1 July, he sent Lieutenant-General George Goring into the city to order Newcastle to be ready to march against the Parliamentarians at 4.00 a.m. the next day.

Meanwhile, the allies were pondering their next move. The Scots were none too anxious to fight and it was decided to march out to Tadcaster. Accordingly, in the early hours of 2 July, the main body of Parliamentarian troops moved out, leaving behind some 4,000 dragoons. By the time Rupert arrived towards 9.00 a.m., the allied column was invitingly strung out, and cavalry charges targeting vulnerable points might have proved decisive. Displaying uncharacteristic caution, Rupert decided to await Newcastle. He had expected to rendezvous with him much earlier, but the marquis had not turned up. It was not until late morning that Newcastle finally appeared – and, even then, he was accompanied only by a column of mounted men. The bulk of the York garrison straggled in during the course of the afternoon. Unable to believe their luck, the allies were able to regroup, unmolested.

The Parliamentarians (some 27,000 men) occupied Marston Hill and adjacent ground. On the right was the cavalry of Sir Thomas Fairfax and Colonel John Lambert. The cavalry of the left wing was commanded by Lieutenant-General Cromwell and Sir David Leslie. The infantry, massed in the centre, were grouped under Sergeant-Major-General William Baillie. Dragoons occupied the extreme flanks. Opposing them were about 17,500 Royalists, occupying level ground to the rear of a ditch. The cavalry of Lord Byron and Lord Molyneux were on the right; that of Goring and Sir Charles Lucas on the left. The heavily outnumbered infantry, under the command of Major-General Henry Tillier (Lord Eythin), comprised several disparate units.

Preliminary manoeuvres having taken all day (it was now approaching 7.00 p.m.), Rupert decided to fight on the morrow and went off to have his supper. Newcastle retired to his coach to smoke a pipe. In the allied lines, there was no such laxness. Having noted that the enemy appeared to be standing down, Leven – in overall command – ordered an attack. Rupert was resting on the grass when he heard a flurry of musket fire to his right: Parliamentarian dragoons were flushing out Royalist musketeers in the vicinity of the ditch.

In the first phase of the battle, Cromwell's cavalry locked horns with the front ranks of Byron's cavalry. At first, Byron was pushed back by the weight of Cromwell's heavy horse, but Rupert brought up his own reserve to bolster the flagging line. At some point, Cromwell suffered a neck wound and left the field temporarily to have it dressed, but Sir David Leslie's light horse succeeded in forging a path between Byron and the adjacent Royalist infantry. Taken in the flank, Byron was broken, as were Rupert and his Lifeguards.

On the Parliamentarian right, Sir Thomas Fairfax was less successful. Having advanced with difficulty over broken ground, he had punched a hole in the Royalist ranks, but a counter-charge made by Goring forced the greater part of his command to withdraw. Finding himself alone within the Royalist ranks, Fairfax removed the white 'signal' from his hat which identified him as a Parliamentarian officer and slipped back to his own lines. He lost no time in locating Cromwell and advising him of the situation.

In the centre, the Parliamentarian infantry was in a bad way. After forging ahead in the initial advance, several units – in particular the Scots – had been forced to retire in some disarray and were now scattered in confusion. Even Lord Fairfax, Leven and, albeit temporarily, Manchester fled the field. Cromwell's nerve held. With the support of Crawford, he began to move across the moor from east to west, systematically rolling up the Royalist infantry brigades before him until he reached what had been Goring's starting position. Goring himself had continued to press Fairfax's cavalry, pursuing them until he reached the Parliamentarian baggage train, which his men plundered. When they returned to the field, expecting to find the enemy dispersed, they encountered Cromwell, who sent them reeling. Soon, the only remaining fully functional Royalist unit was Newcastle's celebrated 'Whitecoat' regiment. Drawing fire, in a despairing effort to give Goring time to regroup, they fought on, refusing all offers of quarter as their fleeing comrades sought to gain the relative safety of the walls of York. By 9.00 p.m., it was all over.

Royalist casualties could be counted in the thousands with Parliamentarian losses as low as three hundred. Rallying as many men as he could, Prince Rupert set out for the south. The proverbial loose cannon, he was free to manoeuvre as he wished. Not so the Marquis of Newcastle. Having beggared himself in the King's cause, the general who had lost his army rode to Scarborough to take a ship into exile.

Within a fortnight, York surrendered. Apart from a few isolated Royalist garrisons, the north of England was now in Parliamentarian hands.

The battlefield today

The battlefield lies on the B1224 between Long Marston and Tockwith, seven miles to the west of York (OS Landranger 105 4952). There is a roadside monument and interpretation panel with a lay by for parking. The public footpath network facilitates a circular walk of this superb, unspoiled site.

Further reading

John Barratt, *The Battle of Marston Moor* (History Press, 2008).

71. Lostwithiel, 21 August–2 September 1644

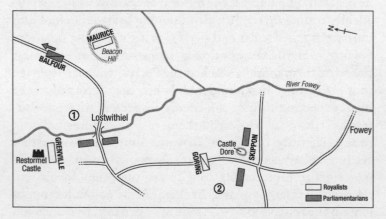

In early June 1644, the Earl of Essex had left Sir William Waller to deal with the army of King Charles I while he marched south-west to challenge Prince Maurice's siege of Lyme. As Essex approached, Maurice withdrew and Essex followed him first to Barnstaple and then to Exeter before pressing on into Cornwall. For some reason, despite Cornwall's Royalist credentials, Essex thought that he would be able to recruit there. It was a bad move, for the king, having beaten Waller at Cropredy Bridge, was soon hot on Essex's trail.

Towards the end of July 1644, Essex reached Bodmin. With no chance of picking up local support and the king now blocking his line of retreat, he then withdrew to Lostwithiel. Initially, there was hope that the Earl of Warwick's Parliamentarian fleet would sail from Plymouth to Fowey with reinforcements, but the men could not be spared. Some 2,000 horse under Lieutenant-General John Middleton did try to fight their way through to Cornwall, but were halted at Bridgwater. Outnumbered by nearly two to one and with no help coming, Essex was in deep trouble.

On 7 August, Charles (his army numbering about 16,000 horse and foot) reached Braddock Down and established his HQ at Boconnoc. Two days later, he invited Essex to surrender, but got the same response as he had received from Waller at Cropredy: Essex had no authority to treat with the king.

During the next two weeks, skirmishing took place as the Royalists tightened their grip. On 21 August, however, they stepped up the pace, taking Beacon Hill to the east of Lostwithiel and Restormel Castle to the north. Restormel was already a ruin, but the Parliamentarian defenders should have been able to hold out. Instead, on the approach of Sir Richard Grenville – brother of Sir Bevil, killed at Lansdown (1643) – they capitulated.

Over the next two days, the fighting deteriorated into a long-range artillery duel between Royalist batteries drawn up on Beacon Hill and Parliamentarian guns sited on the west bank of the River Fowey. Finally, Essex decided to withdraw to Fowey and evacuate his infantry by sea, while Sir William Balfour with 2,000 horse was instructed to break through the Royalist lines and make for Plymouth via Saltash.

The Parliamentarian infantry was gradually withdrawn from 24 August, although two days later, St Blazey, to the south, was occupied by the Royalist cavalry of

Lieutenant-General George Goring. Balfour made his bid for freedom during the early hours of 31 August. Despite being pursued by the Earl of Cleveland, he escaped, suffering relatively few casualties in the process. This spurred the king into action and, at 7.00 am on that day, he entered Lostwithiel. He was determined not to let Essex off the hook and immediately set off in pursuit of the retreating infantry.

There ensued a running battle and Essex did not make it easy for the Royalists, for the landscape was a patchwork of hedges and progress was slow. There was particularly heavy fighting in the neighbourhood of Tywardreath and an Iron Age hill fort, Castle Dore. By 1 September, resistance had collapsed, with the Parliamentarians fleeing in disorder to Menabilly. Sir Philip Skippon sent a message to the king offering peace talks. Skippon was offering to treat with the Royalists because Essex and his staff had commandeered a fishing boat to take them to Plymouth. Charles graciously accepted.

Skippon was lucky. The Parliamentarian foot could, at best, have been compelled to surrender unconditionally or, at worst, have been wiped out. Instead, all 6,000 of them were permitted to leave, minus their heavy guns and personal weapons, on condition that they would not take up arms again until they reached Southampton. In the event, their progress to Southampton turned into a death march. In addition to desertions, attacks by locals and the effects of starvation and disease resulted in only 3,000 of them reaching their destination.

It was certainly a great victory for the king, who had destroyed a second Parliamentarian army, and he lost little time in marching eastwards. However, the Royalists had themselves suffered heavy casualties during the prolonged campaign, and Charles knew that he had to move quickly if he were to take advantage of the breakdown of Parliamentarian power in the south. Essex, who had deserted his command, managed to wriggle off the hook by blaming everybody else.

The battlefield today

Lostwithiel (a personal favourite of mine) is not currently (2014) 'officially' recognized as a battlefield, which is to say that it is not included in the definitive English Heritage listing. Perhaps this is because the action was spread over such a wide area. The town of Lostwithiel is on the A390, seven miles to the east of St Austell (OS Landranger 200 1059). Restormel Castle, an English Heritage property, can be visited. Car parking is available here or in Lostwithiel. Parliamentarian troopers supposedly baptized a horse as 'Charles' in the font of St Bartholomew's Church in the town. On the B3269, towards Fowey, Castle Dore has a stone bearing a plaque that makes mention of the battle.

Further reading

Stephen Ede-Borrett and Derek Stone, *Lostwithiel 1644* (Pike & Shot Society, 2004).

72. 2nd Newbury, 27 October 1644

In the autumn of 1644, Parliament set about solving its man-power problems by bringing together three field armies: those of the Earl of Essex, Sir William Waller and the Earl of

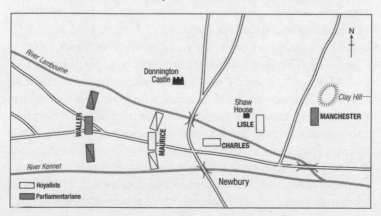

Manchester, amounting to a single force 19,000 strong. The ticklish problem of command was eventually solved when the irascible Essex fell ill, leaving Manchester to assume overall control with Sir Philip Skippon taking command of the infantry and Sir William Balfour the cavalry.

The king, now returned from the West Country, could muster barely 10,000 men. Once again, he set about trying to guarantee the security of Oxford which, among other things, involved raising the siege of Donnington Castle, which lay to the north of Newbury. He entered Newbury on 22 October, and Parliament decided that he should be brought to battle as soon as possible.

On 26 October, the vast Parliamentarian army arrived to find the Royalists in a strong position between the Rivers Kennett and Lambourne. The king occupied the van, with Prince Maurice, supported by the cavalry of Lieutenant-General George Goring and Sir Humphrey Bennet, to his rear at Speen, while, to the north of the Lambourne, Sir George Lisle garrisoned Shaw House and a reinforced garrison occupied Donnington Castle, the siege having been lifted on the king's approach.

The Parliamentarians devised a tortuous plan, whereby Waller would take Skippon's infantry and the cavalry of Balfour and Cromwell on a lengthy flanking march to attack Maurice in the rear. When they engaged Maurice, Manchester was to attack Lisle.

Waller's party set off and spent the night of 26 October at Chieveley. The Royalists were well aware of the manoeuvre and Maurice was ready for them as they approached on 27 October. Skippon took the centre ground with Balfour on the right and Cromwell on the left. At around 3.00 p.m., Skippon moved forward and, despite coming under heavy artillery and musket fire, took Maurice's forward positions. The Royalist infantry was pushed back, but the cavalry put up a stout resistance, holding both Balfour and Cromwell. Finally, the Parliamentarian attack broke down in the failing light.

Waller's offensive had begun too late in the day, and there had been insufficient time to press home the advantage. In any case, Manchester had failed to play his part. It was not until dusk that he made the agreed assault upon Shaw House and Lisle held out. At about 9.00 p.m., the Royalists deposited their stores and heavy guns in Donnington Castle before silently marching away, Charles to Bath, where he planned to meet Rupert, and the main army to Oxford.

The battle had been fought to a draw, with perhaps 500 casualties on each side. The Royalists had been forced to retire, but the weaknesses of the Parliamentarian grand army had been exposed. On 9 November, Charles returned to collect his artillery from Donnington. The Earl of Manchester was still on site and, for a time, it looked as if there would be a 3rd Battle of Newbury, but Manchester stood aside and Charles marched away with his guns.

The battlefield today

The battlefield, most of it hidden beneath Newbury's urban sprawl, is to the north of the town, off the A4 (OS Landranger 174 4668). The remains of Donnington Castle (4669), an English Heritage property, can be visited along with Shaw House (4768) which is open at weekends during the summer. Car parking is available at both sites. (As well as Civil War displays, Shaw House has the famous plaque allegedly marking the spot where a musket ball, narrowly missing King Charles who was within preparing for the battle, lodged itself in the panelling.) Newbury Museum was at the time of my visit in 2014 closed for redevelopment but, hopefully, there will be some battlefield information on display when it reopens.

Further reading
Christopher L. Scott, *The Battles of Newbury* (Pen & Sword, 2008).

UNDER SIEGE

Sieges were a prominent feature of Continental European conflicts, often going a long way towards deciding the outcome of a campaign. In Britain, although armies frequently resorted to siege warfare, the effects were more limited. Success was not unknown, as in the case of Wakefield (1460), when the Yorkists were starved into quitting the safety of the castle. However, this was quite a brief affair. Prolonged sieges, which were almost as demanding for the besiegers as the besieged, were quite another matter. In 1643, the Marquis of Newcastle tied down his whole army in the Siege of Hull. When Lord Fairfax, defending the city, ordered the banks of the River Humber to be cut, the besiegers were flooded out of their earthworks. It was remarked at the time that those without the town seemed likelier to rot than those within to starve.

A protracted siege involved a great deal of spadework (literally) both for the investing forces and the besieged. One of the best surviving defensive earthwork forts, the Queen's Sconce, is to be found at Newark. Covering an area in excess of three acres, it was constructed outside the town walls to the south. A similarly formidable structure, the King's Sconce, was situated to the north. Newark withstood three sieges between 1643 and 1646, to be finally surrendered on the orders of Charles I, who saw more profit in cultivating his enemies than in supporting his friends.

Rarely was the investment of a town or city so tight that the defenders were completely cut off from the outside world. During the Siege of Pontefract Castle (1648–49), a detachment of Royalist horse was able to ride out, proceed to Doncaster, twelve miles distant, and return safely with fifty Parliamentarian prisoners in tow. Similarly, during the Siege of Hull, Sir Thomas Fairfax left the city and successfully crossed the Humber with twenty troops of horse. If those under siege could be provisioned, a siege could last for years. The longest siege in British military history involved Harlech Castle, which became the last Lancastrian stronghold in the country, holding out from 1462 until 1468.

Harlech was provisioned by sea, although a coastal location did not always guarantee success. The Royalist garrison of Scarborough Castle surrendered in July 1645, after a siege of twenty-two weeks, owing to a shortage of water combined with the ravages of scurvy. Bristol, despite having strong defences, was taken by Sir Thomas Fairfax in three weeks. Prince Rupert, who surrendered the city in September 1645, was not, perhaps, the right man for defensive siege warfare. Charles I thought he had given up too easily and sacked him. It could have been worse: Colonel Francis Windebanke, who surrendered Bletchingdon House too quickly to Oliver Cromwell in 1645, was shot.

Holding out for too long also had its problems. After taking Colchester in 1648, Lord-General Fairfax executed Royalists Sir Charles Lucas and Sir George Lisle on the grounds that their tenacity in holding out for over two months was responsible for causing unnecessary bloodshed. The small Parliamentarian garrison of Hopton Castle in Shropshire, under Colonel Samuel More, kept Royalist besiegers at bay for just one month in 1644, but when More finally surrendered, his men were massacred.

Hopton Castle was subsequently slighted. Indeed, a victorious Parliament ordered a good many magnificent castles, particularly in Wales and Yorkshire, to be destroyed so that they would not, in future, constitute a threat.

73. Naseby, 14 June 1645

In May 1645, the main Royalist army, with Charles and Prince Rupert at its head, left the safety of Oxford to campaign in the midlands. By early June, it was being closely

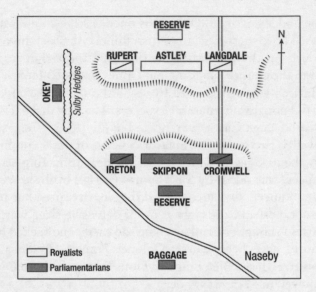

shadowed by Parliament's New Model Army, commanded by Sir Thomas Fairfax, who was determined to bring the king to battle. On the night of 13 June, Fairfax moved in for the kill.

The Royalist army was billeted in Market Harborough and surrounding villages – including Naseby. When word reached Rupert that a party of Royalists had been captured by Parliamentarian troops who had suddenly appeared in Naseby itself, he persuaded Charles to stand and fight.

In his capacity as commander-in-chief of the king's army, Rupert chose an advantageous position on Dust Hill, one and a half miles to the north of Naseby. Accordingly, in the early hours of 14 June, the Royalists, numbering between 7,500 and 12,000 men, deployed along this ridge. On the left, Sir Marmaduke Langdale's Northern Horse straddled the Naseby–Sibbertoft road, while Prince Rupert's cavalry took pride of place on the right wing. Sandwiched between them was Sir Jacob Astley's infantry.

At about the same time, the Parliamentarians, some 14,000 strong, deployed to the south, on high ground closer to Naseby. Lieutenant-General Oliver Cromwell, now Fairfax's second-in-command, led the horse on the right wing, with Colonel Henry Ireton on the left and Major-General Philip Skippon's infantry facing Astley in the centre. Cunningly hidden behind a hedgerow stretching between Ireton and Rupert were Colonel John Okey's Parliamentarian dragoons.

Shortly before 10.00 a.m., Fairfax withdrew Skippon's foot from view and it may be that Rupert, duped into thinking that a full retreat was under way, embarked upon a premature advance. Yet, having determined to fight, there would have been little to gain by further delay and the prince led a cavalry charge which opened the battle. Colonel Okey later claimed to have played a decisive role in the conflict, insisting that much of the sting was taken out of Rupert's advance by the concentrated firepower of his dragoons.

In fact, there is no evidence to suggest that many casualties were inflicted on Rupert's cavalry. For the most part, the enemy sat waiting for them as Rupert, a conspicuous figure in a bright red cloak, swept forward. In what was possibly their finest – and certainly their last – great charge, his men crashed in among Ireton's horse, driving the majority of them from the field.

In the centre, Astley's infantry, striding out purposefully, met with Skippon's hastily recalled lines. Skippon himself was wounded by a musket ball, and although he refused to leave the field, his command was nonetheless deprived of effective leadership. Astley tried to press home his advantage, his men falling on with sword and the butt end of musket, but Ireton, managing to partially regroup, personally led a charge on Astley's right flank in an attempt to relieve the pressure. In the process, Ireton was wounded and fell, temporarily, into enemy hands.

Unfortunately for the Royalists, the efforts of Rupert and Astley were not matched by the performance of Langdale's

Northern Horse – the parochial Yorkshiremen demonstrat-
ing little enthusiasm for fighting away from home. Cromwell
did not wait to meet Langdale's charge, but advanced to meet
him halfway, sweeping the Northern Horse back in disorder. Unlike Rupert, however, he kept his men well in hand.
Leaving three regiments to follow up his success, he led the
remainder of his horse into Astley's left flank.

Meanwhile, the victorious Rupert, as at Edgehill three
years before, was unable to rally his men, who swept on
through the Parliamentarian lines towards Naseby, where
they made a half-hearted attempt to take the enemy baggage train. In this, they were unsuccessful, for it was well
guarded by musketeers. Again, as at Edgehill, the Royalist
mounts were too exhausted to rejoin the battle so, instead of
riding to the hard-pressed Astley's aid, Rupert made his way
to his reserve lines and the king's side, to watch the destruction of Astley's command by Parliamentarian cavalry and
revitalized infantry. While the Royalist reserve may not
have numbered much above a thousand men, it could have
achieved much if used to bolster the centre. As it was, the
men remained immobile while Fairfax threw in his own
reserve.

The outcome was put beyond all doubt by a curious incident. Inclined towards a last-ditch attempt to save the day,
the king placed himself at the head of his own lifeguard, as
if about to lead one final charge. He was stopped by the Earl
of Carnwath, who took hold of his horse's bridle, crying,
'Will you go upon your death in an instant?' In so doing,
he turned the king's steed to the right – away from the
fighting. The reserves, growing increasingly agitated, inter-
preted the manoeuvre as a signal to wheel round and took to
their heels. With Langdale's Northern Horse in retreat and
Rupert's cavalry dispersed, Astley's infantry also fled the
field, although a belated rearguard action stopped the rout
from developing into a massacre.

The short-term results of Naseby were severe enough

for the Royalists: around 1,000 dead, including those slain in a fighting withdrawal to Leicester, and 100 or so camp followers mercilessly butchered by the more zealous Parliamentarians. Five thousand prisoners were also taken – the bulk of them irreplaccable battle-hardened infantry. Similarly, at a time when the Royalists were importing munitions from the Netherlands at twice the cost of London- and midlands-manufactured Parliamentarian weaponry, they could ill afford the loss of their artillery, 8,000 arms and 40 barrels of gunpowder.

In the long term, although Charles himself tried to make light of it, the loss of compromising private papers, which had been with the plundered Royalist baggage train, did much harm to his cause.

The battlefield today
Naseby village is accessed via Junction 2 of the A14, midway between the M1 and Kettering. The battlefield lies to the north of the village, on the Naseby–Sibbertoft road (OS Landranger 141 6880).

Car parking is available in a small lay-by. There are two monuments: a structure on the battlefield itself – the Cromwell Monument – and a second, the Royalist Monument, situated to the north-east of the village on the Naseby–Clipston road (both with information panels). A small museum, situated at the corner of Calendar Lane in Naseby, is open on Sundays and Bank Holiday Mondays between Easter and September – although a new visitor centre is planned. See 'The Naseby Battlefield Project' website for a suggested walking route around the battlefield, together with updates on the proposed visitor centre.

Further reading
Glenn Foard, *Naseby* (Leo Cooper, 2004).

74. Langport, 10 July 1645

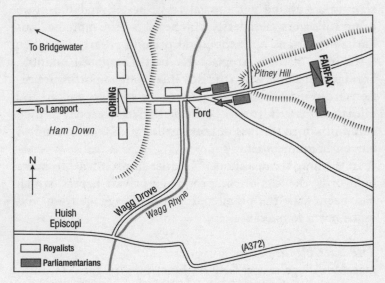

After the Battle of Naseby, it was clear that Parliament was
going to win the war – but when? Those who entertained
hopes that the king would now be obliged to sue for peace
were to be disillusioned, for Stuart obstinacy ensured that
hostilities would drag on for another year.

The West Country was still a hive of Royalist activity, and
Sir Thomas Fairfax was instructed to march south to relieve
Taunton, Parliament's only Somerset stronghold, besieged
by Lord George Goring. It was an untidy campaign. Having
lifted the siege, Goring intended to retreat to Bridgwater.
On 9 July 1645, he fell back on Langport, where he intended
to hold Fairfax while most of his artillery and supplies went
on ahead.

On the morning of 10 July, Goring arrayed his men,
infantry to the fore and cavalry to the rear, on Ham Down,
In addition, 2,000 musketeers were deployed along the
hedges bordering the narrow Langport to Somerton road.
Fairfax, having advanced from Somerton, drew up his forces

on Pitney Hill. He had a numerical advantage, with 10,000 troops against 8,000 Royalists. Having envisaged only a holding action to cover the withdrawal of his guns and supplies, Goring had retained just two pieces of artillery.

At noon, Fairfax commenced hostilities with an artillery barrage which succeeded in pinning down the Royalists, whose own pair of light guns were, in comparison, useless. He then despatched his own musketeers to clear the hedges. Again, the fire of the Parliamentarian heavy guns stopped Goring sending in any support. When the Royalist musketeers had been driven off, 400 Parliamentarian horse, led by Major Christopher Bethel, advanced. First, Bethel had to descend Pitney Hill, then clear the ford over Wagg Rhyne at the bottom before proceeding uphill along the lane (capable of taking a maximum of only four horsemen abreast), in order to take on Goring's cavalry waiting for him on Ham Down.

Bethel made it through, his men emerging from the lane to right and left. The Royalists gave ground and, although a counter-charge momentarily redressed the balance, the lane was now open to allow Parliamentarian reinforcements through. Support in the form of Major John Desborough appeared on the scene to consolidate Bethel's bridgehead. When Fairfax threw in his infantry and musketeers, the Royalists scattered, some to Langport and others to Bridgwater. Those who retired to Langport set fire to the town but Cromwell still managed to steal a scene by catching up with them to take prisoners and supplies. The retreat to Bridgwater was more successful, with the Royalist cavalry fighting a continuous rearguard action.

Goring's casualties were high, with about 300 dead, as opposed to about 30 Parliamentarian dead. Two thousand Royalists were captured. The defeat left Goring broken and dispirited. His attachment to the bottle had long been remarked upon and he now embarked on a 'bender' which drove the morale of his surviving troops to an all-time low.

And yet, even now, the king felt that final victory was not beyond reach. With Montrose chalking up a string of victories in Scotland and with the port of Bristol still in Royalist hands, he continued to insist that there was hope.

The battlefield today

There is no monument, but the landscape has not changed much, making it a profitable battlefield to visit. Ordnance Survey maps place the battle site at Huish Episcopi, but the generally accepted site is a little further north, on the B3153, one and a half miles to the east of Langport (OS Landranger 193 4427). If you park opposite St Mary's Church on the A372, you can walk up to the battlefield via Wagg Drove. (The battle is known locally as 'The Battle of Wagg Drove'.) There is a Langport and River Parrett Visitor Centre, with parking, by the bridge in Bow Street.

Further reading

Hugh Norris, *The Battle of Langport* **(British Library Historical Print Editions, 2011).**

75. Rowton Heath, 24 September 1645

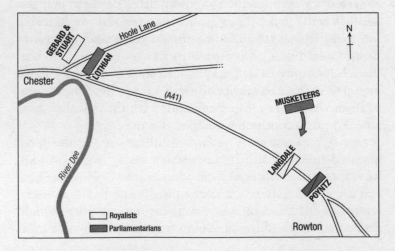

Charles I observed that Prince Rupert's surrender of Bristol on 11 September 1645 was the greatest trial that befell him during the Civil War. His faithful nephew was publicly chastised, relieved of his duties and ordered to leave the country. Gratitude was not a prominent attribute of the Stuarts. Bristol's loss redoubled the importance of Chester as a point of entry for a long-hoped-for Irish army, but it, too, was under siege. The king marched to its relief.

Like many Civil War sieges, the noose around Chester was slack. When Charles arrived on 23 September, he was able to enter the city, unchallenged, from its western approaches. He was accompanied by 500 horse, the bulk of his army – some 2,500 men under Sir Marmaduke Langdale – having been hived off to approach Chester from the south-east and take the Parliamentarian besiegers in the rear.

Colonel Michael Jones, in charge of the siege, made a plea for help to Major-General Sydenham Poyntz. A relative newcomer, Poyntz was a soldier of fortune, having fought on the continent for twenty years before returning to England in 1644. In the spring of 1645, he was appointed commander of Parliament's forces in the north. When Poyntz received Jones's message, he was already on his way, riding throughout the night of 23 September from Whitchurch.

Langdale had intended to advance on Jones's positions in the suburbs of Chester but, learning of the approach of Poyntz, he turned to face him at a point on Whitchurch Road between Hatton Heath and Miller's Heath. Poyntz hoped to take the Royalists by surprise. However, at about 7.00 a.m. on 24 September, he came under fire from Langdale's dragoons. Forced to charge before all his men were assembled, Poyntz was repulsed. Langdale sent a messenger to the king in Chester, requesting support.

At 2.00 p.m., Jones extracted a party of horse and musketeers from his besieging force and set off to support Poyntz. In the late afternoon, apparently unaware that he had by this time been outflanked by Jones's relief force, Langdale withdrew to Rowton Heath and Poyntz moved in to attack once more. As Langdale moved forward to meet the attack, he was subjected to fire from Jones's musketeers, whose accurate volleys put the horse to flight.

From within Chester, the king had despatched a force commanded by Sir Charles Gerard and Lord Bernard Stewart, in pursuit of Jones, but they were successfully challenged at Hoole Heath by Colonel James Lothian, who had been left in charge of the siege. Meanwhile, those in the rear of Langdale's ranks made for the safety of Chester, but as they approached, they ran into Lothian. Attempts by Stewart and Gerard to regroup only added to the confusion and, until the light began to fail, Parliamentarian musketeers continued to do considerable damage. Stewart himself was mortally wounded.

The Royalists had suffered yet another major reverse, suffering casualties of around 1,800, killed, wounded or captured. Charles hurriedly withdrew into Wales, the siege of Chester was tightened and the war entered its fourth year.

The battlefield today

Rowton Heath, where the main encounter took place, is on the A41, three miles to the south-east of Chester (OS Landranger 117 4464). It is said that the king watched the disaster unfold from what is now called King Charles Tower in Chester, which houses Civil War displays including a plan of the battle. There is also now a small monument with an information panel in the centre of Rowton. According to tradition, a small building in a field near the junction of Whitchurch Road and Rowton Lane was utilized to treat the wounded.

Further reading

John Barratt, *The Battle of Rowton Heath and the Siege of Chester* **(Stuart Press, 1995).**

76. Torrington, 16 February 1646

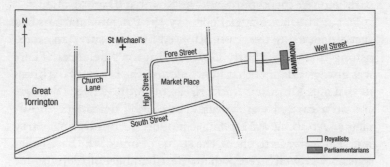

During the winter of 1645–46, Parliamentarian forces were engaged in mopping up Royalist pockets of resistance, particularly in the south-west, where the Prince of Wales was in nominal command. Sir Thomas Fairfax, commander-in-chief of Parliament's New Model Army, was attempting to take Exeter. He was ready to launch a final assault when he learned that Lord Hopton, appointed by the Prince of Wales as commander-in-chief of Royalist forces in the west, was on his way to launch what he hoped would be a surprise assault on the besieging forces. On 10 February 1646, Fairfax set off to seek him out.

Hopton reached Torrington on the same day. When Fairfax arrived on the evening of 16 February, he found the place well fortified. At that time, Torrington consisted of little more than three streets with a church and the ruins of an old castle. Hopton, protected by the River Torridge to the west, had thrown up earthen barricades, manned by infantry and cavalry, at all the entrances to the town. The remainder of his cavalry were deployed on a common to the north, with 200 dragoons occupying Stevenstone House which stood to the east. In fact, his problem was that he had an excess of horse, some 3,000 as opposed to only 2,000 infantry. Fairfax – a veteran of urban warfare – was leading 10,000 men and he needed somewhere to muster them, so he sent some of his horse to commandeer Stevenstone House's parkland. At their approach, the Royalist dragoons fled.

By the afternoon of 16 February, the Parliamentarians had succeeded, using the cover afforded by enclosures, in establishing themselves fairly close to Hopton's defences. There was always a danger that he would use the hours of darkness to disengage himself and retreat over the River Torridge, and so a careful watch was kept on the defenders' movements. At about 9.00 p.m., a modest reconnoitring party was sent forward to check the status of one of the barricades (possibly at Well Street) where there had been no activity for some time. Fairfax gave credit to Colonel Robert Hammond (in later years, the king's jailer on the Isle of Wight) for this initiative. Others have nominated Cromwell but, although he shared in the battle, it is unlikely that he performed a decisive role. Had he done so, he would have made sure that everyone knew about it.

As it happened, the barricade was still manned and the group was fired upon. Hammond sent forward more troops in support, the mêlée soon developing into a general engagement. Fierce hand-to-hand combat, or what was called fighting 'at push end of pike and butt end of musket', followed. It must have been a bizarre and terrifying spectacle, illuminated, presumably, by blazing torches. It is recorded that the Royalist horse in the town did repulse two concerted assaults before retreating – prompting most of the infantry to abandon their positions and flee across the river at what is now the New Street bridge. Hopton brought in the rest of his cavalry, stationed on the common, but the narrowness of the streets rendered their task impossible.

Hopton may well have been captured but for a freak accident. Having had one unfortunate experience with gunpowder in the aftermath of the Battle of Lansdown (1643), and given that it had been raining, he had taken care to place the eighty barrels currently in his possession in what he thought was a safe, dry place: the Church of St Michael. However, the

Parliamentarians decided to herd their prisoners inside and the cache was accidentally ignited, the massive explosion that followed killing and injuring many men on both sides. In the ensuing confusion, Hopton managed to pull together what remained of his cavalry and fall back across the Torridge. (Parliamentarians later claimed that the powder in the church had been deliberately ignited by a man named Watts, 'a desperate villain' hired by the Royalists for the job.)

The battle was unique in that it had been fought from start to finish during the night. Fairfax estimated that only 400 of Hopton's infantry escaped death or capture. Over the next four weeks, Hopton moved ever further south, the remnants of his army gradually melting away, as men drifted off to their homes. When Fairfax offered honourable terms for his surrender, he agreed. On 20 March 1646, he capitulated, effectively bringing to an end the Royalist campaign in the south-west.

The battlefield today

Great Torrington is on the A386, nine miles to the south-west of Barnstaple (OS Landranger 180 4919). A cobbled mound outside St Michael's Church is said to mark the mass grave of those killed in the gunpowder explosion – an event commemorated by a plaque within, which notes that the church was rebuilt in 1651. The Black Horse, in High Street, was reputedly used by Fairfax after the battle. Car parking is available in the town. The remains of Stevenstone House are to the east of Great Torrington, off the B3227.

Further reading

John Wardman, *Forgotten Battle: Torrington 1646* (Fire & Steel, 1996).

77. Stow-on-the-Wold, 21 March 1646

After the Royalist defeat in the west, only the south midlands remained to the king. Even though he was bottled up in

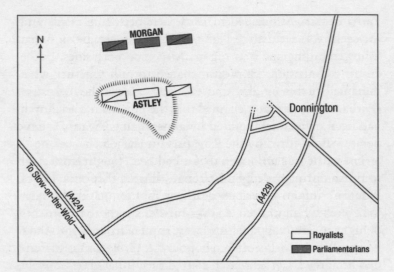

Oxford, he still had vague hopes of Queen Henrietta Maria being able to send help from France. Furthermore, Lord Astley had raised 3,000 men and, by mid-March, had set off from Bridgnorth to join forces with him. Parliamentarian forces were soon in pursuit, the Governor of Gloucester, Colonel Thomas Morgan, and Colonel John Birch mustering some 2,000 men.

On 20 March, still thirty miles short of their objective, Astley and his weary troops stopped to pass the night at Donnington, near Stow-on-the-Wold. Astley had counted on being met by such cavalry as Charles was able to release from Oxford but, by now, he must have suspected that they were not coming. To add to his woes, during the hours of darkness, Morgan and Birch, having followed at a respectful distance, were reinforced by Sir William Brereton and 1,000 horse from Chester.

The next morning, Astley decided to fight it out, deploying on high ground to the west of Donnington. Astley himself was in the centre with the foot, flanked by the cavalry of Sir Charles Lucas on the right and that of Sir William Vaughan on the left. When the Parliamentarians approached, they drew up in a similar formation, Colonel Birch occupying the centre, Sir William Brereton on the right and Colonel Morgan on the left.

It was the Parliamentarians who took the initiative, Morgan mounting an attack on Lucas, whose lines held. Lucas was even able to launch a counter-attack of his own. Astley's leadership skills were no doubt largely responsible for his men maintaining their position when they came to grips with the Parliamentarian centre. The breakthrough was made by Brereton. Although, like Astley and Lucas, Vaughan was an experienced officer, his command was over-whelmed by sheer weight of numbers. Once he had routed Vaughan, Brereton was able to turn on Astley's left flank. When Lucas's horse were also finally broken, Astley kept the infantry together and retreated into Stow-on-the-Wold, where the fighting continued in the streets until, finally, Astley was captured. Casualties may have been compara-tively light on both sides, with up to 1,000 Royalist prisoners subsequently held in St Edward's Church.

On 27 April, Charles slipped out of Oxford and on 5 May, at Southwell, he surrendered to the Scots. Nevertheless, several Royalist strongholds refused to follow the example of their king and continued to hold out. The last bastion to fall was Harlech Castle, which capitulated on 13 March 1647.

The battlefield today

Donnington is off the A429, two miles to the north of Stow-on-the-Wold. A public footpath leads to a battlefield monument with an interpretation panel (OS Landranger 163 1828). The battle is also commemorated in a memorial in St Edward's churchyard in Stow-on-the-Wold – and on the head of the market cross. The church contains a memo-rial to Sir Hastings Keyte, a Royalist officer who was killed in the battle. Stow is one of a growing number of battles of which the exact location is currently being questioned. The battle may have been fought a little further south, the action centring on the A424, closer to Stow-on-the-Wold.

Further reading
Ron Field, *Stow-on-the-Wold 1646* **(Design Folio, 1992).**

CAMPAIGNS OF MONTROSE

78. Tippermuir, 1 September 1644

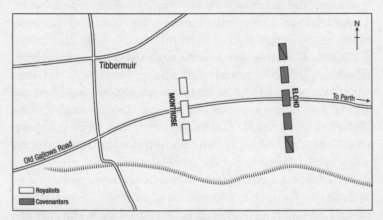

After the Royalist defeat at Marston Moor (1644), Charles I appointed the Earl of Montrose as his Lieutenant-General in Scotland. Montrose, who had opposed the king in the Bishops' Wars, at Brig o' Dee (1639) and Newburn (1640), was now a committed Royalist and remained so for the rest of his life.

Montrose raised the Royal Standard at Blair Atholl on 28 August 1644. He was joined by Alasdair MacColla and a thousand men from Ireland and also by a smattering of Scottish clansmen – largely Stewarts and Robertsons. All were lightly armed and there was no cavalry or artillery.

This modest army marched along the River Garry towards Perth, gathering more support along the way, including a contingent of lukewarm Covenanters led by Lord Kilpont, expanding their strength to around 3,000. To the west of

Perth, on the plain of Tippermuir, a Covenanter army under Lord Elcho, waited for them.

Elcho commanded about 3,500 foot and some 800 horse. His men were well armed and he had nine pieces of artillery. At 7.00 a.m. on 1 September, they deployed along gently sloping ground, the Earl of Tulliebardine in the centre, flanked on the right by Lord Elcho and on the left by Sir James Scott. For the Royalists, MacColla occupied the centre with Montrose on the right wing and Lord Kilpont on the left.

As the Royalists advanced, Tulliebardine sent forward a skirmishing party which was easily put to flight, the horse creating some confusion as they retreated into the Covenanter ranks. Lacking the resources to engage in any sophisticated manoeuvres, Montrose ordered a charge. MacColla rushed forward, his men firing their muskets once when the enemy came within range, before closing with them and using musket butts, swords, pikes and even stones to belabour them.

To withstand such an assault, troops had to be experienced and disciplined. The majority of the Covenanters were neither and they soon broke ranks. It is said that the fighting was at its most intense between Scott and the men led by Montrose, who fought for possession of the higher ground. When Scott was overcome, resistance collapsed. The ensuing flight and pursuit was a bloody one, lasting from 8.00 a.m., when the battle ended, until darkness fell. Several hundred Covenanters lost their lives, while Royalist casualties were very low.

Thus, Tippermuir became Montrose's first victory. It was momentous because it had been achieved against a greater number of opponents who were in possession of artillery and cavalry. Montrose also obtained precious supplies from Perth, which was pillaged by the clansmen. Some of the latter departed with their booty, and there was little enthusiasm for supporting the royal cause among the city's inhabitants. Furthermore, another Covenanter army, led by the Earl of Argyll, was already on its way.

The battlefield today

The battlefield is to the south-east of the village of Tippermuir, today called 'Tibbermuir' (OS Landranger 52 0623), four miles to the west of Perth. Old Gallows Road, along which the Covenanters would have advanced (and retreated), crosses the A9 by Noah's Ark campsite, and you can follow it, on foot, through the centre of the battlefield.

There is no monument. However, in Perth itself, on the wall of a bungalow at the corner of Needless Road and Wilson Street, is a plaque marking it as the site of a stone which once commemorated the spot where many fleeing Covenanters were cut down. Car parking is available at the Park & Ride site at Broxden Roundabout, where the M90 terminates.

Further reading

Paul Philippou and Rob Harris, *Battleground Perthshire: Two Thousand Years of Battles, Encounters and Skirmishes* **(Tippermuir Press, 2009).**

79. Aberdeen, 13 September 1644

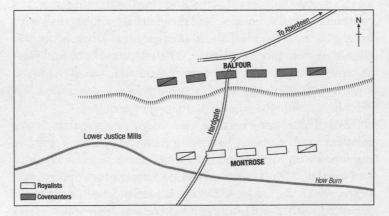

After his victory over the Covenanters at Tippermuir, the Earl of Montrose marched north. The seriousness of the threat he posed to the Covenanters is reflected in the eventual £20,000 reward posted for his capture. En route to Aberdeen, his supporter, Lord Kilpont, was murdered by a Covenanter sympathizer and Kilpont's men promptly deserted. This reverse was offset by the arrival of Nathaniel Gordon with forty or fifty horse. Gordon was destined to play an integral part in the creation of the Montrose legend.

The Royalists reached Aberdeen on 12 September. The next morning, Montrose ordered the town to surrender, threatening the inhabitants with no quarter if they refused. They did refuse, a 2,500-strong Covenanter force deploying on high ground across Hardgate, the main road from the south-west, overlooking Montrose's position in front of the Howburn.

Commanded by Lord Balfour of Burleigh, the Covenanters, as at Perth, were largely inexperienced levies. Three hundred horse were divided between the right and left flanks, with 2,000 infantry comprising pikemen and musketeers in the centre. For the Royalists, Alasdair MacColla led around 1,500 infantry, his flanks protected by as few as seventy horse – Sir William Rollo on the left and Nathaniel Gordon on the right. Montrose was in the rear. Both sides had some artillery, the Royalists having acquired their guns at Tippermuir.

At about 11.00 a.m., the battle began with an artillery exchange and an attempt by the Covenanters to occupy buildings that lay between the two armies. This was followed by a half-hearted attack by the horse of the Covenanter right wing, who withdrew after a discharge of pistols. Two attacks by the horse of the Covenanter left similarly came to nothing. One party accomplished rather more, undertaking a flanking manoeuvre via a sunken lane. Although it succeeded, the plan was not followed through, giving Montrose the opportunity to retrieve the situation, and the detachment of horse and foot was destroyed.

In the centre, MacColla's advancing Irish were charged by a party of Covenanter horse led by William Forbes. Instead of buckling, the Irish made a path for them, and then turned to fire a musket volley at their backs. Then, as Nathaniel Gordon led a charge which broke the Covenanter left wing, MacColla fell upon the Covenanter infantry with sword and dirk. It was the 'gentlemen of quality' and those who had most to lose among the Covenanters who quit the field first, after which everyone turned and ran back towards the town, hotly pursued by the Royalists.

The most controversial aspect of the battle was in the aftermath, when the Royalists behaved very much in accordance with their leader's earlier threat. Covenanter accounts depict an orgy of murder, rape and pillage and, while one has to allow for exaggeration, it is certain that excesses did occur. About 150 Covenanters died in the battle, while almost 100 townsfolk may have been slaughtered afterwards.

For Montrose, a second Covenanter army had been destroyed and his reputation as a general was growing, although, crucially, he was not yet attracting substantial support, and a third army led by the Marquis of Argyll was still on his track.

The battlefield today
The battlefield, completely urbanized, is centred on Hardgate and is roughly bounded by Union Street (A901) and Willowbank Road (A93) (OS Landranger 38 9305). Use the city centre car parks.

Further reading
Chris Brown, *The Battle of Aberdeen 1644* (Tempus, 2002).

80. Fyvie, 28 October 1644

For some weeks after the Battle of Aberdeen, the Royalist army of the Earl of Montrose managed to keep a step ahead of the Marquis of Argyll and his Covenanters. On 27 October, after much meandering, Montrose arrived at Fyvie Castle, twenty-five miles to the north-west of Aberdeen. He thought

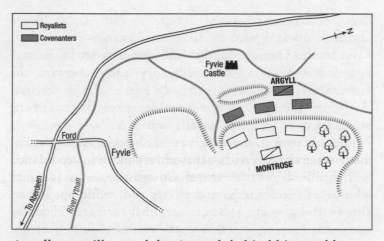

Argyll was still several days' march behind him, and he was surprised when, the following morning, he learned that his pursuers were only two miles away and closing rapidly.

Montrose was without his lieutenant, Alasdair MacColla, who was recruiting in the west, although MacColla's reliable kinsman, Magnus O'Cahan, was present. A shortage of ammunition was remedied by the melting down of all the castle's pewter plate. It would have been fatal for Montrose to allow himself to be pinned down inside the castle walls, and so he deployed on a hill to the east, his men developing a series of existing earthworks for defence. As at Aberdeen, his infantry numbered about 1,500, while his horse cannot have amounted to more than 50.

Argyll commanded perhaps 2,500 infantry and around 800 horse, but the broken landscape, which included trees, a stream and a gulley, prohibited a formal deployment. Thankful to have finally run his quarry to ground, he lost no time in attacking the Royalists' entrenched positions. Initially, the Covenanters had the better of a close encounter, managing to establish themselves on the lower slopes of the hill. Reinforcements were sent forward but before they could secure the beachhead, they were driven off by a counter-attack led by O'Cahan.

A second concentrated attack of Covenanter horse and foot almost ended in disaster. Montrose tried to lure them into an ambush, but his intended trap, set in the surrounding woodland, was sprung too early, allowing the Covenanters to retire to their own lines. Later in the day, Argyll tried to outflank the Royalists on their left, but the attacking force was successfully driven off by the horse of Nathaniel Gordon, supported by musketeers. At length, the Covenanters had to withdraw for the night.

The offensive was renewed the next day – 29 October – but Argyll seems to have been reluctant to indulge in further frontal assaults, settling instead for a more sedentary approach, keeping the Royalists under fire and, perhaps, hoping to tempt them down. He met with no success and was eventually forced to withdraw once more. On the following morning, short of provisions and realizing that he was not getting anywhere, Argyll decided to retreat towards Aberdeen, giving Montrose the opportunity to slip away.

Fyvie must be counted as another victory for Montrose. Casualties were in the dozens rather than in the hundreds, and it is classed as a minor battle. However, he had repulsed the main Covenanter army and given notice that something more would be needed to defeat him. Troops would have to be withdrawn from England, thus, in theory, reducing the pressure on the king. Shortly after the battle, a grateful monarch made him the Marquis of Montrose.

The battlefield today

Fyvie Castle is off the A947, twenty-five miles to the northwest of Aberdeen (OS Landranger 29 7739). Since the mid-1980s, the castle has been in the care of the National Trust for Scotland and is open (with car parking) to the public. An earthwork, Montrose's Camp, the remains of a network of defensive ditches prepared by the Royalists, lies to the east of the castle. A few artefacts, probably originating with the Covenanter army, are on display in the castle.

Further reading
Stuart Reid, *The Campaigns of Montrose* (Mercat Press, 1990).

81. Inverlochy, 2 February 1645

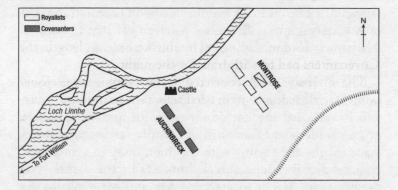

Throughout the 'closed season' of 1644/45, when armies usually went into winter quarters, the Royalist army of the Marquis of Montrose kept on the move. In part, this was through necessity, for it had no real base, but such mobility did give Montrose an edge over his enemies. They never knew where he would turn up next. More often than not, Montrose himself did not know. Mid-January 1645 found him heading north, up the Great Glen, towards Inverness – and, ultimately, to one of his most celebrated adventures.

Inverness had a strong Covenanter garrison, while Montrose's strength was continuously being eroded as his Highlanders slipped away to head home. Soon, he was left with only 1,500 men. To compound his problems, 3,000 Covenanters, led by the Marquis of Argyll, were to his rear, at Inverlochy. However, a situation which would have constituted a crisis to most men was viewed by Montrose as an opportunity. Abandoning his march on Inverness, he turned around and, in the depth of winter, marched over thirty miles across some of the most inhospitable ground in the country. In a little under three days, he reached his goal:

Inverlochy. His men were tired and hungry but, as always, this failed to dull their fighting spirit.

Disappointingly, Argyll was not taken by surprise, although, while his army was ready to give battle, Argyll was not. Owing to an injury he had sustained, he had retired to a ship on Loch Linnhe, leaving Duncan Campbell of Auchinbreck to take charge. As head of Clan Campbell, Argyll was able to call on men who would surely prove a match for Montrose's Highland and Irish warriors.

Before dawn on 2 February 1645, Auchinbreck positioned a small force of musketeers in Inverlochy Castle, which anchored his left wing, comprising a mixed force of Lowlanders and Campbells. A similar arrangement was made for the right wing, with the main body of Campbells, commanded by Auchinbreck himself, in the centre. For the Royalists, Montrose assigned Alasdair MacColla to the right wing and Magnus O'Cahan to the left while Montrose himself opposed Auchinbreck in the centre.

O'Cahan was sent in first, with the usual instructions not to fire muskets until the last possible moment, thereby inflicting the most damage. The Lowlanders were unable to withstand the devastating volley and the force of the charge with which they were hit almost immediately afterwards. They broke, sweeping the supporting Campbells away with them. MacColla achieved the same result on the Covenanter left. As expected, Auchinbreck's centre proved more difficult to intimidate and withstood Montrose's initial onslaught yet, with both Covenanter wings in disarray, it was only a matter of time before it was overcome.

Many refugees sought the safety of the castle, but the Royalist horse of Sir Thomas Ogilvie cut off their line of retreat. The unpopularity of the Campbells was confirmed by the fact that 1,500 of them, including Auchinbreck, were slaughtered in a prolonged pursuit. Montrose, as always, stressed that he was powerless to stop the killing. In this case, it was probably true. Again, Montrose claimed to have suffered only a handful of casualties, which included Ogilvie who was mortally wounded, probably by musket fire from the castle.

It has been said that the Covenanters were overawed by the appearance of Montrose, having expected to contend with a far more modest force. If so, it demonstrated the air of invulnerability which now surrounded him.

The battlefield today
Inverlochy is on the A82, to the north of Fort William (OS Landranger 41 1175). Much of the battleground is now covered by the Rio Tinto Alcan Smelting works, which was responsible for placing a memorial plaque at a viewpoint near the Inverlochy Castle Hotel. Car parking is available at Inverlochy Castle.

Further reading
Stuart Reid, *The Campaigns of Montrose* (Mercat Press, 1990).

82. Auldearn, 9 May 1645

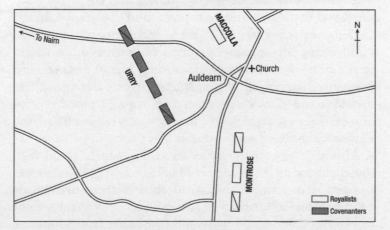

On the evening of 8 May 1645, the Royalist army of the Marquis of Montrose was encamped at the village of

Auldearn. A Covenanter army led by Sir John Hurry was at Inverness, blocking Montrose's path to the Highlands. Having been reinforced to the extent that he could field around 3,500 infantry and 350 horse, Hurry felt confident that he could deal Montrose a mortal blow. An overnight march from Inverness led him to Auldearn, where he hoped to take the Royalists by surprise. He didn't, because it had been raining and his musketeers tested their damp weapons by firing them, thereby alerting Montrose to their presence.

Accustomed to reacting quickly, the Royalists were able to deploy before Hurry's arrival. Despite being able to muster only 2,000 infantry and 350 horse, Montrose spread his men thinly. Alasdair MacColla with 400 men, took up a position at Boath House to the north of the village. Another body of infantry was positioned to MacColla's left, in what was the centre of his line, while Montrose and the horse deployed in a concealed position to the far left.

Moving up from the south-west, Hurry advanced on the forces he was able to see – MacColla's contingent and what he thought were the troops of the Royalist left wing, with the Royal Standard cunningly planted in their midst. In the Covenanter van were the infantry regiments of the Earl of Loudon and Sir Mungo Campbell of Lawers; immediately to the rear were the regiments of the Earls of Lothian and Buchanan, supported by the Moray Horse. Between these divisions and Hurry's own reserves stood a contingent of northern levies, flanked by the infantry regiments of the Earls of Sutherland and Seaforth.

Although Montrose had ordered his men to stand fast, thereby drawing in the enemy, MacColla charged out to meet Loudon and Lawers. Notwithstanding their undoubted courage, MacColla's men were driven back by sheer weight of numbers. A second sally met the same fate. Montrose had to unleash his cavalry, and Lord Gordon's horse broke cover, charging the Covenanter forward right flank. Taken completely by surprise, the Covenanter horse broke and scattered. The crucial manoeuvre of the battle now occurred. The commander of Moray's Horse either misinterpreted an order from Hurry or gave the wrong order to his men, who wheeled in to their left to bear down on their own infantry. MacColla grasped the opportunity to rush forward to make a third and final assault. More Royalist horse joined in the fray, but Lawers' and Lothian's regiments tried to make a fight of it. At length, however, Sir Mungo Campbell was cut down and they were overwhelmed.

Hurry's entire army fled and was pursued as far as Inverness, suffering heavy casualties along the way. Montrose estimated the total of Covenanter dead at 3,000. A more realistic total would be half that number. Again, sources sympathetic to Montrose claim Royalist losses to be a mere handful, although they must have been approaching three figures, given that MacColla took severe punishment in the opening round of the battle.

At this stage, Covenanter losses could be made good, while recruitment was a continuing headache for Montrose. The Royalists were winning battles, but they endured a hand-to-mouth existence which rendered the capture of supplies significant. Hence, in the present instance, Hurry's baggage train was eagerly plundered. The downside of such windfalls was that many Highlanders tended to view the seizure of booty as the objective of a campaign and, thus enriched, would gratefully make their way home.

The battlefield today

Auldearn is on the A96, two and a half miles to the south-east of Nairn (OS Landranger 27 9165). Make for Boath Dovecote, where there is car parking and, at the top of the hill, an interpretation panel. Some of the dead were interred in Auldearn Churchyard, but there is only one marked grave. Although the village has expanded over the years, the area in which the battle took place is quite compact, and had all British battlefields remained as undisturbed as Auldearn, we would have little cause for complaint.

Further reading
Stuart Reid, *Auldearn 1645: The Marquis of Montrose's Scottish Campaigns* **(Osprey, 2003).**

83. Alford, 2 July 1645

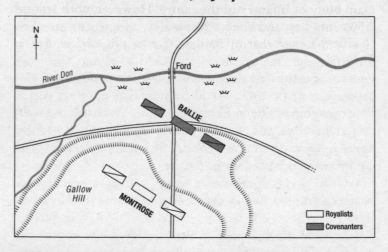

The Royalist victory over the Covenanter army at Auldearn opened up the Highlands to the Marquis of Montrose, and he lost no time in repairing thither. Lieutenant-General William Baillie, whose second-in-command, Colonel John Hurry, had been beaten at Auldearn, took up the chase. On the evening of 1 July 1645, Montrose was camped at Alford, twenty-four miles to the west of Aberdeen. With Baillie only four miles behind and closing, Montrose had to face another battle.

On the morning of 2 July 1645, Montrose occupied Gallow Hill, on the south bank of the River Don at what is today Bridge of Alford. At that time, there was only a ford, and it was here that Baillie was expected to appear. Baillie duly arrived and Montrose, concealing much of his strength to the rear of the hill, allowed him to cross over. When the crossing had been made, Montrose brought his men forward.

The cavalry of Lord Gordon, supported by Nathaniel Gordon's infantry, took the right flank and Viscount Aboyne, probably supported by Magnus O'Cahan's infantry, the left. In the absence of Montrose's trusted lieutenant, Alasdair MacColla, it is unclear who took command of the main body of infantry in the centre. However, with around 2,500 infantry and some 250 cavalry, Montrose's strength closely matched that of Baillie. The latter's deployment is uncertain, but the cavalry of Lord Balcarres occupied the left flank, as the Covenanters drew up on the plain between Montrose and the Don.

Although it is likely that Montrose told his men to maintain their positions, Lord Gordon opened the battle by rushing forward with his cavalry to attack Balcarres. The Covenanters stood firm and fierce hand-to-hand fighting followed. However, while Balcarres received no support, Nathaniel Gordon's foot, laying their muskets aside, ran forward with their dirks and began to disable the Covenanter horses, severing hamstrings and cutting open bellies. As Aboyne, with similar support from O'Cahan, crashed into the Covenanter right wing, Gordon forced his way through to take the enemy in the rear. Finally, Montrose, commanding the Royalist reserve, emerged on to the field and the Covenanters were routed.

Baillie sustained casualties of 700 dead. Once again, while the Royalists claimed that they themselves lost only four men, their own casualties must have been high. One death hit them particularly hard. As Lord Gordon was galloping around to the rear of the Covenanters, he was shot in the back. His infuriated followers ensured that the pursuit of the fleeing Covenanters was particularly harsh – and Montrose could now look forward to extending his influence to the lowlands.

The battlefield today

Modern Alford is on the A944, twenty-four miles to the west of Aberdeen (OS Landranger 37 5815). Car parking is available in Haughton Country Park to the north of the village. The Gordon Stone, marking the spot where Lord Gordon fell, is to the south of the adjacent Murray Park (26 1161). Some sources suggest that Baillie crossed the Don at Montgarrie, placing the battle to the east of the generally accepted location.

Further reading

Stuart Reid, *The Campaigns of Montrose* (Mercat Press, 1990).

84. Kilsyth, 15 August 1545

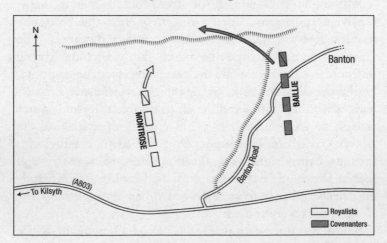

Following the defeat at Auldearn, a new Covenanter army was cobbled together for General William Baillie. Its strength was nearly 8,000 combined foot and horse, and Montrose – who, at a pinch, could muster 3,500 men – was anxious to tackle it before it grew any bigger.

With Baillie at Perth, Montrose marched from Dunkeld, camping at Kilsyth on 14 August 1645. Baillie lost no time in advancing on the Royalist position, reaching Hollinbush, only three miles distant, the same evening. Here, despite outnumbering Montrose by more than two to one, he intended to wait until expected reinforcements arrived. Montrose, of course, was eager to engage the Covenanters before this happened. Luckily for him, the Committee of the Estates (representatives of Scotland's governing body), accompanying Baillie, felt that the Covenanter force was sufficient to overcome the Royalists, although, ominously, the cavalry – 800 Covenanter horse against 500 Royalist horse – were fairly evenly matched. Accordingly, the next morning, Baillie moved up to the village of Banton, overlooking the Royalist camp. Balcarres' cavalry was on the right, with Loudoun's on the left and Lauderdale's and Home's in the centre.

Montrose was occupying high ground to the west, his deployment also taking in a portion of low-lying land or 'meadow' separating the two armies. His chosen deployment is unclear, but Nathaniel Gordon may have occupied the left wing, the Earl of Airlie the right and Alasdair MacColla the centre. On Montrose's orders, all removed their plaid and fought in their shirts.

The Committee of the Estates now instructed Baillie to commence an outflanking manoeuvre, by occupying high ground to his right. He obeyed and ordered Balcarres and Lauderdale to lead off, together with a group of musketeers under Major John Haldane. Perceiving Baillie's intention, Montrose sent a party of Royalist musketeers up the hill to occupy some buildings and enclosures. Contrary to orders, Haldane also moved off to engage them, Home and Loudoun veering off course to offer their support. In turn, MacColla broke ranks and led his men into the fray.

Balcarres and Lauderdale, having continued on, now moved to attack, to be met by Nathaniel Gordon, who was soon under pressure against superior numbers. Viscount Aboyne, who had been placed in reserve, galloped to

Gordon's rescue and, with the additional support of the Earl of Airlie, drove the Covenanters back. In the enclosures, Home's and Loudoun's regiments were also overcome by MacColla, and Baillie tried to bring up his own reserves – levies from Fife who, having no stomach for a fight, fled the field. Almost without knowing it, Baillie had been beaten. Joining in the retreat, he barely made good his escape.

While Royalist casualties were probably relatively light, the Covenanters may have lost upwards of 4,000 men. Not only was Montrose master of the field, but he was now master of Scotland, for there was no army left to oppose him.

The battlefield today

The battlefield is off the A803, ten miles to the east of Kirkintilloch (OS Landranger 64 7378). Exit from Junction 4 of the M80/A80. Car parking is available at Colzium House, which has an unusual curling-stone-shaped monument to the battle in its grounds. There is a museum with battlefield displays within, but special arrangements have to be made to view it – see the Colzium Estate website. The centre of the battlefield is occupied by a reservoir (Banton Loch), but it is possible to explore the surrounding area via the footpath/minor road system. A more recent additional battlefield monument is situated on the south bank of the loch. Note some of the names of local topographical features: Slaughter Howe, Baggage Knowe, Bullet Knowe, which have their origins in the battle.

Further reading

Stuart Reid, *The Campaigns of Montrose* (Mercat Press, 1990).

85. Philiphaugh, 13 September 1645

On 6 September 1645, General Sir David Leslie and 6,000 men reached Berwick, having marched north to deal with the Marquis of Montrose. Despite his famous victory at

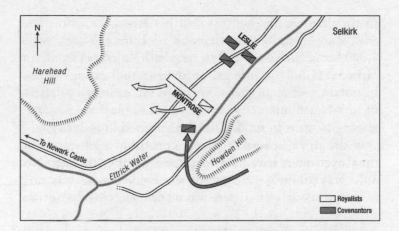

Kilsyth a month before, Montrose was now on the defensive. He had hoped to march into England and had advanced as far as Jedburgh. Now he was cut off from his preferred fighting country in the Highlands. Furthermore, he commanded barely 2,000 men. He could depend upon the loyalty of Magnus O'Cahan's Irish contingent, but 1,200 new levies brought in by the Earl of Douglas were untried, and Alasdair MacColla, not wishing to fight in England, had departed. In any event, he had to retreat and somehow evade Leslie's Covenanter army.

On 12 September, Montrose and the few cavalrymen under his command entered the town of Selkirk and settled in for the night. The infantry camped over a mile to the west on Philiphaugh, in woodland bordering Ettrick Water. It is said that Montrose was at breakfast on the morning of 13 September, when he received the news that Leslie was almost upon him. In the early days, this situation would not have arisen, for Montrose would have slept in the field with his men and would have taken personal responsibility for posting scouting parties.

To ensure speed, Leslie had abandoned his infantry, moving south with some 4,000 cavalry, dragoons and mounted infantrymen. Approaching Selkirk undiscovered in the darkness, he had divided his army, the main force advancing along the north bank of Ettrick Water, while 2,000 horse circled around to the south, to cross the river at Howden Hill. Montrose galloped down to the haugh to find his infantry camp in chaos. Speedily, he organized a defence of sorts. Such infantry as he was able to muster – probably about 500 men in total, Douglas's men having scattered – was deployed behind a ditch, constructed the previous evening, with Harehead Hill protecting the left flank and 120 horse the right.

Upon his arrival, Leslie launched two assaults on the Royalist right, but the Covenanters were beaten back both times. Leslie turned his attention to O'Cahan's Irish, many of whom fought to the death. When the second column of Covenanter horse arrived from the south bank, however, the Royalists were overwhelmed. Montrose and some of his cavalry were able to escape, but the infantry was doomed. Those who surrendered on promise of quarter were subsequently marched to nearby Newark Castle, to be slaughtered in the courtyard, their bodies buried on land which was afterwards known as Slain Men's Lea. A further 300 camp followers were cut down when the baggage was plundered.

The king was en route to join Montrose when the news of Philiphaugh reached him. Instead of turning back, as he did, he could have kept going, for Montrose was far from finished. He was able to muster some 500 survivors of the battle and would spend the winter months canvassing for support. By the spring of 1646 he was ready to begin campaigning once more. By that time, however, Charles had surrendered to the Covenanters and ordered Montrose to lay down his arms. The Marquis sailed into exile soon afterwards.

The battlefield today

Philiphaugh is on the A708, one mile to the west of Selkirk (OS Landranger 73 4428). The starting point for today's visitor is the Philiphaugh Estate's Salmon Viewing Centre, where

information about the battle can be obtained, including a
phone app which provides a guided tour linked to a series of
information panels along the A708. A plaque commemorating
the dead of the battle has also been introduced. The 'original'
memorial cairn is in Harehead Wood. Slain Men's Lea and
Newark Castle, in the grounds of Bowhill House (check website for opening times), can also be viewed. In Selkirk itself,
the Haliwell House Museum contains some battlefield artefacts, while a building in West Port displays a plaque of the
'Montrose slept here' variety. He may well have done so.

Further reading
Stuart Reid, *The Campaigns of Montrose* **(Mercat Press, 1990).**

SECOND CIVIL WAR

86. St Fagans, 8 May 1648

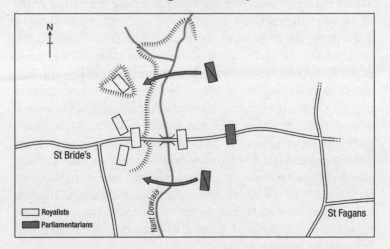

After his surrender at Stow-on-the-Wold (1646), the Royalist,
Lord Astley, had prophesied that the victors would fall out.
And so they did. Charles I was able to exploit differences
between the English Parliament and the Scots, while divisions within Parliament itself began to manifest.

There were also problems with the army. Money was not available to pay it and surplus troops refused to disband until they had received money owing to them. In Wales, the situation developed into open rebellion. Colonel John Poyer, Governor of Pembroke Castle, and his men were owed several months' back pay. When Parliament refused to meet the demand, Poyer declared for the king. His action provided a focus for Welsh Royalists, of whom there were many, and he soon acquired an army of about 8,000 men. Sir Thomas Fairfax despatched Cromwell to deal with the rising.

Parliament already had a small army operating in South Wales. Commanded by Colonel Thomas Horton, and about 2,700 strong, it undertook a march to block an advance by Poyer upon Cardiff Castle. On 4 May 1648, Horton reached the village of St Fagans, four miles to the west of the castle, commanding a crossing of the River Ely. He arrived just ahead of Poyer, who had intended camping there that night en route to the castle.

Perhaps Poyer should have attacked immediately, but another malcontent, Major-General Rowland Laugharne, arrived to take command. Throughout the following day, much skirmishing took place, but there was no sense of urgency in the rebel ranks until it was learned that Cromwell was on the way. Their response was to fall back a few miles, only to reappear on the radar on the morning of 8 May, having crossed the Ely further downstream – a move which enabled them to draw up on high ground spanning the road to St Brides, to the north-west of St Fagans. Marshalling his troops, Horton rode out to confront them, deploying on high ground opposite the Royalists, the two sides separated by a stream known as Nant Dowlais.

Although he was heavily outnumbered, Horton commanded experienced, disciplined troops, including Colonel John Okey who, like Horton himself, was a veteran of Naseby (1645). The Royalist army, on the other hand, contained as many as 4,000 poorly armed 'clubmen'. Laugharne did manage to manoeuvre 500 cavalry into a position behind Horton's lines, but Horton chose to ignore them, forming up his men into three divisions, himself in the centre with the infantry, Colonel Okey's dragoons on the right and Major Barton's cavalry on the left. Forward parties of infantry and horse were deployed in front of the main body.

Laugharne appears to have made the first move by sending forward 500 infantry, accompanied by a few horse, across the Nant Dowlais. They were met by Horton's advance guard and pushed back, facilitating a general Parliamentarian advance. Okey forced the Royalist left to give ground, although it was heavy going, with every hedge fiercely contested. Laugharne kept throwing more and more men into the fight, but the disciplined troops of the New Model Army kept to their task.

On the Parliamentarian left, Barton's cavalry was also pressing forward. The Royalist infantry was unable to hold them, and fresh Royalist horse which Laugharne introduced could not stem the advance. In fact, Laugharne's plan, involving the cavalry sent to outflank the Parliamentarians, had failed. Nothing more is heard of the flanking party, which probably withdrew instead of attacking Horton's rear. Instead, it was the Royalists who were flanked when Barton crossed the stream and swung in towards the centre. The Royalist resolve finally broke and they quitted the battlefield in disarray.

The Parliamentarian pursuit was lengthy and determined. From time to time, groups of fleeing Royalists would turn and make a last stand but, in the end, over 2,000 were captured. The dead numbered in excess of 200. Laugharne and Poyer took refuge behind the walls of Pembroke Castle, while Horton moved on to Tenby Castle, held for the Royalists by Colonel Rice Powell. For once, Cromwell arrived too late to claim the credit, although he flexed his muscles by taking charge and laying siege to Pembroke.

Parliament announced days of thanksgiving in celebration

of the victory at St Fagans. The majority of the rebel prisoners were released, although 240 of their number were shipped to the West Indies. Poyer, Laugharne and Powell, when they were eventually taken, were made to draw lots for their lives. Poyer drew the short straw (or, more accurately, the blank sheet of paper) and was shot.

The battlefield today
St Fagans is off the A4232 (OS Landranger 171 1077), four miles to the west of Cardiff city centre. Exit from Junction 33 of the M4. The battlefield is to the north-west of the village. The long-defunct Barry Railway branch line was routed through the site and the course of the Nant Dowlais was altered. However, Cardiff City Council has produced a leaflet (available for download via their website) describing a circular walk, taking in the battlefield. Car parking is available at the National History Museum (signposted).

Further reading
David Webb, *The Battle of St Fagans 1648* **(Stuart Press, 1998).**

87. 1st Preston, 17/19 August 1648

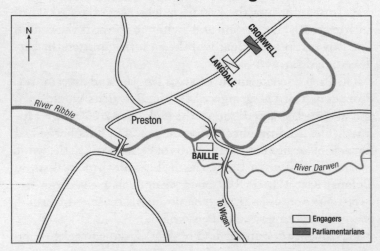

In December 1647, Charles I entered into the 'Engagement' with the Scots. In return for their attempting to put him back on his throne, he promised to establish Presbyterianism for a period of three years. Throughout the early months of 1648, there were several loosely coordinated Royalist uprisings in England and finally, on 8 July 1648, the Duke of Hamilton led an 'Engager' army across the border.

In response, Parliament was able to spare only 4,000 troops under Major-General John Lambert. All Lambert could do was to try to contain the invasion force until more troops were freed up. Had Hamilton acted with urgency, he might have prospered, but he lingered for a month while his army of Scots and die-hard Royalists grew to 18,000 men.

At last, Hamilton pushed his way south, into Lancashire, by which time Lieutenant-General Cromwell was marching from Wales to link up with Lambert. They met on 13 August, at Knaresborough, to create an army still only 9,000 strong. However, Hamilton's force was being dissipated. He left 3,000 experienced veterans under Major-General George Munro in the north of Lancashire while, during the course of his march south, many more troops slipped away. More significantly, he had permitted his army to become dangerously strung out over a distance of fifteen miles.

By the evening of 16 August, Hamilton's infantry had reached Preston. Most of his cavalry, under Lieutenant-General John Middleton, had ridden on ahead to Wigan. Hamilton sent the veteran Royalist campaigner Sir Marmaduke Langdale out to Ribble Moor to guard the road into Preston from the northeast while the main body of Engagers prepared to cross the River Ribble and the River Darwen.

On the morning of 17 August, Langdale took up a strong defensive position on Ribble Moor. The Parliamentarians had arrived, but it took Cromwell until mid-afternoon to deploy his men. When he had done so, Langdale was quickly overrun, his men retreating to Preston. Disagreements within the Engager command had led to the continued movement of infantry across the Ribble Bridge, while Langdale was left to fend for himself. When he appeared with the remnants of his command, the Parliamentarians were already attacking the bridge. Lieutenant-General William Baillie, commanding the Engager infantry, deployed musketeers to defend the bridge but, having to advance over open ground, they were driven back by Parliamentarian musketeers. Baillie was eventually pushed back from both the Ribble Bridge and the Darwen Bridge at Walton-le-Dale. As darkness fell, to grant a little rest, the Parliamentarians advanced to seize the enemy baggage train.

Hamilton decided to march away under cover of darkness and rendezvous with Middleton's cavalry, which had been sent for from Wigan. During this night march, undertaken in foul weather, many more Engagers deserted. Worse still, Middleton returned along a different road and the groups missed one another. In the early morning of 18 August, Middleton blundered into Cromwell's troops. He galloped off in pursuit of his own infantry and was harassed by Cromwell's cavalry every inch of the way.

When Middleton caught up with Hamilton's column, it was decided to continue marching as far as Warrington, where a stand would be made. Towards evening, the infantry rearguard reached Wigan. Forming a defensive line in Market Place, they mistook their own cavalry for those of Cromwell and attacked them at point of pike. The horse, in turn, in their anxiety to escape their pursuers, trampled them underfoot. In fact, an exhausted Cromwell had decided to rest for the night.

The next morning, he set off again, encountering many Scots who had fallen out of line to plunder any habitation in their path. Ahead, Hamilton had decided to ride ahead with the Engager cavalry to prepare defences in Warrington. To give him time, Baillie's infantry would fight a delaying action at the village of Winwick.

Baillie's chosen site was a good one – a point where the road ran through a high-sided pass. At midday on 19 August, Cromwell's advanced guard attacked the position but could make no headway. Even when reinforcements came up, Baillie's infantry stood its ground for several hours. Then some local inhabitants showed Cromwell a way around the enemy position. This outflanking manoeuvre, in unison with another frontal assault, finally broke the defenders, some of whom withdrew to make a last stand near St Oswald's Church in Winwick. Baillie and the rest stumbled into Warrington to find that Hamilton had fled across the River Mersey. There was nothing for it but to surrender.

Cromwell reported that his troops had killed 2,000 Engagers and captured another 9,000. Nearly all the Engager army leaders were eventually captured, bringing a swift end to the Second Civil War.

The battlefield today

The battle, in its entirety, was fought between Preston and Warrington. Ribble Moor (OS Landranger 102 5429), the scene of Langdale's encounter with Cromwell, is now covered by a housing development. Ribble Bridge is now Walton Bridge, carrying the A6. South Ribble Borough Council have devised a riverside walk here, starting from the Park & Ride site (see the SRBC website). Darwen Bridge now forms part of the B6258, Chorley Road. The holding action at Winwick took place to the north of the village on the A49, near Hermitage Green Lane. A plaque on the wall of 90 Church Street, Warrington, proclaims that, after the battle, Cromwell composed his despatches to Parliament near that spot.

Further reading

Stephen Bull and Mike Seed, *Bloody Preston: Battle of Preston 1648* (Carnegie Publishing, 1997).

THIRD CIVIL WAR

88. Carbisdale, 27 April 1650

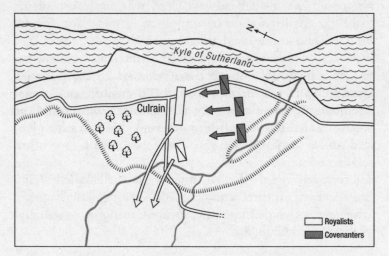

After the execution of Charles I in 1649, Charles, Prince of Wales, assumed the mantle of the Royalist cause. As a first step in securing his rightful position as Charles II, he turned to the exiled Marquis of Montrose. Having performed miracles for the father, Montrose was now expected to do likewise for the son.

In March 1650, Montrose duly arrived in Orkney, setting up a base at Kirkwall. In addition to taking command of some Danish troops who had arrived some months earlier, he raised some local support from the islands, giving him a total force of 1,500 men. It was precious little, but had he not discomfited the Covenanters with a similar number? All the same, ships carrying much-needed supplies were lost at sea and, even as he was making preparations to head to the mainland, he knew that Charles was making overtures to the Scottish government.

Montrose arrived at John O'Groats on 12 April. Hampered by heavy cannon and the need to canvas for support, his advance inland was uncharacteristically slow. By 27 April, he had reached Carbisdale, on the Kyle of Sutherland, forty miles to the north of Inverness. He was hoping to receive reinforcements, but no one came and, by now, he must have realized that he was not simply going to take up where he had left off five years before.

Montrose was aware that the Covenanters were on his trail, but he could not tell their numbers or their precise location. In fact, a force of around 700 men under Colonel Archibald Strachan was only a few miles to the south, at Wester Fearn. The Royalists were camped in a narrow glen, in a well-entrenched position, with a wooded hill to their rear. As Strachan approached, he displayed the cunning that had once been the hallmark of Montrose, by concealing the main body of his force while sending forward a single troop. Montrose responded by ordering his small force of cavalry to advance while the infantry made for the hill.

Without warning, Strachan unleashed his entire army. The Royalist horse were overwhelmed as the Covenanter cavalry charged for the hill. The Danes, disorganized as they were, tried to make a stand after being rallied by Colonel John Hurry (now fighting for Montrose), but the Islanders simply fled. It is thought that over 400 Royalists were killed, with only minimal casualties on the Covenanter side.

Montrose managed to escape. Wounded, he wandered for four days before being taken by Neil MacLeod of Ardvreck Castle and handed over to Strachan. On 21 May, he was hanged on a gibbet at the Market Cross in Edinburgh, written off by Charles as collateral damage in the latter's quest for power.

The battlefield today

The battlefield is on a minor road off the A836, fifteen miles to the west of Dornoch (OS Landranger 21 5695. The name 'Carbisdale' exists only in the twentieth-century Carbisdale Castle, currently (2014) a youth hostel. The settlement of

Culrain and a railway line covers part of the area, but the battlefield is largely unspoilt. There is car parking and a viewpoint between Culrain and the castle.

Further reading
Stuart Reid, *The Campaigns of Montrose* **(Mercat Press, 1990).**

89. Dunbar, 3 September 1650

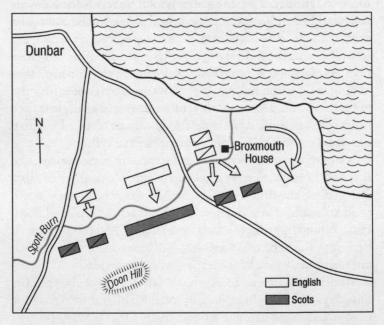

The future Charles II did something his deceased father had always refused to do: he subscribed to the National League and Covenant, promising to establish Presbyterianism in England if the Scots would help him restore the crown to the Stuart dynasty. The English Parliament decided not to await another invasion but to strike first. Lord Fairfax (Sir Thomas had succeeded to the title in 1648 upon the death of his own father) refused to participate, resigning as commander-in-chief of the New Model Army. Cromwell gratefully stepped into his shoes. Whether they would fit remained to be seen.

Cromwell's army, 16,000 in number, crossed the border on 22 July 1650. In terms of invasions of Scotland – and despite the strengths of the New Model Army – it was the same old story: local food supplies destroyed; deaths from disease; an enemy, ably led by Lieutenant-General David Leslie, that dodged and weaved. Finally, an exasperated Cromwell withdrew to Dunbar, a port through which he received seaborne supplies. When he arrived, he found Leslie's 22,000-strong army ranged across Doon Hill.

At first, Cromwell though he might settle down before Dunbar and await reinforcements. However, Leslie, pressured by extremists among accompanying clergy (and perhaps also a victim of his own scorched-earth policy), needed a quick resolution and, on 2 September, he came down from his unassailable position. In the late afternoon, from the grounds of Broxmouth House, Cromwell and his trusted cavalry commander, Major-General John Lambert, watched his descent to the lower slopes.

The problem with Leslie's position was that his left flank was cramped by the Spott Burn and a deep ravine, while his right flank did not extend to the sea. Both Cromwell and Lambert thought that it might be possible to roll up the Scottish army by launching an attack on its exposed right flank. The Parliamentarians had drawn up below the Scots in standard formation: infantry flanked by cavalry. During the night, while the Scots sought what shelter they could from driving rain, Lambert transferred most of the cavalry to the Parliamentarian left wing. Lambert himself would lead the projected cavalry advance, with Cromwell and two infantry brigades under Colonels Pride and Overton bringing up the rear. In the centre, General George Monck would command the main body of infantry. The Parliamentarian right, with only a few horse, was bolstered with a concentration of artillery.

At 4.00 a.m. on 3 September, the battle began. The cavalry on the right launched a feint attack which was followed by the advance of Monck's infantry and Lambert's cavalry on the left. The Scots responded promptly, meeting Monck and forcing him back by sheer weight of numbers. Lambert, too, found himself hard-pressed as he ran into a far superior force, but Cromwell and Pride and Overton followed up at the right time to provide the necessary support. The Scots, poorly officered, were unable to withstand the inroads made by the Parliamentarian horse and, as if on cue, their lines recoiled along their entire length. The Scottish cavalry fled, leaving their infantry to its fate. By 6.00 a.m., the victory was complete.

Only 4,000 Scots escaped. Cromwell claimed that 3,000 were killed and 10,000 captured, for the loss of only 20 or so of his own men. About half the prisoners were released. The remainder were marched to Durham. Many died of disease and starvation, the remainder being shipped to the colonies. Even so, Leslie and 4,000 of his men had evaded Cromwell's grasp and remained at large. The Third Civil War was far from over.

The battlefield today

The battlefield straddles the A1, one and a half miles to the south-east of Dunbar. Take the A1087 for Dunbar and park in the generous lay-by adjacent to Broxmouth House. There is a monument (OS Landranger 67 6976), which has to be approached via the cement works service road. Doon Hill (OS Landranger 67 6875) is usually recommended as a viewpoint. The grounds of Broxmouth House (now an exclusive hotel and leisure complex) contain the grave of Sir William Douglas, killed in the battle, and Cromwell's Mount, a mound on which Cromwell and Lambert may have hatched their plan.

Further reading

Peter Reese, *Cromwell's Masterstroke: Dunbar 1650* (Pen & Sword, 2006).

90. Inverkeithing, 20 July 1651

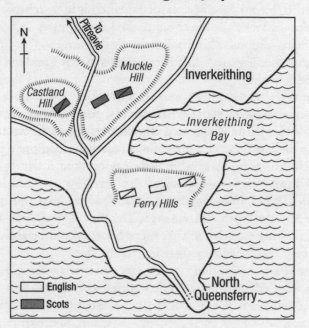

One could be forgiven for inferring that Cromwell's celebrated victory at Dunbar (1650) ended the Scottish campaign. In fact, nearly a year later, he was still trying to make headway against Sir David Leslie's reconstituted army.

In July 1651, Leslie's army was concentrated at Torwood, preventing the English, based at Linlithgow, from advancing further into Scotland. Cromwell decided to outflank the enemy by sending a force across the Firth of Forth from South Queensferry to North Queensferry. On 17 July, Colonel Thomas Overton took some 1,600 horse and foot over the water and succeeded in establishing an entrenched position in the Ferry Hills. In response, Leslie despatched Sir James Brown of Fordel and Lieutenant-General James Holbourn with 3,600 men to block Overton's route inland.

On 19 July, Cromwell sent 3,000 further troops under

the command of Major-General John Lambert to reinforce Overton. It took Lambert a full day and night to achieve this objective, but by the morning of 20 July his men had taken up their positions. There was no time to spare, for the Scots, fast approaching, occupied the lower slopes of Castland Hill and Muckle Hill.

Lambert, now in overall command, then observed Holbourn turn, either to withdraw, given the strength of the English force, or to occupy the higher slopes of Castland Hill. In response, Lambert sent forward Colonel John Okey's horse to harass him. As hoped, the Scots halted, turned and, infantry flanked by cavalry, deployed for action. They numbered about 4,000, having been joined by some 500 clansmen – Macleans led by Sir Hector Maclean of Duart. When he learned that more Scots would be arriving, Lambert took the brave decision to attack.

The Parliamentarians – Okey on the right, Colonel Leonard Lydcot on the left, flanking the infantry – duly descended from the Ferry Hills, passed through the isthmus and advanced on the enemy position. Scottish lancers charged forward, penetrating Lydcot's ranks, before being checked by a combination of counter-charge (led by Lambert himself) and musket fire. The determined ascent continued in the expectancy that the Scots would hurl themselves downhill at any moment, but it did not happen. Instead, in the face of the Ironsides' exemplary discipline, Holbourn lost his nerve and led his infantry from the field. Brown was wounded and captured. The cavalry was overcome and, as at Dunbar, a brutal pursuit began. The Macleans appear to have beaten a fighting retreat as far as Pitreavie Castle, where they made a last stand. The survivors begged for admission to the castle, but were refused.

Lambert assessed enemy losses as 2,000 killed with 1,400 taken prisoner, while his own casualties were 8 or 9 killed and several wounded. Whatever the truth of the matter, the deadlock had been broken and Cromwell moved on to Perth, which surrendered to him on 2 August. Leslie did not care because he had already begun a march south into England.

The battlefield today

One might think that this is a fairly compact battlefield, but it covers an area of nearly three miles on OS Landranger 65. However, there are possibilities for development and these are gradually bring explored. In 2001, a memorial cairn to the Macleans who died in the battle was erected at Pitreavie Castle (OS Landranger 65 1184) and this may be viewed, together with information panels. The castle itself is in private hands. To the south, there has always been a good viewing point on Ferry Hills (OS Landranger 65 1381), accessible via a footpath from Ferryhills Road. At the time of writing, archaeologists are excavating Overton's Ferry Hills earthworks. Car parking is available at the A90/Hope Street Park & Ride site.

Further reading

Stuart Reid, *Crown, Covenant and Cromwell: The Civil Wars in Scotland 1639–51* (Frontline Books, 2012).

91. Worcester, 3 September 1651

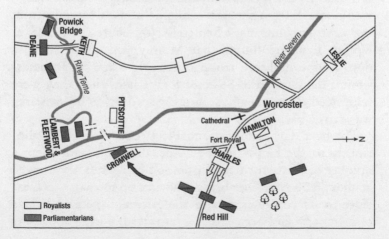

When Cromwell's army outflanked Sir David Leslie through Major-General John Lambert's victory at Inverkeithing (1651), the Scots turned south to invade England. With Charles Stuart – already recognized by them as King Charles II – in tow, they hoped to gather Royalist support as they progressed and to add to their 9,000 foot and 4,000 horse. This did not happen. Instead, they were shadowed by some 12,000 Parliamentarians under Major-Generals Lambert and Charles Fleetwood. On 24 August, Cromwell caught up with his colleagues to form an army of some 28,000 men.

At the same time, Charles and Leslie were resting at Worcester, where Charles hoped to be joined by Royalist supporters from Wales and the south-west. Leslie, who had been morose from the outset, had little appetite for the venture. He and his cavalry, deployed to the north of the city, would take no part in the coming battle. Nonetheless, efforts were made to strengthen the city defences, particularly at Fort Royal, an entrenched earthwork on the exterior of the south-east corner. In addition, Sir Edward Massey was sent to destroy bridges, over the Severn at Upton and over the Teme at Bransford and Powick.

Approaching Worcester via Evesham, Cromwell decided to divide his army. One half, under Fleetwood and Lambert, would attack from the east while he himself came in from the west. Arriving on 2 September to secure the bridge at Upton, Lambert found that Massey had only partially destroyed it. Eighteen troopers got across and took possession of the Church of St Peter & St Paul. When they were reinforced, Massey, whose brief was to hold the crossing, was driven back.

The next day, Lambert and Fleetwood proceeded laboriously to the banks of the Teme, dragging with them a number of boats for use as pontoon bridges. They arrived at about 3.00 p.m. One bridge they set up to span the Teme close to its confluence with the Severn; a second bridge of boats was laid across the Severn itself, a little above the

Teme. Meanwhile, Colonel Richard Deane attempted the bridge at Powick. As at Upton, a small portion had been left in place, but Royalist Colonel George Keith put up a stout resistance. Lambert and Fleetwood also met strong opposition from Colonel Pitscottie.

Meanwhile, to the west of the city, Cromwell had drawn up the rest of his army in the meadows, out of range of the Royalist artillery. Perceiving the difficulties his forces were facing to the east, he led three brigades across the Severn bridge of boats, outflanking the Royalists who were finally forced back into the city via Severn Bridge at St John's.

In the city itself, Charles took advantage of the weakening of the force facing him to emerge from Sidbury Gate to lead an attack on the Parliamentarian position on Red Hill, while the Duke of Hamilton assaulted Perry Wood. Leslie and his cavalry remained immobile but, even in his absence, the Royalists began to gain ground. Then Cromwell wheeled back across the Severn to counter-attack. The fighting was fierce, but the Scots, short of ammunition and growing increasingly dispirited, eventually gave ground and, despite Charles's attempts to rally them, retreated at push of pike behind the city walls.

Fort Royal was successfully stormed and its artillery turned on the city. Lambert was in control of the St John's Bridge and the only avenue of escape was to the north, by St Martin's Gate. After what had been twelve hours of fighting, the battle was effectively over, with the desperate Scottish infantry looking to Leslie to lead them home.

The Parliamentarian victory was almost total. Cromwell claimed to have lost not above 200 men, whereas up to 3,000 Scots and Royalists were killed and 10,000 taken prisoner. The Duke of Hamilton was mortally wounded while Leslie was captured and ultimately imprisoned until the Restoration. Charles did manage to escape, embarking on his famous flight to safety. Like his father before him, and like more Stuarts to follow, he had demonstrated that in order to secure the throne of England, he would fight to the last drop of Scottish blood.

The battlefield today

The Battle of Worcester covered a large area, much of which is now urbanized. Only the southern portion, at Powick Bridge, is on partially open ground. A battlefield city centre trail (downloadable from the Worcester City Council website) takes in the site of Fort Royal and The Commandery museum. A plaque in the cathedral commemorates the Duke of Hamilton, while the exterior walls of St Peter's Church in Powick bear the marks of musket shot. There is a small monument to the Scots at Powick Bridge, although plans are afoot to provide something more imposing. A viewpoint, with interpretation panels, is located to the east of Powick, at the junction of the A38 and A4440 (OS Landranger 150 853516). Car parking options include city centre car parks; a car park at the viewpoint; and a parking area adjacent to the A449 roundabout at Powick Bridge. Exploration is facilitated via the public footpath network.

Further reading

Malcolm Atkin, *The Battle of Worcester 1651* (Pen & Sword, 2004).

The Covenanter Wars

92. Drumclog, 1 June 1679

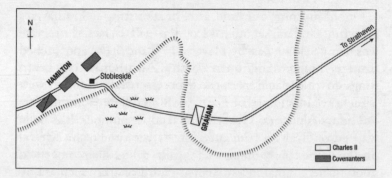

The Restoration of 1660 led, inevitably, to dissatisfaction in Scotland, for King Charles II wished to see a return to an Episcopalian church, insisting that Presbyterianism was 'no religion for a gentleman'. An essentially conciliatory policy led to most Scots falling into line, isolating a hard core of diehards who preferred to roam the open countryside, presiding over open-air services known as conventicles.

In 1671, conventicle preaching was made a capital offence, owing to government fears that coventicles would be used as a tool for the promotion of political unrest – as they were, with armed 'congregations', several hundred strong, roaming the hills. Such government troops as existed to enforce the law were always overstretched. In Glasgow, for example, the Earl of Ross commanded a garrison of just 240 men.

Matters came to a head in May 1679, with the murder of James Sharp, Archbishop of St Andrews. His assassins joined forces with Sir Robert Hamilton, an eccentric activist and advocate of violence. On 29 May, Hamilton and a group of armed supporters arrived in Rutherglen, where they presided over a conventicle in the market square.

An officer of dragoons, Captain John Graham of Claverhouse, whose task it was to break up conventicles wherever he found them, arrived at Rutherglen on 31 May and then moved on to Hamilton, where he heard that a large conventicle was to take place the following day at Loudon Hill, near Drumclog.

On the morning of 1 June, after breakfasting at Strathaven's Slate Inn, Graham set out for Loudon Hill. In fact, the service was being held on nearby Harelea Hill and, as he approached from the high ground to the north, Graham may have heard songs of praise and perhaps even the words of the fiery preacher, James Douglas, borne aloft on the morning air.

The worshippers, several thousand in number, had been warned of Graham's advance for, by the time of his arrival on the scene, the women and children had been moved to safety. There remained an armed guard of sixty men led by Hamilton. A further 200 poorly armed but committed able-bodied members of the congregation stood ready to defend their right to worship.

Instead of being faced with a peaceful meeting that would disperse hurriedly, leaving him free to pick up the ringleaders at his leisure, Graham was met with armed resistance. His own force of 150 dragoons and infantry was heavily outnumbered, and the Covenanters had occupied a position on high ground, occupied today by Stobieside. Furthermore, in order to tackle them, he would have to advance over some very boggy land.

Having sent a rider back to Glasgow for reinforcements, Graham demanded the insurgents' surrender. When this was not forthcoming, he sent in a skirmishing party. Instead of scattering as he had hoped, the rebels formed an advance party of their own, the two sides exchanging one or two volleys of musket fire before the rebel skirmishers withdrew. This left Graham with no choice but to order a general advance. He must have realized that his dragoons would be rendered largely ineffective by the nature of the terrain, but he gambled on throwing the rebels into disarray. He could not have guessed that the rebels, throwing caution to the winds, would respond by launching a fast and furious assault of their own.

As Graham himself later reported, the amateur rebel infantry began its advance, guided, perhaps, by local men who knew how to negotiate the mire. The dragoons stood their ground, but their fire cannot have been confined to disciplined volleys, for the rebels seem to have experienced little difficulty in coming to grips with them. Moreover, William Cleland (a minor poet), leading the rebel infantry, managed to outflank the government force on its left. In the resulting confused mêlée, Graham's horse was wounded by a pitchfork-wielding rebel, prompting it to bolt and carry its rider from the field. Despite the severity of the wound that Graham claimed it had sustained, the animal carried him three miles to Hillhead, where he commandeered his trumpeter's horse to take him on to Glasgow.

In his absence, his men stood little chance. Deducing that Graham had fled voluntarily, the rank and file followed suit, although a number were surrounded and butchered. At Strathaven, hostile villagers were on the alert, for they attempted to block the road, forcing the pursued survivors to fight their way through. Darkness had fallen by the time they reached Glasgow, accompanied by the requested reinforcements, whom they had met on the road.

As far as casualties are concerned, Graham may have lost around ten dead, with many more wounded, while rebel losses, according to the victors, may have stood at three to six dead. The importance of the battle lay in the confidence that it gave the Covenanters in terms of their effectiveness as a fighting force. Having defeated regular troops, they now felt capable of marching on to Glasgow.

The battlefield today

The battlefield is approached via the Hallburn Bridge junction of the A71, running between the M74 (Junction 8) and Kilmarnock, five miles east of Strathaven (OS Landranger

71 6239). There is an imposing monument at Stobieside.
Follow the road around into the village of Drumclog and
stop at Drumclog Memorial Kirk. Named in remembrance
of the battle, the kirk has a stained glass window depicting
the Covenanters and a copy of their banner. The remains of
an earlier monument can be seen in the churchyard. On the
A71 at Caldermill is The Trumpeter's Well where, according to legend, the trumpeter, whose horse was taken by
Graham, was caught by the rebels and killed. Loudoun Hill
Visitor Centre, adjacent to Loudoun Hill Inn on the A71, is
a good starting point for exploring on foot. Strathaven also
has a tourist office with free leaflets providing historical
background to the area's Covenanter associations and information on the battle.

Further reading
William Aiton, *A History of the Rencounter at Drumclog and
Battle at Bothwell Bridge* (**Ulan Press, 2011**).

93. Bothwell Bridge, 22 June 1679

Emboldened by their victory at the minor Battle of
Drumclog on 1 June 1679, the Covenanter army under

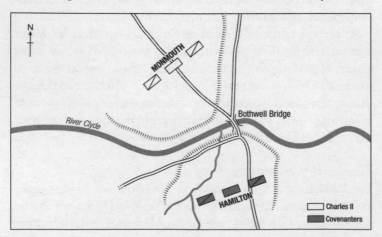

Robert Hamilton resolved to march directly on Glasgow, which they reached at about 10.00 a.m. on 3 June.

Government troops had barricaded the streets and coordinated Covenanter attacks were beaten off. Hamilton had made up his mind to withdraw when the commander-in-chief of the army in Scotland, the Earl of Linlithgow, ordered a retreat to Stirling, and the regulars marched away, enabling Hamilton to move in and take control.

James, Duke of Monmouth, was sent north to replace Linlithgow, and the time that it took to raise an army capable of confronting the Covenanters provided them with an opportunity to organize. Instead, they spent the coming weeks arguing among themselves.

In total, Monmouth could call on some 5,000 men, mainly comprising groups of hastily raised militia, but Monmouth was an experienced soldier, as were his officers who included the Earls of Airlie and Home and John Graham of Claverhouse, humiliated at Drumclog and now out for revenge.

The Covenanters, having withdrawn from Glasgow, were encamped on the opposite bank of the River Clyde, at the town of Hamilton. They had barricaded the bridge spanning the river at Bothwell. A narrow structure with a central gate tower, its approach on the Hamilton side was commanded by houses and walled enclosures. Although the Covenanters numbered around 6,000, they were thrown into a panic when lookouts observed the approach of Monmouth's army on the evening of 21 June.

On the following morning, a force of 400 Covenanters manning the barricade began to exchange fire with the government troops. A discussion within the main Covenanter army, drawn up about half a mile from the bridge, resulted in an effort to parlay, and there was a lull while both sides conferred. Monmouth insisted that the Covenanters must lay down their arms and surrender unconditionally. He gave them half an hour to acquiesce, and when it was clear that they were not going to do so, he brought his artillery up to the bridge. The two sides exchanged fire and Monmouth's gunners were driven back. Unfortunately, the Covenanters did not exploit this advantage and a stalemate ensued, both sides exchanging musket fire for two hours.

Finally, with ammunition running short, the defenders were forced to retire to the main body, enabling the government troops to cross the bridge and deploy on the south bank, experiencing no harassment from the rebels as they did so. Monmouth now brought his artillery back into operation, initially against Hamilton's left wing. Several of Hamilton's officers appear to have abandoned the field at an early stage, resulting in much indecision and confusion. According to some reports, the rebel cavalry gave a good account of itself before falling back and creating more turmoil within the infantry ranks.

Suddenly, in the absence of officers to command them and with the government guns continuing to play upon them, the entire rebel force threw down its arms, turned and fled. A surviving Covenanter later observed that the right wing stood fast, 'but not so long as to put on a pair of gloves'. The government troops were quick to engage in pursuit. Prominent among the hunters was Graham of Claverhouse or 'Bloody Clavers', as he was known, owing to the ardour with which he persecuted Covenanters.

At the end of the day, 800 Covenanters had been killed and, despite Graham's display of zeal, more than 1,000 were taken prisoner. The churchyard of Edinburgh's Greyfriars Church was infamously used as a temporary open-air prison. Most prisoners were later freed, although, to set an example, there were a few executions. Others were transported to the colonies, one transportation vessel being wrecked off the Orkneys, with the loss of most of the 257 convicts on board. Although a hard core of extremist Covenanters, including Hamilton, remained at large, the defeat at Bothwell Bridge effectively put paid to their dalliance with armed rebellion.

The battlefield today

The bridge of the battle occupied the same position as the present-day bridge spanning the River Clyde (OS Landranger 64 7157). Exit from Junction 6 of the M74 for Hamilton. Public car parks are situated off Bothwell Road. The bridge, with a battlefield monument on the Bothwell side, is one mile to the north.

Further reading

William Aiton, *A History of the Rencounter at Drumclog and Battle at Bothwell Bridge* (Ulan Press, 2011).

The Monmouth Rebellion

94. Sedgemoor, 6 July 1685

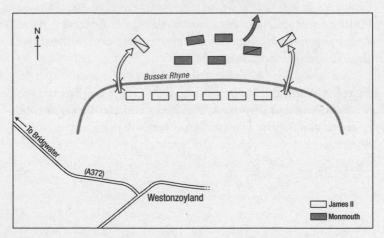

In 1685, Charles II died, to be succeeded by his brother, James II, a committed Roman Catholic who, it was feared, might lead England back to Rome. Although Charles had been unable to provide a legitimate heir to the throne, he had sired at least fourteen illegitimate children, one of whom was James, Duke of Monmouth. The previous year, Monmouth had been driven into exile for his involvement in the 'Rye House Plot' to murder his father. Now he returned, claiming to be the rightful king.

Monmouth landed at Lyme Regis on 11 June 1685, attracting around 3,000 men to his cause. Many of them lacked weapons, and a shortage of pikes led to the improvisation of scythe blades tied to rough-hewn staves. (As it happened, even bespoke pikes would have proved unsatisfactory for, at long last, warfare had begun to revolve around the use of gunpowder as opposed to the blade.) Furthermore, hoped-for support was not forthcoming, while a secondary landing in Scotland by the Duke of Argyll was a failure.

Having failed to take Bristol and having bypassed Bath,

the rebels were running out of steam. In the early hours of 27 June, at Norton St Philip, to the south of Bath, they were heartened by a victory over the Duke of Grafton. His 500 horse – an advance guard of the Earl of Feversham's Royalist army – were ambushed by rebel musketeers in a hedged lane approaching the village. Following this success, Monmouth moved north, to Bridgwater.

The decision suited Feversham, who saw the advantages to be gained by forcing Monmouth to fight on the boggy expanse of Sedgemoor. He arrived at Westonzoyland, to the south of the moor, on 5 July. It is said that his army was spotted by Monmouth from the tower of St Mary's Church in Bridgwater. Situated to the rear of Bussex Rhyne, one of the dykes that drained the moor, Feversham's camp was well chosen. He and his cavalry had set up their HQ in the village, with the infantry in forward positions behind the dyke. Another portion of his force, the Earl of Pembroke's Wiltshire militia, was almost two miles away, at Middlezoy, while a forward post, commanded by Sir Francis Compton, occupied Chedzoy.

Much has been made of Monmouth's decision to risk all by launching a surprise night-time assault. However, only by riding the crest of the wave of rebel enthusiasm, always a short-lived phenomenon, could he hope to succeed: hence his desperate gamble. The rebel force numbered around 4,000 men, as opposed to Feversham's 1,800 foot and 700 horse, who slumbered, unaware of the enemy's proximity. Only two factors militated against Monmouth's plan: the rebels were insufficiently disciplined to undertake an orderly night march, and the landscape was peppered with treacherous drainage ditches.

Some time after 11.00 p.m. on 5 July, the rebel army moved out of Bridgwater in a north-easterly direction along the old Bristol road, with the intention of descending on Westonzoyland from an unexpected direction. Somehow, they avoided a party of Royalists scouting the route. They swung to the south at Peasey Farm, crossing a ditch, Black

Rhyne, with the help of their guide, a local man named
Godfrey. Having given Compton's outpost at Chedzoy
a wide berth, they approached another ditch, Langmoor
Rhyne, which Godfrey experienced some difficulty in
negotiating. At this juncture, a shot rang out. Possibly, a
rebel had accidentally discharged a firearm. Whatever the
source, Compton was alerted and a rider was despatched to
rouse the Royalist camp. It was now essential for Monmouth
to press forward to catch Feversham before he was fully prepared. Having crossed Langmoor Rhyne, the rebel cavalry,
led by Lord Grey of Warke, galloped forward to try to find
the two crossing points – the upper and lower plungeons
– of the Bussex Rhyne. Espied by the Royalists, they were
subjected to volleys of musket fire from the regulars. To the
dismay of the rebel infantry struggling along behind, Grey
panicked and led his men swiftly from the field.

Bussex Rhyne was found to be almost dry, but instead of
hurling themselves across, on the right of the Royalist line,
the rebels halted to begin an exchange of musket fire. Only
half of the rebels carried muskets and Monmouth, realizing that there could be only one outcome, did his utmost
to encourage them to advance. He did manage to bring up
three pieces of ordnance, which inflicted some damage on
the Royal Scots, facing them. Major-General John Churchill
(later Duke of Marlborough) reinforced the Royal Scots
with men from the Royalist left and the increased firepower
took its toll on the rebels. Nevertheless, they stood firm,
even when attacked on both flanks by Royalist cavalry that
advanced across the upper and lower plungeons. Then, as
night gave way to day, Feversham ordered his infantry forward. The rebels finally broke and ran – but without their
leader, for Monmouth had already slipped away.

Over a thousand rebels died on the battlefield. In company with Grey, Monmouth headed for the south coast, but
was apprehended hiding in a ditch. Grey saved his own life
by informing on Monmouth who, in turn, hoped to cheat

the executioner by informing on others. On 15 July 1685, however, the duke was beheaded in an execution noted for its inefficiency, five or six blows of the axe being required to do the job; even then, it was necessary for the executioner to use a knife to completely separate the head from the trunk.

The surviving rebel rank and file were even less fortunate for, as common men, many were destined to meet traditional traitors' deaths by being hanged, drawn and quartered. The man entrusted with meting out punishment was Lord Chief Justice Jeffreys, whose reputation for brutality would be consolidated by his conduct at the infamous 'Bloody Assizes'.

Three years after the failed rebellion, James II was deposed in the bloodless 'Glorious Revolution', and was permitted to escape to France. Jeffreys, who also tried to escape, was taken, disguised as a seaman, at London's Wapping Old Stairs. He died a prisoner in the Tower of London while awaiting trial.

The battlefield today

'Sedgemoor', a geographical expression as opposed to a place name, is not readily identifiable in gazetteers. The nearest settlement is Westonzoyland, on the A372 between Bridgwater and Langport. Roadside parking can be found in the village. The battlefield lies to the north of the village (OS Landranger 182 3535). A monument to the battle is situated on Langmoor Drove and a battlefield information panel may be found at nearby Bussex Farm. St Mary's Church in Chedzoy (with parking) houses a small battlefield visitor centre, while a comprehensive network of public footpaths facilitates exploration of the battlefield.

Further reading
John Trincey, *Sedgemoor 1685* (Pen & Sword, 2005).

The Jacobite Rebellions

THE '89

95. Killiecrankie, 27 July 1689

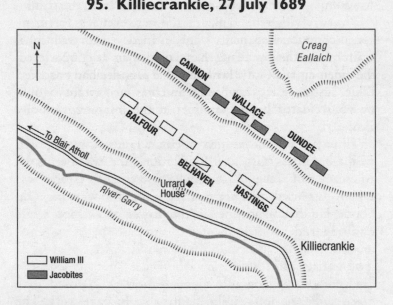

King James II, having successfully seen off the challenge to his reign of the Duke of Monmouth at Sedgemoor (1685), was deposed just three years later. In the 'Glorious Revolution' of 1688, William of Orange became King William III. Immediately, the exiled James began a campaign to recover his kingdom. So began the series of risings known as the Jacobite Rebellions, in which Highland clans, loyal to the House of Stuart, played a key role. The first such rising was the '89 in which James, with French help, landed in Ireland. In Scotland, Highlanders came out in support.

Spearheading the Scottish challenge was James Graham of Claverhouse, Viscount Dundee, who had been active in the Covenanter Wars a decade earlier. A popular, charismatic figure, he toured the Highlands gathering support until he commanded some 2,500 men, including a contingent under Colonel Alexander Cannon, sent from Ireland. Pitted against Dundee was Major-General Hugh MacKay, a Highlander who had emigrated to Holland to become one of William's military advisers. MacKay spent three months chasing Dundee around the Highlands before finally running him to earth at the Pass of Killicrankie, near Pitlochry.

McKay reached the eastern end of the pass at 11.00 a.m. on the morning of 27 July. He knew that Dundee had occupied Blair Castle at the western end and was well aware that his own 5,000-strong army passing through this narrow defile, almost three miles long and bordered by precipitous slopes on either side, would present an easy target for an ambush.

Proceeding with great care, he reached the hamlet of Aldclune at 4.00 p.m. As his men rested by the River Garry, Dundee's army, having circled the high ground from Blair Castle, appeared on the hillside above them, on their right flank. McKay ordered his men to wheel to the right, sending them up the hillside until they attained a section of level ground, just above Urrard House, and deployed in lines three deep. Brigadier-General Barthold Balfour commanded on the left, Colonel Ferdinand Hastings on the right. One hundred horse under Lord Belhaven stood a little to the rear behind three small pieces of artillery. The Jacobites were spread more thinly, Colonel Cannon commanding on the right and Dundee on the left. Some horse, forty in number, led by Sir William Wallace of Craighie, occupied the centre.

Time passed and the Jacobites showed no sign of making a move. Fearing a night attack, McKay tried to draw them down, mounting sorties and using the few light guns he had with him to pepper their lines, but Dundee held his men back until 7.00 p.m. Only then, with an hour or so of daylight left, were the Highlanders given the order to charge. It was ideal ground for them, and they gathered momentum as they ran. MacKay's troops stood firm, holding their fire. They managed to rake the enemy ranks with up to three volleys, creating significant gaps in the line. The remaining Highlanders kept running, giving the government troops no time to fix bayonets. Much of the government right wing was swept away. Mackay's brother was killed attempting to make a stand, although some of the infantry remained on the field, helplessly watching their comrades being swept away as on a tidal wave. The left wing, although suffering considerable damage from the fearsome Highland swords, might have stood its ground but for Belhaven's horse. Sent forward in an attempt to outflank the Highlanders, they panicked – possibly at the approach of Dundee and the Jacobite horse – and galloped back through their own infantry, adding to the confusion.

Both MacKay and Dundee put their lives at risk by riding openly on the battlefield, MacKay in efforts to rally his men and Dundee by leading the Jacobite cavalry. MacKay was lucky but Dundee was not. Hit by a musket ball, he fell, mortally wounded. Unaware of their loss, his men pursued the government troops down to the road, butchering them as they thronged together. Under fire from Urrard House, which the Highlanders had occupied, MacKay gathered whatever troops remained on the field, to organize something of an orderly retreat, fording the Garry and, ultimately, making his way to safety.

The pursuit, apart from the slaughter at the pass, was not quite so devastating as it might have been, many of the pursued owing their lives to the Highlanders' interest in MacKay's well-stocked supply train. Even so, government casualties were terrible enough, with the number of dead estimated at around 1,200. The Jacobites also suffered heavily, with perhaps 700 dead, a figure that included several of their leaders – a price they often paid for leading from the front. Most significantly for the Jacobite cause, however, Dundee himself lay dying on the battlefield, his demise creating a vacuum that could not be filled, condemning the '89 rising itself to a slow and lingering death.

The battlefield today

The battlefield is on the A9, which cuts through the middle of the battlefield, four miles to the north of Pitlochry (OS Landranger 43 9063). Car parking is available at the Pass of Killiecrankie Visitor Centre – geared both to nature studies and to the provision of information about the battle. On the battlefield itself, you will find: an updated Urrard House; Tomb Clavers (also known as the Graham Monument), a cairn with a plaque marking the site of a mass grave; and the Claverhouse Stone, a standing stone supposedly marking the spot where Dundee was killed. Ask at the Visitor Centre for directions to: The Soldier's Leap (where one of McKay's men jumped eighteen feet across the River Garry); Balfour's Stone (marking the grave of Brigadier-General Balfour, killed in the battle; and Trooper's Den, where the first casualty of the battle occurred – a government horseman shot by a sniper. Dundee's body was taken for burial to nearby Blair Atholl, where a monument can be seen in the ruins of St Bride's Church. Blair Castle (open to the public) has Dundee's breastplate on display.

Further reading

Stuart Reid, *I Met the Devil and Dundee: The Battle of Killiecrankie 1689* (Partizan Press, 2009).

96. Cromdale, 1 May 1690

Highland support for the Jacobite Rebellion of '89 petered out after a disastrous raid on government troops occupying Dunkeld, led by Colonel Alexander Cannon, who had replaced Viscount Dundee after the latter's death at Killiecrankie (1689). In the spring of 1690, Cannon himself was replaced by Major-General Thomas Buchan, who arrived from Ireland to breathe new life into the movement – by leading 1,200 Highlanders (all that could be mustered) in a guerrilla campaign south towards the Lowlands. He hoped

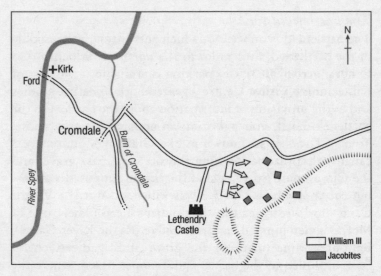

to recruit as he progressed, but ending up losing, through desertions, a third of the men he started out with.

The government garrison at Inverness was commanded by Sir Thomas Livingstone, who was able to put 1,200 men into the field. He had been kept informed of Buchan's movements and was particularly interested to learn that he was moving – against all advice – into flat, open country. Setting off in pursuit, he made a forced march which, by the evening of 30 April 1690, led him to Castle Grant, from where he could see Buchan's campfires at Cromdale, on the other side of the River Spey. Livingstone had not expected to catch up with the Jacobites so quickly and his men were inclined to maintain a respectful distance, but he decided to press on in the expectation of taking the slumbering enemy by surprise.

Buchan's force was spread out over a mile. Two hundred of his best troops had been despatched to guard the Spey's fording points, in particular the ford by Cromdale's kirk where, it seems, many of them were at rest. Some were billeted in the village while others were camped in the open, with Buchan himself occupying Lethendry Castle.

At about 3.00 a.m. on 1 May, Livingstone set up a feint

attack on the ford by the kirk, while the main body of his men crossed at another ford a little downriver. When those within the kirk realized what was happening, they managed to ring the bell to warn the main camp, where panic soon reigned. Livingstone lost no time in taking full advantage of the situation, charging through the village and on towards groups of Highlanders who could be seen running naked towards the hills. It was reported that even Buchan was caught unarmed and in night attire.

Livingstone tried to cut off the line of retreat to the east but, when the initial shock of the surprise attack had worn off, many of the Highlanders, armed with swords and shields, offered stern resistance. The fighting was fierce, with the Jacobites slowly but surely being pushed back. Apparently, they were saved from annihilation by a dense mist that descended from the hills to render an extended pursuit impossible although, to the west, some Camerons and McLeans who had fled across the Spey were run to earth the following day near Aviemore.

Officially, the Jacobites lost up to 400 men killed, while Livingstone's losses were limited to a handful of horses, although some sources describe the losses on both sides as heavy. In this connection, it is well to remember that, when cornered, the Highlander was particularly dangerous. During the Jacobite rebellions, many casualties among government troops were sustained in the course of over-zealous pursuits.

Cromdale essentially brought the '89 Jacobite rising in Scotland to a close. Ireland had been the main focus of the rebellion and it was here, on 1 July 1690, that the forces of William III vanquished James II at the Battle of the Boyne.

The battlefield today

Cromdale (with car parking) is off the A95, three miles to the east of Grantown-on-Spey. The Jacobite campsite is about two miles to the east of the village, along a track, The

Haughs (OS Landranger 36 0928). The fording point by the kirk is now a bridge. The current kirk has an exterior memorial plaque to the battle. Lethendry Castle has been reduced to a single ruined tower. The Piper's Stone to the east of Claggernich Wood allegedly marks the spot where a badly wounded piper continued to play until he expired.

Further reading

T. Livingston, *A True and real account of the defeat of General Buchan and Brigadeer Cannon, their High-land Army, at the Battel of Crombdell upon the 1st of May; 1690* (Early English Books Online).

PART SIX:
THE EIGHTEENTH CENTURY

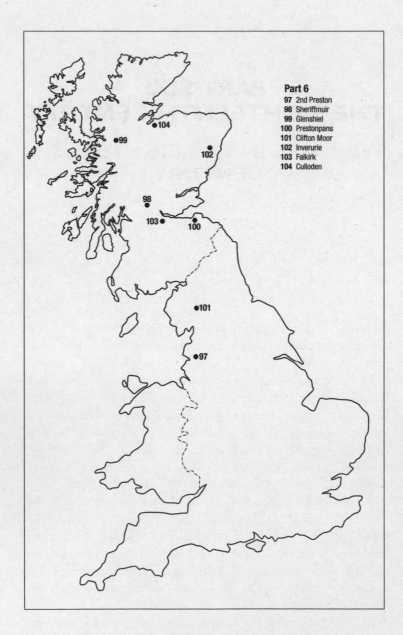

Part 6
97 2nd Preston
98 Sheriffmuir
99 Glenshiel
100 Prestonpans
101 Clifton Moor
102 Inverurie
103 Falkirk
104 Culloden

WARFARE IN THE EIGHTEENTH CENTURY

In terms of developments in warfare, the latter part of the seventeenth century sits more comfortably with the eighteenth century.

Parliament's New Model Army was disbanded in 1660, but the idea of a professional army had caught on. In Restoration England, Charles II reintroduced regiments of professionals – forerunners of the units that fought at Sedgemoor (1685). Towards the end of the seventeenth century, the standing army was about 7,000 strong, but this number increased twentyfold during the War of the Spanish Succession, which gave John Churchill, Duke of Marlborough, his most famous victory, at Blenheim (1704). Once again, Britain was becoming a player to be reckoned with on the battlefields of Continental Europe. In 1743, just three years before Culloden, George II became the last British monarch to lead his troops into battle at Dettingen, during the War of the Austrian Succession.

In some respects, the organization of this new band of

professionals (still supplemented, where required, by foreign mercenaries) was inferior to that of the New Model.
For example, the principle of promotion on merit was
largely replaced by a system whereby commissions were
purchased. But the army was, at last, well armed, trained,
provisioned and operating under iron discipline, as opposed
to the scratch rebel armies of the Jacobite rebellions which,
by rights, should never have stood a chance.

As a direct result of the Act of Union in 1707, the English
and Scottish armies (including existing units such as the Scots
Guards) were merged. The recruitment of Scots, particularly
Highlanders, into this new British Army was disrupted to
some extent by the Jacobite Rebellions, although the first
Highland regiment, the Black Watch, was formed in 1740.

By the time of the '89 Jacobite Rebellion, the pike had
disappeared from the battlefield, and the new-fangled bayonet, which replaced it, contributed to the English defeat at
Killiecrankie (1689). In its earliest incarnation, the bayonet
had to be screwed into the muzzle of a musket, a fiddly process that also meant that muskets could not be fired once
bayonets had been fixed. The defeated English commander at
Killiecrankie, Major-General Hugh Mackay, subsequently
invented a system whereby the bayonet was attached to the
musket barrel via rings, but this, too, was soon replaced by
the socket system.

Unlike the pike, the bayonet was the last line of defence.
At Culloden (1746), the Duke of Cumberland expected his
infantry to have to depend heavily upon their bayonets. As
things turned out, the Jacobite army was largely destroyed
long before it reached the Hanoverian lines. The flintlock
musket ('Brown Bess'), replacing the matchlock, was more
reliable, although powder still had to be kept dry. Long-
range accuracy still left much to be desired, but concentrated
fire delivered at short-range could be devastating.

The Highlanders at Culloden suffered most from the
Hanoverian artillery fire. Standard shot was hard to endure,

but they were also subjected to grapeshot – canvas bags packed with small shot which disintegrated upon firing, spreading their projectiles into the massed enemy ranks.

Cavalry was still used to protect artillery positions and to cover the infantry flanks, but body armour had disappeared from the battlefield, and light swords, still worn by officers, were playing an increasingly ceremonial, as opposed to combative, role. Culloden confirmed that battles could be won at a distance, by superior firepower. This would be demonstrated time and again in the colonial wars of the nineteenth century.

The Jacobite Rebellions

THE '15

97. 2nd Preston, 12/14 November 1715

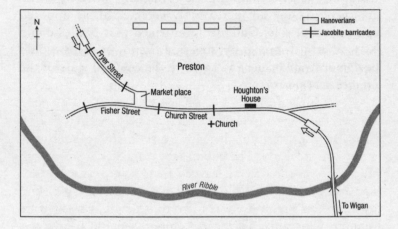

William III died in 1702. He was succeeded by Anne, daughter of James II. When Anne died, in 1714, she was succeeded by George, Elector of Hanover, descended from Elizabeth, daughter of James I. Supporters of James Edward Stuart, son of the exiled James II (who had died in 1701), rose to the occasion, declaring for James Edward in September 1715.

Leading the '15 insurrection was John Erskine, Earl of Mar, Secretary of State for Scotland, who felt he was getting a raw deal from the new administration. Drumming up support among the Highland clans – in particular the Mackintoshes and Clan Chattan – he was able to raise the Jacobite standard on 6 September 1715, at Kirkmichael. The master plan was for Mar to lead the rising in Scotland, while James Edward, with French support, landed in the south-west of England and Thomas Forster, MP for Northumberland, gathered support in the north of England.

On 22 October 1715, at Kelso, Forster met with a party

of Lowlanders, led by Viscount Kenmure and Mackintosh of Borlum who, against his will, had been sent south to join them. The combined force, with the inexperienced Forster as their commander-in-chief, crossed into England on 1 November 1715. The following day, they reached Penrith, having dispersed some local militia and deprived them of some welcome supplies. By 7 November, however, when they reached Lancaster, they had to face up to the fact that the hoped-for inundation of support had not materialized. Two days later, they set out for Liverpool on a march that would take them via Warrington and Preston.

At Preston, which he reached on 11 November, Forster was cheered by the arrival of a party of Catholic gentry and their tenants, even though many of the latter were armed only with pitchforks. His euphoria was tempered somewhat when, later in the day, he learned that the government had sent General Charles Wills, with 2,500 troops, to assault the town. Forster's response was to go to bed, and it was left to Kenmure to organize a defence. Kenmure sent out an advance party towards Wigan and mounted a guard at Ribble Bridge.

On the morning of 12 November, when Wills was advancing on the bridge, Forster ordered the guard that had been placed on it to retire into the town. More men occupying another sound defensive point, Sir Henry Haughton's house between the bridge and the town, were also withdrawn. Wills couldn't understand it. When he arrived at the bridge to find it unguarded, he thought that the defenders must be waiting in ambush along the high banks bordering the road running the half-mile or so between bridge and town.

In fact, Forster, with around 1,700 men, was holed up in the town centre, several barricades having been thrown up across the main streets. One barricade was at the eastern end of Church Street. In support – for this barricade would surely bear the brunt of any attack – was a force stationed in St John's churchyard. To the east, Fisher Street was blocked by a barricade, and another to the north-west defended Fryer Street.

Accounts of the subsequent action are confused, but it seems that, as expected, the government troops launched their first assault on the Church Street barricade. Some 200 men under the command of Brigadier-General Philip Honeywood attacked the barricade head-on. They were met with heavy fire both from the barricade and from adjacent houses that the Jacobites had occupied. Despite suffering heavy losses, Honeywood, who was himself wounded, persisted and eventually two houses were commandeered, although, in the absence of artillery support, no real progress could be made. Brigadier-General James Dormer led an assault on the Fryer Street barricade, though with little success, and eventually he had to withdraw. Several houses were set alight in this quarter, but fortunately the flames did not spread into the central area. Nightfall brought an end to the fighting, although snipers on both sides were busy throughout the hours of darkness.

The following morning, after another assault on Church Street, Lieutenant-General George Carpenter arrived to reinforce Wills, who now had sufficient men to seal off the town and prepare a major assault. When faced with the prospect, Forster lost his nerve. During the afternoon, without reference to anyone else, he sent a messenger to Wills to request terms for surrender. Wills merely ordered the defenders to lay down their arms. Heated discussions among the various Jacobite factions went on all day. It was not until 7.00 a.m. on the morrow that the surrender took place. The officers and noblemen, 75 English and 143 Scots, were lodged, under guard, in Preston's inns. The rank and file, 1,000 Scots and 400 English, were bundled into the church.

Government casualties had been heavy, with up to 300 killed and wounded. Forty or so of the defenders had been killed or wounded. Later, a further 34 (including Kenmure) were executed and over 500 transported to the colonies. The architect of the tragic farce, Thomas Forster, escaped to France to live out the remainder of his life.

The battlefield today

The action took place in the centre of Preston (OS Landranger 102 5429). Like many another city, Preston has suffered from the construction of an inner ring road, but the old street pattern can still be discerned: notably Church Street, Market Place (Market Square), Fisher Street (Fishergate) and Fryer Street (Friargate). St John's Church has been rebuilt, but the Harris Museum in Market Square houses some relics of the battle. Use the city centre car parks.

Further reading

Daniel Szechi, *1715: The Great Jacobite Rebellion* (Yale, 2006).

98. Sheriffmuir, 13 November 1715

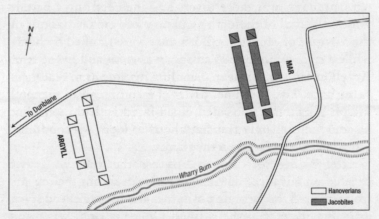

The Earl of Mar, instigator of the Jacobite Rebellion of 1715, arrived in Perth at the end of September 1715 and remained there while a steady stream of recruits increased his army to around 10,000 men. The government forces in Scotland were headed by John Campbell, 2nd Earl of Argyll, an experienced commander whose 3,000 troops, stationed at Stirling Castle, were outnumbered by more than two to one.

Eventually, Mar decided to move south to invade the lowlands. He left Perth on the morning of 10 November, spending the evening at Auchterarder. On 12 November, he moved on to Braco, about five miles from Dunblane, which General Alexander Gordon was sent forward to occupy, with a view to gaining Argyll's attention while Mar crossed the River Forth. Gordon did not reach Dunblane, for he discovered that Argyll, not content to sit and wait in Stirling, had beaten him to it and was camped two miles to the east of the town at Kippenross. Mar brought up the rest of his men to Kinbuck. Thus, the two armies spent the night of 12 November divided by the uneven ground of Sheriffmuir.

At daybreak on the morning of 13 November, the Jacobites deployed before Sheriffmuir, facing west. Their first line, consisting of ten battalions of Highlanders, was led by Alexander Gordon. The second line, also comprising ten battalions, was more divers and included three battalions of the Earl of Seaforth's infantry and two battalions of the Marquis of Huntley's. Both lines were flanked by horse while a reserve, about 800 strong, was stationed to the rear. Argyll, meanwhile, was marshalling his troops in readiness to advance. His first line, under the command of General Joseph Wightman, consisted of six infantry battalions, but he could muster only two battalions to form a second line. Dragoons were placed on the flanks.

After riding forward to observe the enemy, Argyll ordered an advance, but it was early afternoon before his troops neared the Jacobite position and he experienced some difficulty in reforming his lines. Only his right wing was properly formed when he came under attack. Furthermore, he observed that the Jacobite right wing stretched well beyond his own left wing. Following an initial exchange of musket fire and determined to take advantage both of the overlap and the Hanoverians' disorganization, Mar attacked. Argyll followed suit, ordering an advance on Mar's left wing.

For over two hours, the advantage moved back and forth, with ground being lost and then won back through charge and counter-charge. Finally, on the enemy right wing,

Argyll managed to push back the rebels, who retreated over the River Allan. On Argyll's left wing, however, his own troops were suffering a defeat similar to that which he had inflicted on the rebel left. Here, the Hanoverians, struggling to deploy, were broken by a Highland charge. In their retreat, they carried with them the supporting dragoons. Mar was quick to follow in a pursuit that lasted for half an hour. When he received news of the defeat of his own left wing, he came back to the battlefield and regrouped. Argyll, who had also returned, fully expected the Highlanders to move in for the kill. Instead, Mar merely watched as Argyll gradually retreated into Dunblane. The next day, after passing an anxious night, Argyll discovered that the Jacobites had gone, leaving him in possession of the battlefield.

Hanoverian casualties were something over 200, killed, wounded or captured, while Jacobite casualties were probably three times this number. Although the encounter might best be described as a draw, a contest drawn, as far as Mar was concerned, was as good as a battle lost, for he needed nothing less than a decisive victory to maintain the impetus of the rebellion.

While matters were drawing to a premature and unspectacular close, James Edward was attempting to organize a passage to Scotland. The Duke of Orleans, Regent of France during the minority of Louis XV, was unsympathetic, and so it was without the men and materials he needed that James arrived at Peterhead on 22 December, far too late to accomplish anything. A few weeks later, accompanied by the Earl of Mar, he went back into exile.

The battlefield today

The battlefield of Sheriffmuir is well off the beaten track, on the minor road that runs between the A9 near Blackford and Glen Road, Dunblane (OS Landranger 57 8202). The Gathering Stone (57 811022), protected by an iron grille, marks the spot from which Argyll allegedly studied the

Jacobite deployment. There is a roadside monument to the Macrae Clan (57 816019) and a more recent monument erected by the 1745 Association. Dunblane Museum has a little information about the battle. There is a public car park in Springfield Terrace, Dunblane, or (preferably) there is a little off-road parking by the Macrae Monument. The Sheriffmuir Inn (57 827021) is also well worth a visit.

Further reading
Daniel Szechi, *1715: The Great Jacobite Rebellion* **(Yale, 2006).**

THE '19

99. Glenshiel, 10 June 1719

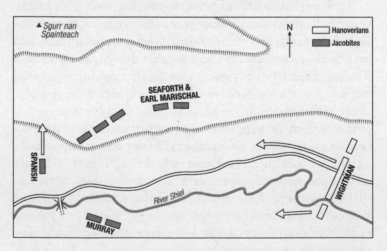

By 1719, Britain was at peace with France but at war with Spain, and the Spanish, albeit temporarily, became eager sponsors of the Jacobite cause, and instigators of another attempt to place James Edward Stuart on the English throne. On 7 March 1719, an invasion force of 27 Spanish ships carrying the Duke of Ormonde and 5,000 troops set sail for England. Like the famous Armada, two centuries before, the fleet was scattered by a storm; only two frigates, bound for Scotland, with 300 Spanish troops and a small group of Jacobites led by the Marquis of Tullibardine and George Keith, Earl Marischal, managed to land. This modest force sailed around the west coast of Scotland, entering Loch Alsh and establishing itself in Eilean Donan Castle to await the arrival of the Highland clans which, it was hoped, would flock to the banner.

The enterprise had got off to a bad start and the situation deteriorated even further. On 10 May, while the main body of troops were away recruiting, British warships attacked the castle, reducing it to rubble and capturing the Spanish garrison together with the expedition's ammunition and supplies. The Jacobites, now without a base, were able to muster only about 1,000 men. Some clansmen had arrived in answer to the call: MacGregors (led by the famous 'Rob Roy' MacGregor); Mackinnons; Camerons; Murrays (led by Lord George Murray); and Mackenzies (joining William Mackenzie, Earl of Seaforth, who had returned from exile), but it was not enough.

On 5 June, Major-General Joseph Wightman was despatched from Inverness to deal with the rising. Arguably, his force was light, comprising 850 foot and 120 dragoons, although he did have four mortars. It took him five days to reach the position chosen by the Jacobites for their defence – the narrow pass of Glenshiel, some twelve miles due east of Eilean Donan Castle.

The rebel army occupied a sound position, but it lacked the numbers to form a strong defensive line. On the extreme right, on a hill to the south of the road, were the Murrays. To their rear, on another hill on the north bank of the river, was the Spanish contingent. Then, beyond a ravine, the rest of the force was arrayed, with Seaforth and Earl Marischal on the far left. The road, between the Spaniards and Lord George Murray, had been barricaded and earthworks thrown up as an additional line of defence.

During the late afternoon of 10 June, Wightman deployed his men on both sides of the river, well to the west of the rebel positions. The right wing on the north bank included loyal clansmen: those of Sutherland, Ross, Fraser and MacKay. The south bank included men of Clan Munro, while the dragoons and the mortars occupied the road.

Instead of attacking along the line, as the Jacobites expected, Wightman first assaulted the rebel right wing to dislodge Lord George Murray. After subjecting him to mortar fire, he ordered Munro's and an accompanying English regiment on to the offensive, forcing Murray to retreat. Next, he turned his attention to the rebel left. Although Seaforth was well entrenched, he was soon under pressure from an advance by Wightman's grenadiers. Eventually outflanked, and with Seaforth wounded, the MacKenzies also retreated. The rebel response was to weaken their centre-left by sending men over to bolster Seaforth's crumbling position. Wightman now ordered a general advance. Throughout, the Spaniards had been pinned down by the mortars. As they, too, now came under attack, they had to join what was developing into a general retreat up the mountainside.

By 9.00 p.m., the battle was at an end. Estimates of Jacobite casualties range from as few as 10 to as many as 100 killed and wounded. Wightman's casualties were high: 21 killed and 121 wounded – 15 per cent of his total force. While the surviving highlanders drifted away to their homes, the Spaniards were left with no alternative but to surrender.

The defeat at Glenshiel signalled the end of James Edward Stuart's aspirations. The next time the Highland clans came out, it would be for his son, Charles Edward, the 'Young Pretender'.

The battlefield today

The battlefield is on the A87 twenty-eight miles to the west of Invergarry (OS Landranger 33 9913). Among the most isolated of battlefields, the location is well marked and a

path from a lay-by leads to a stone wall bearing explana-
tory panels about the battle. Sgurr nan Spainteach, the 'Peak
of the Spaniards' (OS Landranger 33 9914) was named after
the Jacobites' allies. Eilean Donan Castle (OS Landranger 33
8825) is open to the public.

Further reading
John Sadler, *Scottish Battles* **(Birlinn Ltd, 2010).**

THE '45

100. Prestonpans, 21 September 1745

The year 1745 brought new hope for those who wished to
see a return to the Stuart dynasty. There was a new claimant,
Charles Edward Stuart, the 'Young Pretender'; there was a
new English king, George II, and there was a new genera-
tion of Scots to be fired with enthusiasm for what had long
been a lost cause.

In other respects, it was business as usual, for Britain was at war with France and it suited the French to renew the 'auld alliance'. Unfortunately, a strongly supported expedition mounted the previous year had come to grief in storms and, thereafter, Louis XV limited himself to providing largely moral backing. Therefore, when Charles Edward landed on Eriskay on 23 July 1645, it was with one ship, a handful of companions and little in the way of either arms or cash.

Surprisingly, several clans came out in support. The Jacobite position was helped by the fact that only 3,000 government troops, commanded by Major-General Sir John Cope, were stationed in Scotland. Charles marched south, recruiting along the way. On 17 September, he entered Edinburgh. He had appointed as Lieutenant-Generals of his army James Drummond, Duke of Perth, and Lord George Murray, who had been pardoned for his role in the '19.

Cope had marched into the Highlands in an attempt to nip the rising in the bud – much as Wightman had done in the '19 – but, unlike Wightman, he failed to take the initiative. He was reduced to catching up with his quarry by taking his army by sea from Aberdeen to Dunbar. As he marched eastwards from Dunbar, the Jacobites left Edinburgh to meet him. After some jockeying for position, Cope deployed at Prestonpans, his right flank protected by the walls of two estates, Preston House and Bankton House, his front by a ditch and marshland. The Jacobites deployed to the south, on high ground beyond Tranent. Cope's army now numbered about 2,300, that of the Jacobites about 2,500.

During the night of 20/21 September, with the aid of a local sympathizer, the Jacobite army managed to cross the marshland to take up a position to the west of Seton. Towards daybreak on 21 September, Cope realized what was happening and wheeled his army about to face due east. Two squadrons of dragoons occupied the right flank – Whitney's regiment to the fore and Gardiner's regiment to the rear – with two squadrons of Hamilton's dragoons on the left. The infantry comprised companies from the regiments of Murray, Lascelles, Guise and Lee. Artillery was also squeezed in on the right.

On the right of the Jacobite front line were Clanranald's MacDonalds, with Glengarry MacDonalds, Keppock MacDonalds, men of the Duke of Perth, Stewarts of Appin and Lochiel's Camerons. A rear line comprised, from right to left, men of Atholl, Robertsons, Maclachlans and MacDonalds of Glencoe.

At dawn, the Jacobites attacked across what was a recently harvested cornfield. The Camerons, facing Cope's guns and mortars, should have had the hardest time of it, but the gun crews were inexperienced and their fire had little effect. Whitney advanced to halt the Camerons before they reached the artillery. A burst of Jacobite musket fire wounded Whitney and killed several of his men, and the squadron wheeled about, riding over their own artillerymen, who immediately abandoned their posts. Gardiner's dragoons now advanced, but went the same way as Whitney's, Colonel Gardiner suffering a gunshot wound.

On the Jacobite right, the MacDonalds created similar panic in the Hanoverian ranks. Their advance, while menacing, was at once uniform and orderly, and it was this precision as much as anything that succeeded in overawing their opponents. When Hamilton's dragoons turned tail, the foot was left to bear the brunt of the onslaught. Many of the Camerons had quitted the field in pursuit of Gardiner's dragoons but some, again displaying exemplary discipline, turned in on the Hanoverian infantry. Riding up and down the line, Cope did his best to rally his men, but the sword-wielding clansmen, now advancing en masse, struck such terror into their hearts that they fled regardless.

Cope's strong defensive position had turned into a death trap, with his men, infantry and dragoons alike, being slaughtered as they fell back to the walls of Preston House and Bankton House – the latter being Colonel Gardiner's home. Gardiner, who had already been shot, was cut down by an axe as he tried to rally the troops, most of whom now thought only of surrender.

Within a quarter of an hour, the Hanoverian army had been all but destroyed. In addition to the loss of their baggage train, over 200 men were dead, 400 wounded and 1,400 captured. The Jacobites lost between 20 and 30 dead and about 70 wounded. Lord George Murray ensured that the wounded of both sides received medical attention while Cope, with 450 survivors, fell back on Berwick, allegedly becoming the first general in history to arrive before news of his own defeat. On 22 September, Charles made a triumphant return to Edinburgh, where he squandered the advantage gained at Prestonpans by spending the next six weeks in a hectic round of social engagements.

The battlefield today
The battlefield of Prestonpans is on the A198, eleven miles to the east of Edinburgh (OS Landranger 66 4074). It is a battle that has caught the local popular imagination and, at the time of writing (2014), a visitor centre is planned. In 2010, a 'Prestonpans Tapestry' was completed – see the Prestonpans Tapestry website for current location. There is a viewing point with interpretation panels, and a memorial cairn nearby. A monument to Colonel James Gardiner is to be found to the rear of Bankton House, along the path skirting the railway line, off Johnnie Cope's Road, the route along which the Hanoverian survivors retreated. Car parking is available at the railway station. Despite the existence of battlefield plans, drawn by actual participants, it has been suggested that the action took place a third of a mile east of the accepted location.

Further reading
Martin Margulies, *The Battle of Prestonpans 1745* (NPI Media Group, 2007).

101. Clifton Moor, 18 December 1745

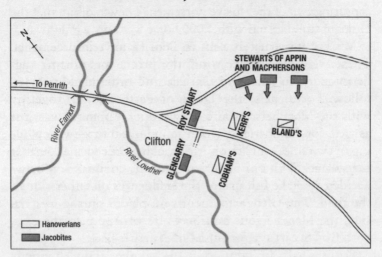

The heady days of the Jacobite victory at Prestonpans (1745) were short-lived. A march into England, as far south as Derby, quickly turned sour as the English demonstrated little enthusiasm for the cause. Charles Edward Stuart, the 'Young Pretender', reluctantly turned back towards Scotland. Laying the blame squarely on his senior officers, he became increasingly fractious. With a Hanoverian army in pursuit, Lord George Murray wanted to speed up the retreat by lightening the baggage train, but the prince would not hear of it. Hence, on the morning of 18 September 1745, Charles had reached Penrith while Murray was still struggling with heavy wagons three miles in the rear, having already been harassed by enemy horsemen.

At about noon, a body of horse, who were taken to be local militia, appeared in front of Murray on high ground near Clifton Hall. The front of the column came to a halt and, without waiting for orders, men of Roy Stuart's regiment charged up the hill. Murray sent forward men of the Glengarry regiment in support. The Scots reached the top of the hill just in time to find the militia retreating. The baggage train moved on and, at Clifton, Murray sent it forward while he scoured the area, capturing two of the elusive horsemen. They told him that the Duke of Cumberland with 4,000 horse was only a mile away.

Murray immediately sent to Penrith for reinforcements. These were not forthcoming, the prince announcing that he intended to march to Carlisle and ordering Murray to follow. Fortunately, the Duke of Perth arrived, together with the MacPhersons and Stewarts of Appin. It was just as well, for Cumberland's men soon hove into view, deploying in two lines on Clifton Moor, half a mile to the south of the village. With only 1,000 men at his command, Murray decided to make full use of the enclosures on either side of the road. The Glengarry men were placed on the western side, the MacPhersons and Stewarts of Appin to the east, with Roy Stuart's regiment a little further back.

Within half an hour, 500 of Cumberland's dragoons – detachments of Bland's, Cobham's and Kerr's – had dismounted and were advancing on foot. By now, it was dark and they too were able to use the enclosures for cover. Murray decided that the best form of defence would be to attack. This required careful management, for he was only too aware of the difficulties of coordinating action between the disparate clans. He explained to the Glengarrys that they should attack when they saw the MacPhersons, whom he would be leading, rise up.

When Murray gave the signal, all his men attacked at the same time, according to plan. Bland's regiment occupied a strong position behind a hedge and ditch and, as the MacPhersons came on, their lines were raked by what Cluny McPherson later described as 'a most warm fire'. After discharging their own muskets, the MacPhersons threw them down and came on with drawn swords. Hacking their way through the hedge, they put the dragoons to flight, the ditch 'all filled up with their dead bodies'. On the other side of the road, the Glengarrys kept up a withering fire on Cobham's and Kerr's regiments until they too retreated.

Casualties were probably comparatively light on both sides, despite Cluny MacPherson's claims that 150 government troops were killed and a great many wounded. The battle must be counted as a Jacobite victory, for it enabled them to proceed, unhindered, on their way to Scotland.

The battlefield today

Clifton is on the A6, three miles to the south of Penrith (OS Landranger 90 5327). The village sign proclaims the battle to have been the last fought on English soil – and why not, for it has as good a claim as any to the title. A wall enclosing the Kelter Well (one of Cumbria's holy wells), on the main road opposite the aptly named Cumberland Close, acts as a memorial to the battle. There is also a small stone monument and a new plaque, by The Rebel Tree (beneath which Jacobite dead are allegedly buried) at the southern end of the village, at the bottom of Town End Croft. The churchyard of St Cuthbert's has a stone memorial to the men of Bland's Regiment who were killed in the battle. If patronizing the George and Dragon, use the car park. A tower, in the care of English Heritage, near the church is all that remains of Clifton Hall which (in company with most other dwellings) was ransacked by the Jacobites.

Further reading

Christopher Duffy, *The '45: Bonnie Prince Charlie and the Untold Story of the Jacobite Rising* (**Weidenfeld & Nicolson, 2003**).

MARCHING ORDERS

Throughout the centuries, all armies on active service seem to have spent much of their time marching. Clothes and shoes quickly wore out, and battlefield corpses were often stripped naked for this reason. One of Prince Rupert's most valuable prizes during the Civil Wars was 4,000 pairs of shoes, taken at York in 1644.

The poor condition of the roads drastically curtailed the life of a pair of shoes. The road network itself often dictated where a battle might be fought. Many battles were fought in proximity to the major Roman roads such as Watling Street, Ermine Street, Iknield Street and Fosse Way. These were often the only roads capable of taking columns of men, artillery trains and (where they existed) supply wagons. In the Highlands of Scotland, it was almost impossible to move armies around at all. From the 1720s, in the wake of the early Jacobite rebellions, General Wade and, later, General Caulfield constructed between them over 1,000 miles of Highland military roads. (Ironically, during the '45 Rebellion, Wade was unable to challenge the rebels on their march south owing to the poor condition of the roads in England.)

During the course of a long march, there was never enough shelter. Even a well-organized army, such as that commanded by Cromwell in the Dunbar campaign of 1650, lacked tents. Sir Thomas Fairfax spent his declining years crippled with rheumatoid arthritis and confined to a wheel-chair, a circumstance he put down to years of camping out during the Civil Wars. Wherever possible, troops on the move commandeered the homes of unfortunate civilians. Needless to say, such enforced hospitality was often abused. It was often better for civilians to cut their losses by extending the hand of friendship. So, when the Jacobite army of '45 reached Derby, the officers were given billets in the houses of the gentry, while the Highlander rank and file were offered bread, cheese and beer and were accommodated in outhouses. The '45 army had to march in two divisions, separated by half a day's march, because otherwise there would have been insufficient accommodation for everyone along the way. Whenever an army on the march did camp for the night, there would sometimes be fierce competition for the best billet. The Battle of Edgcote (1469) was lost because the joint Yorkist commanders fell out over who was entitled to first choice of lodgings.

An army's movements were usually (although not exclusively) limited to the campaigning season, or the summer months, very few battles being fought during the winter. Grass had to be available to feed the horses that accompanied all armies, while the armies themselves would often supplement supply train provisions by foraging. The subsequent loss of livestock and crops could be catastrophic for the civilian population. On the march near Swindon in 1643, for example, the Earl of Essex took 1,000 sheep and 60 head of cattle 'from malignants and papists' for the maintenance of his army.

Essex's army was rarely well supplied. It should have been, because Parliament was able to raise taxes, whereas the king's expenses had to be met through the generosity of Royalist gentry. To their credit, they rose to the occasion. When the Duke of Newcastle, once one of the wealthiest men in the kingdom, went into exile after Marston Moor (1644), he had just £90 left in his pocket.

102. Inverurie, 23 December 1745

Following its abortive invasion of England, Bonnie Prince Charlie's Jacobite army marched back on to Scottish soil on 20 December 1745. New hope began to replace disappointment as provisions were requisitioned and new recruits – loath to fight in England, but happy to take up arms at home – arrived.

Charged with the responsibility of recruiting in Aberdeenshire during the prince's English adventure was Lord Lewis Gordon. Some 800 men had been forced into service and money had been demanded of Aberdeen's citizens. In response to requests for aid from the hard-pressed Aberdonians, the loyalist John Campbell, Earl of Loudoun,

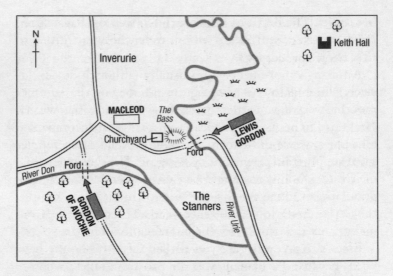

despatched MacLeod of MacLeod and 400 clansmen from Inverurie. On the same day that Charles arrived back in Scotland, MacLeod reached Inverurie, about twelve miles from Aberdeen, where he was joined by a mixed force of Munros, led by George Munro of Culcairn, Mackenzies and Grants.

Lewis Gordon had retreated into Aberdeen, where his strength had mushroomed. In particular, he had acquired 300 Farquharsons and 150 piquets from Irish regiments in the French service, in company with Lord John Dummond, recently arrived by sea. Gordon also learned that, far from being concentrated at Inverurie, the loyalist forces lay scattered throughout the locality. For their part, MacLeod and Munro made no attempt to obtain intelligence about Gordon's intentions; they simply presumed that he would be going south to join the main Jacobite army. In fact, Gordon had other plans.

At 9.00 a.m. on 23 December, 900 men, divided into two columns, marched out of Aberdeen – not to the south, but to the north-west, in the direction of Inverurie. Eventually, one column, led by Gordon of Avochie, swung to the west to approach Inverurie via the south bank of the River Don. The other, led by Lewis Gordon, continued on the main road before proceeding via Keith Hall to a ford on the River Urie.

MacLeod had no idea what was afoot. During the afternoon, he became aware of activity in the grounds of Keith Hall, but he made no attempt to investigate or to take the sensible precaution of securing the ford over the Urie. At 4.00 p.m., Lewis Gordon's column was free to come streaming down the hill towards the river, creating panic in the town, where 300 of the loyalists were billeted.

To their credit, the MacLeods reacted quickly, firing upon the Jacobites as they forded the Urie although, positioned on the eastern edge of the town, they were too far away to do much damage. Had they taken possession of 'The Bass' – an area consisting of two mounds, the remains of a motte and bailey castle – and an adjacent churchyard, they might have checked the advance. Instead, a forward party of Lewis Gordon's men was able to occupy both vantage points.

Arriving on the banks of the Don, the second Jacobite column also sent forth a detachment, forcing the Macleods to defend on two fronts. Their attempts at resistance appear to have been limited to a series of sallies which failed to stem the assault. Faced with the advance of both columns, they began to fall back through the town. The action was not prolonged, owing largely to the shortness of the day. With 'night coming on apace', it was remarked, neither side 'could see to level their pieces' and the MacLeods abandoned the fight, retreating northwards out of Inverurie and on to the River Spey. Estimates of the casualties sustained by the armies vary, but may not have amounted to many more than a dozen killed on each side.

This minor battle is now almost forgotten, lost in the greater scheme of things, but the Jacobite victory left them in control of Aberdeen, enabling them to continue their fundraising efforts for the cause.

The battlefield today

Inverurie is situated on the A96, twelve miles to the north-west of Aberdeen. The battlefield is off the B993 at the junction of Inverurie and Port Elphinstone (OS Landranger 38 7820). The fording points of the Urie and Don are now road bridges. The Bass and the churchyard remain and, a little upstream from the latter, there is a battlefield memorial cairn and an interpretation panel. Use the public car parks in Inverurie.

Further reading

Peter Marren, *Grampian Battlefields* (Mercat Press, 1993).

103. 2nd Falkirk, 17 January 1746

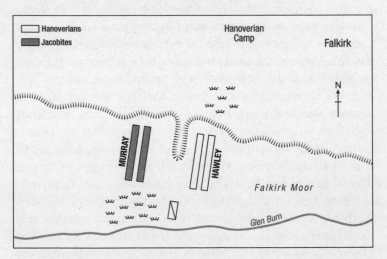

When the army of the 'Young Pretender' returned to Scotland following its doomed foray into England, it was thought possible that Prince Charles would make for Edinburgh. With this in mind, Lieutenant-General Henry Hawley led a Hanoverian army north from Newcastle, arriving in Edinburgh on 6 January 1746. Meanwhile, the Jacobites had laid siege to Stirling Castle. Prince Charles was staying at

Bannockburn House, while Lord George Murray and part of the army was stationed nine miles away, at Falkirk.

Both sides were keen to fight. Hawley, making slow progress, decided to march on to Stirling. On the evening of 16 January, Hawley's army was camped to the west of Falkirk, Hawley himself lodging at Callendar House, home of the Jacobite, Lord Kilmarnock. His opinion of the Highlanders was such that he did not believe they would take the initiative. He was wrong, for the prince's army had been hurriedly assembled and, on Murray's advice, would move towards Falkirk Moor, a ridge of high ground to the south-west of the town.

At about 2.00 p.m. on the afternoon of 17 January, with the Jacobite army clearly in view, Hawley was forced to acknowledge his error and ordered his men to break camp. His dragoons were sent on ahead of the infantry to beat the enemy to the high ground. The Hanoverian artillery got stuck in mud and could not be moved up the hill – an 'offence' for which the officer in charge, Captain Cunningham, was later cashiered. (The Jacobite guns were also labouring far in the rear, so that neither side would have the benefit of artillery.)

Both sides reached the moor at about the same time, deploying in the midst of torrential rain. With a ravine to the north and marshland to the south, outflanking actions by either side looked improbable. The Jacobite army, 8,000 strong, was organized in two lines with a reserve of horse in the rear. Hawley also drew up his men in two lines. The most vulnerable regiments, the Argyll Militia and the Glasgow Volunteers, which had helped swell Hawley's numbers to 8,000, were placed in relatively sheltered positions, the former in front of the ravine, the latter on the left wing, behind six squadrons of dragoons.

At about 4.00 p.m., before the Jacobite regiments of foot had quite finished deploying, Hawley ordered his dragoons to attack. Convinced that the Highlanders could not withstand the charge of three regiments of mounted men, he was determined to prove it. Lord George Murray, commanding on the Jacobite right, led out his own men to meet the dragoons, who were moving slowly forward. He waited until they were almost upon him before giving the order to fire. The resulting volley instantly broke all three regiments. Those who remained in their saddles fled, trampling their own infantry underfoot. One small party, retaining some measure of discipline, pressed forward only to have their horses cut out from under them.

Murray was struggling to keep the Highlanders in some sort of order, for the MacDonalds broke ranks to charge the Hanoverian left wing. The Hanoverian regiments in the centre and to the right countered, but were met with stern resistance. The entire Jacobite front line, supported by part of their second line, now moved on to the attack and Hawley's infantry gave way much as the dragoons had done a few moments before.

The fighting now became more confused. The Highlanders had cast their muskets aside and, as was their custom, fell to with their swords. Only three Hanoverian infantry regiments on the extreme right, and to some extent standing apart from the main action, held firm. Undoubtedly, they staved off complete disaster, for they were even able to direct fire at the flanks of the Highlanders pursuing their fleeing comrades. Thus, much of the Hanoverian army – carrying Hawley along in its wake – was able to retire into Falkirk.

The Highlanders, it seems, failed to follow up their advantage through sheer amazement, unable to believe that the enemy had crumbled so easily. Surely, the retreat must be a feint, designed to lure them into a trap? Murray tried to persuade them otherwise, fearing that Hawley would take the opportunity to regroup. He need not have worried, for when he entered Falkirk, he found that all the government troops had fled, abandoning precious stores of equipment and supplies.

Jacobite casualties in the battle were 32 dead and 120 wounded. Government losses were given as 280 killed, wounded or missing. (The Highlanders stripped the dead so completely that the bodies were described from a distance as looking like a flock of white sheep at rest on the hill.) Like Cope after Prestonpans (1745), Hawley blamed the 'scandalous cowardice' of his infantry for his defeat. He had dozens of his men either hanged or shot. The Jacobite high command also expressed concern over the poor discipline of its own men and, to the prince's disgust, the clan chieftains insisted on retreating to the Highlands with a view to regrouping in the spring.

The battlefield today

The battlefield is to the south of Falkirk, off the B803 (OS Landranger 65 8778). Car parking is available in Bantaskine Estate public park. A battlefield monument is also to be found on the corner of Greenbank Road, not too far from the Estate entrance (868789). Stained glass windows depicting Prince Charles Edward Stuart, Lord George Murray and Lord John Drummond, once belonging to the long-demolished Bantaskine House, are preserved in Falkirk's Howgate Shopping Centre. The grave of Sir Robert Munro, killed in the battle, can be seen in Falkirk's Old & St Modan's Church. Callendar House (8979) is open to the public.

Further reading

Geoffrey B. Bailey, *Falkirk or Paradise! The Battle of Falkirk 1746* **(John Donald, 1997).**

104. Culloden, 16 April 1746

After his defeat at Falkirk, the Hanoverian general, Henry Hawley, was replaced by the Duke of Cumberland, although the Duke allowed him to lead the horse in the Culloden campaign. Wisely, the new commander-in-chief ignored

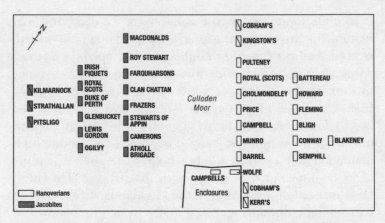

critics who argued that he should move swiftly and spent several weeks organizing the most formidable army ever to be assembled against the Jacobites.

The Jacobites themselves were moving ever further north. At the beginning of April 1646, their army was dispersed around Inverness. Prince Charles Edward, having established himself at Culloden House, was usually to be seen amusing himself in the town. When it was learned that the Hanoverians were on the move, frantic attempts were made to muster all available Jacobite forces, and the night of 14 April saw the bulk of Charles's army camped on Culloden Moor. Lord George Murray, the prince's commander-in-chief, did not relish the prospect of being brought to battle on this rough tract of open ground, far more suited to artillery than the Highland charge, but Charles was persuaded otherwise, in particular by his toadying quartermaster, John William O'Sullivan.

The following day, it was proposed to launch a night attack on the Hanoverians who, by that time, had reached Nairn, just ten miles away. The plan ended disastrously for, after marching all night, the Jacobites had to turn back at daybreak when slow progress left them still two miles short of their objective. They arrived back at Culloden exhausted and just in time to deploy on the moor to receive Cumberland, who had now taken to the road.

The Jacobites, 5,000 men representing 26 clans, formed their battle lines. The MacDonalds glumly made their way to the left of the front line while, to their chagrin, Murray's Atholl Brigade took pride of place on the right. A second line was flanked by Clan Ogilvie on the right and Brigadier Walter Stapleton's Irish piquets on the left. A third line, consisting mainly of light cavalry, remained in the rear, ready to commence mopping-up operations when the Hanoverian lines collapsed – as they surely would do.

Deploying on the moor with speed and precision, Cumberland's immaculately drilled troops, 8,000 in number, looked most unlikely to break. The front line comprised six regiments of foot, flanked by cavalry and dragoons. A second line also consisted on six infantry regiments, with three regiments in reserve.

It is said that the first shot of the last battle to be fought on British soil came at about 1.00 p.m. from a Jacobite gun, and that it narrowly missed the Duke of Cumberland. If true, then the shot must have been a lucky one, for the Jacobite artillery, consisting of twelve pieces positioned in the centre and on the flanks, was operated by inexperienced men. Cumberland's artillery, under the command of Brevet-Colonel William Belford, comprised ten three-pounders, spread in pairs along the front line, with six mortars in two batteries of three to the rear. When Belford returned fire, the effect upon the tightly packed Jacobite ranks was devastating. Such was the accuracy that Prince Charles was forced to move out of harm's way, to the rear of the right flank.

For at least a quarter of an hour, the Jacobites remained immobile, moving only to close the gaps punched in their ranks by Belford's guns. Perhaps Charles was waiting for the Hanoverians to attack. If so, then he waited in vain, for Cumberland was quite satisfied to see the enemy being cut to pieces at a distance. Under pressure from Lord George Murray, Charles finally gave the order to advance.

In preparation for the dreaded Highland charge,

Cumberland added a reserve regiment to each of his lines. The extreme left of the battlefield was bordered by a wall, part stone and part turf, and one regiment (Wolfe's) was removed from the second line to take up position in front of the wall, at right angles, so as to catch the advancing Highlanders in a crossfire.

When it came, the belated Highlander assault was not quite the fearsome spectacle as of old. The centre led off, with the Atholl Brigade on the right following up. The uneven course of the wall forced the latter to their left while the Jacobite centre, for some reason, veered to the right. As the converging clansmen neared the Hanoverian lines, Belford's guns were being loaded with grapeshot – a lethal cocktail of lead ball, nails and jagged metal – to bring about greater carnage, heightened even further by concentrated musket fire.

Despite sustaining heavy losses, the assailants finally made contact with the Hanoverian front line, Barrell's and Munro's on the extreme Hanoverian left bearing the brunt of the onslaught. Barrell's were forced back on to Semphills in their rear, but Semphill's stood firm. Those Highlanders who had fought their way through found themselves surrounded, with Barrell's and Munro's regrouping to their rear while Wolfe's regiment kept up a continuous fire.

Had the Jacobite charge been coordinated and launched immediately, Cumberland might have had his work cut out to contain it, but his artillery tore the heart out of the attack. Most of the clans never came to grips with the enemy, taking flight following the fearful damage created by the Hanoverian artillery. On the far left, the MacDonalds were left stranded. In an attempt to draw the infantry facing them out into the open by taunting them, MacDonald of Keppoch led a series of swift dashes halfway down the field, which succeeded only in drawing more deadly fire. Finally, when they were passed by the clans of the centre and right, in full retreat, the MacDonalds turned and ran. It was left largely to Keppoch, his brother, Donald, and a handful of officers to salvage a little honour by running on to their deaths.

With most of the Highlanders in flight, Hawley was able to unleash his horse, the loyalist Campbells having made a gap in the wall to facilitate their movement on the right. Murray tried to organize some resistance, but was unable to do more than bring some semblance of order to the retreat, which was covered, in part, by Stapleton's Irish piquets who were among the last to leave the field. Prince Charles was reluctantly led away to achieve what would prove to be a remarkable escape into a lifetime of exile.

The battle, which lasted less than one hour, was over, enabling Cumberland to initiate a systematic programme of bloody revenge, earning himself the additional title of 'The Butcher'. Jacobite casualties were in the region of 1,500 dead and wounded. Many of the latter were despatched by the victors as they scoured the battlefield for survivors. Hanoverian dead were stated to be around 50 in number, although the true figure is probably nearer 300.

The era of the Jacobite rebellions was over. To make doubly sure, the government put in place a series of harsh short- and long-term measures. One hundred and twenty prisoners were executed and 936 were transported to the colonies. All Highlanders were compelled to surrender their weapons, the wearing of tartan was forbidden and the power of the clan chieftains was severely curtailed.

The battlefield today

The battlefield is on the B9006 (off the A9), five miles to the south-east of Inverness (OS Landranger 27 7445). There are several memorials scattered about, in particular the main memorial cairn and the Cumberland Stone, allegedly the spot from which the Duke of Cumberland watched the battle. In addition, there are two buildings of interest: King's Stables Cottage, where dragoons were picketed after the battle, and Old Leanach Cottage, which served as a museum for the battle until 1983, when a purpose-built visitor centre was opened. This, in turn, has been superseded by a nine-million-pound, state-of-the-art visitor centre – check the Culloden Battlefield and Visitor Centre website for current entrance fees, which include car parking. Culloden House (7246) is now a hotel.

Further reading

Stuart Reid, *Culloden Moor 1746: The Death of the Jacobite Cause* **(Osprey, 2002).**

SELECT BIBLIOGRAPHY

Adair, John, *Battle of Cheriton 1644* (Roundwood Press, 1973).

Barrett, C. R. B., *Battles and Battlefields in England* (Innes & Co., 1896).

Brooke, Richard, *Visits to Fields of Battle in England of the Fifteenth Century* (John Russell Smith, 1857).

Brotchie, T. C. F., *The Battlefields of Scotland* (T. C. and E. C. Jack, 1913).

Bryant, Sir Arthur, *The Age of Chivalry* (Collins, 1963).

Burne, Alfred H., *The Battlefields of England* (Methuen & Co. Ltd, 1950).

——, *More Battlefields of England* (Methuen & Co. Ltd, 1952).

Carlton, Charles, *Going to the Wars: The Experience of the British Civil Wars 1638–1651* (Routledge, 1992).

Chandler, David, *Sedgemoor 1685* (Anthony Mott, 1985).

Firth, C. H., *Cromwell's Army* (Methuen & Co. Ltd, 1902).

——, *Oliver Cromwell and the Rule of the Puritans in England* (Putnam, 1908).

Fraser, Antonia, *Cromwell Our Chief of Men* (Weidenfeld & Nicolson, 1973).

Gardiner, Samuel R., *History of the Great Civil War 1642–1649*, Vols I–IV (Longmans, Green and Co., 1888).

George, H. B., *Battles of English History* (Methuen & Co. Ltd, 1896).

Grainge, William, *The Battles and Battlefields of Yorkshire from the Earliest Times to the End of the Great Civil War* (Hunton, 1854).

Green, Colonel Howard, *Guide to the Battlefields of Britain & Ireland* (Constable, 1973).

Hyde, Edward, Earl of Clarendon, *History of the Great Rebellion & Civil Wars in England*, Vols I–VIII (Clarendon Press, 1826).

Kendall, Paul Murray, *Richard III* (George Allen & Unwin Ltd, 1955).

Kinross, John, *The Battlefields of Britain* (David & Charles, 1979).

Leadman, Alex D. H., *Battles Fought in Yorkshire* (Bradbury, Agnew & Co. Ltd, 1891).

Mackenzie, W. M., *The Battle of Bannockburn* (James Maclehose & Sons, 1913).

Marren, Peter, *Grampian Battlefields* (Mercat Press, 1990).

Phillips, C. E. Lucas, *Cromwell's Captains* (William Heinemann Ltd, 1938).

Oman, Sir Charles, *Warwick the Kingmaker* (Macmillan, 1891).

——, *A History of the Art of War in the Middle Ages* (Methuen, 1898).

——, *A History of the Art of War in the Sixteenth Century* (Dutton, 1937).

Prebble, John, *Culloden* (Martin Secker & Warburg Ltd, 1961).

Ramsay, Sir J. H., *Lancaster & York* (Vols I–II) (Clarendon Press, 1892).

Reid, Stuart, *All the King's Armies* (History Press, 2007).

Rogers, Colonel H. C. B., *Battles & Generals of the Civil Wars 1642–1651* (Seeley Service & Co. Ltd, 1968).

Seymour, William, *Battles in Britain 1066–1547* (Sedgwick & Jackson, 1975).

——, *Battles in Britain, 1642–1746* (Sedgwick & Jackson, 1975).

Smurthwaite, David, *Ordnance Survey Complete Guide to the Battlefields of Britain* (Webb & Bower, 1984).

Tomasson, Katherine and Francis Buist, *Battles of the '45* (B. T. Batsford Ltd, 1962).

Toynbee, Margaret and Peter Young, *Cropredy Bridge 1644* (Roundwood Press, 1970).

Wedgwood, C. V., *Battlefields in Britain* (Collins, 1944).
——, *The King's War 1641–1647* (Collins, 1958).
Woolrych, Austin, *Battles of the English Civil War* (B. T. Batsford Ltd, 1961).
Young, Peter, *From Hastings to Culloden* (G. Bell and Sons, 1964).
——, *Edgehill 1642* (Roundwood Press Ltd, 1967).
——, *Marston Moor 1644* (Roundwood Press Ltd, 1970).
——, *Naseby 1645* (Century Publishing, 1985).

Doubtless, readers will be trawling the web for further information, but don't miss the following sites:

- The Battlefields Trust
- English Heritage
- Historic Scotland
- The Towton Battlefield Society
- The Musselborough Conservation Society
- The Battle of Cheriton Project
- The Tywardreath Battlefield Project
- The Richard III Society
- The Cromwell Association
- The 1745 Association
- The British Civil Wars, Commonwealth and Protectorate 1638–60
- The English Civil War Society
- The English Civil War Society of America
- The Sealed Knot
- The Simon de Montfort Society
- Flodden 1513 Ecomuseum
- The 1st Marquis of Montrose Society
- Caliver Books
- Battlefield History TV
- Pegasus Entertainment
- American Libraries: Free Books

The 'American Libraries: Free Books website' is invaluable, providing access to a wealth of copyright-free material, including a number of the older books listed in the Select Bibliography. Primary source material can also be found here, notably:

- *The Paston Letters*
- *Holinshed's Chronicles*
- *Warkworth's Chronicle*
- *Historie of the Arrivall of Edward IV*

All of the above are contemporary sources for the Wars of the Roses period. For the Civil Wars, search online for individual names, such as Sir Ralph Hopton; Sir Thomas Fairfax; Sir Henry Slingsby. This will lead to volumes of memoirs and contemporary biographies.

INDEX